NORTHERN CALIFORNIA AND LAKE TAHOE

Dear Reader,

Northern California is one of America's most diverse vacation destinations. From its stunning natural landscapes to its towns built on culture and wine, this part of the Golden State truly offers something for the whole family to enjoy.

I have my personal biases, of course, having enjoyed more than a few memorable moments in certain spots within the region. I love the world-famous aquarium in Monterey, for instance, but I have just as much fondness for the wild sea lions that congregate at the end of the wharf in Santa Cruz. I appreciate all the fine wines that come out of Napa and Sonoma but have relished some divine tasting experiences at lesser-known vineyards far from those two storied counties. And while most people visit San Francisco for a look at the spectacular Golden Gate Bridge or the infamous Alcatraz, I'm just as content wandering up and down the hilly streets, enjoying fresh crab at hole-in-the-wall restaurants and rummaging through the colorful shelves at eclectic bookstores.

No matter what indulgences you prefer to plan for your own vacation, I hope you will find all the information you need in *The Everything® Family Guide to Northern California and Lake Tahoe.*

Kim Kavin

THE
EVERYTHING
— Family Guides —

Everything® Family Guides are designed to be the perfect traveling companions. Whether you're traveling within a tight family budget or feeling the urge to splurge, you will find all you need to create a memorable family vacation. Review this book to give you great ideas before you travel, and stick it in your backpack or diaper bag to use as a quick reference guide for activities, attractions, and excursions. You'll discover that vacationing with the whole family can be filled with fun and exciting adventures.

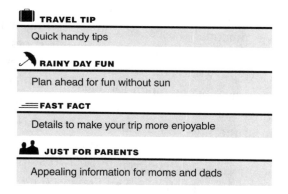

TRAVEL TIP

Quick handy tips

RAINY DAY FUN

Plan ahead for fun without sun

FAST FACT

Details to make your trip more enjoyable

JUST FOR PARENTS

Appealing information for moms and dads

When you're done reading, you can finally
say you know **EVERYTHING**®!

PUBLISHER Karen Cooper

DIRECTOR OF ACQUISITIONS AND INNOVATION Paula Munier

MANAGING EDITOR, EVERYTHING SERIES Lisa Laing

COPY CHIEF Casey Ebert

ACQUISITIONS EDITOR Lisa Laing

ASSOCIATE DEVELOPMENT EDITOR Elizabeth Kassab

EDITORIAL ASSISTANT Hillary Thompson

Visit the entire Everything® series at *www.everything.com*

THE
EVERYTHING®
FAMILY GUIDE TO
NORTHERN CALIFORNIA
AND LAKE TAHOE

A complete guide to San Francisco,
Yosemite, Monterey, and Lake Tahoe—
and all the beautiful spots in between

Kim Kavin

Avon, Massachusetts

For Auntie Sue, the California Girl

• • •

An Everything® Series Book.
Everything® and everything.com® are regis-
tered trademarks of F+W Media, Inc.

Published by Adams Media, an F+W Media Company
57 Littlefield Street, Avon, MA 02322 U.S.A.
www.adamsmedia.com

ISBN 10: 1-59869-714-5
ISBN 13: 978-1-59869-714-8

Printed in Canada.

J I H G F E D C B A

Library of Congress Cataloging-in-Publication Data
is available from the publisher.

This book is available at quantity discounts for bulk purchases.
For information, please call 1-800-289-0963.

Contents

Top 10 Things to Do in
Northern California and Lake Tahoe

1. Enjoy lunch with moving scenery onboard the Napa Valley Wine Train.

2. Come face-to-face with sharks, eels, and stingrays at the Monterey Bay Aquarium.

3. Chow down at the World's Largest Salmon Barbecue on the Mendocino Coast.

4. Look for the more than 1,000 species of plants and animals that live in Redwood National Park.

5. Join the 30,000 or so Bard fans with beach blankets and picnic baskets at the annual Shakespeare at Sand Harbor Festival on Lake Tahoe's East Shore.

6. Let your hair blow in the wind in a rented convertible along the Pacific Coast Highway.

7. Take a beginner's rock-climbing class at Yosemite National Park.

8. Pan for gold nuggets and rich memories in the American River.

9. Take a free walk full of stunning scenery across San Francisco's Golden Gate Bridge.

10. Hoot and holler at a Sacramento Valley three-day rodeo, the largest in the United States.

Acknowledgments

Literary agent Jacky Sach of Bookends LLC brought me this project and helped me to see it through. She never fails to think of me when writing opportunities arise, and I am always grateful for chances to work with her.

This is my fourth *Everything® Guide* for Adams Media, and everyone at the company continues to impress me with their hard work and collegial attitudes. Lisa Laing, in particular, has been a terrific supporter of mine.

My good friend and fellow journalist Dave Sheingold shared his personal expertise about San Francisco, and I owe thanks to the whole Garrett family—Kevin, Kara, Casey, and Riley—for opening their Santa Cruz home to me and sharing their local knowledge.

My parents, Marc and Donna Kavin, and my sister, Michelle Kavin, are wonderful supporters of everything I do—and excellent distractions when I need a break from writing. I love and appreciate them dearly.

Last on this list but first in my heart is Sean Toohey, who always understands when I am still typing long past midnight. He is the partner of my dreams.

Introduction

Where, exactly, is northern California?

It's a debate that rages within the Golden State itself. Some locals feel that northern California—AKA NoCal to hipsters and cool kids—encompasses nothing south of the San Francisco Bay area. Other people believe northern California refers only to the well-developed areas along the Pacific coast. Still others say the region is far more vast, comprising all the land from San Luis Obispo County north to the Oregon border, plus all the land from the Pacific Ocean across to the state of Nevada.

For the purposes of this book, that last definition is the one that applies. The best family vacations can't be held to strict geographical distinctions, and no place will make you feel more prone to wandering just a bit farther down the path than northern California. There are seashores and mountain vistas, epicurean hubs and rural outposts, pristine redwood forests and glistening cities alike. None of these places is more "northern California" than the next, so try as many as you can to experience the best this region has to offer.

Heck, the state motto is "Eureka!" It means "I have found it!" Just imagine all that awaits you on a vacation where you take the time to explore far and wide.

In most cases, your northern California vacation will start in a city. The best-known regional cities are San Francisco and Sacramento, each of which boasts an international airport. While neither of these cities enjoys as much tourism as the entertainment mecca of Los Angeles in the south, both have incredible amounts of family-friendly sights and activities to offer. If you prefer the feel of smaller cities, you'll likely find your way to places like San Jose, Sausalito, and Santa Cruz, which are lesser known but continue to charm visitors from around the globe.

After you explore northern California's cities, you'll likely want to make your way to its next-most-popular tourism area: Wine Country. Napa and Sonoma counties are known the world over for their vineyards full of Chardonnay and other varietals, and more than a few fine restaurants have sprung up in those areas to satisfy your urge to eat as much as you drink. In places like San Luis Obispo and Santa Barbara counties, too, wineries are an option for your vacation itinerary.

If sitting around filling your belly all day doesn't sound appealing, fear not: This area also offers some of the best hiking, biking, and general sightseeing in the entire United States. National parks from Yosemite to the Redwood National Forest are among the most widely renowned ecological areas in northern California, and there are countless other fantastic state and regional parks to explore as well. If you want to stay away from the biggest crowds, you can tour inland ranges such as the Trinity Mountains and Mount Shasta. There's even a volcanic park if you prefer your peaks to be of the formerly erupting variety.

Then again, you may be more of a water baby than an inland hiker, and once more, northern California comes through in high style. From Lake Tahoe, which straddles the state's border with Nevada, to the Pacific Ocean shoreline, you'll find more water sports fun than in almost any other state. The Pacific Coast Highway is legendary, and rightfully so—it offers some of the most scenic drives in all of the Americas, with countless beaches along the way where you can surf, play carnival games, and spot sea lions at play. Monterey, in particular, is a fantastic choice for nature lovers, with its world-famous aquarium providing hands-on, educational fun for the whole family.

Even better, if learning is one of your vacation goals, northern California boasts a large number of active university campuses and museums, including one dedicated to the state's history of mining and minerals. Should your interest in the gold rush be piqued, you can take your family out to Gold Country to pan for nuggets, just as the area's first American settlers did in the mid-1800s.

Between then and now, as you can plainly see, northern California has developed into a region filled with every kind of tourism activity you can imagine. In the following pages, you'll get an introduction to them all—along with all the information you need to plan the perfect vacation for your family.

Northern California

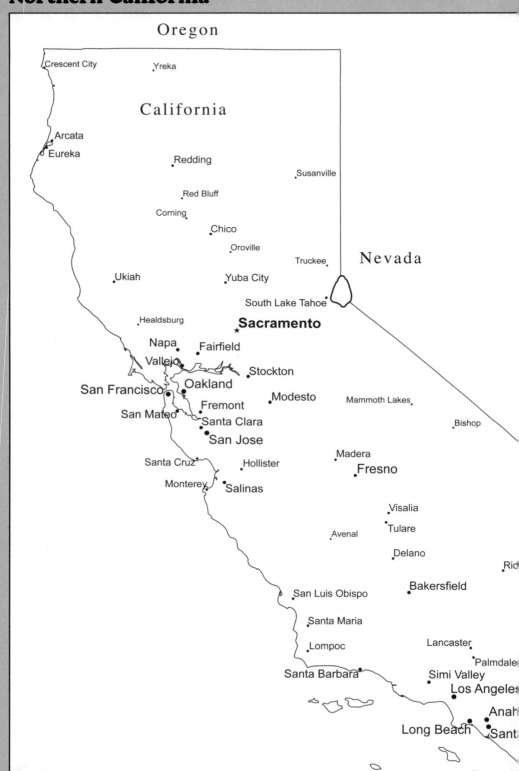

CHAPTER 1

California, Here You Come!

YOU HAVE A LOT OF CHOICES when it comes to selecting a destination for your family's vacation. One of the great things about the northern California and Lake Tahoe region is that it offers the best of many different worlds. Whether you want a cosmopolitan, world-class city experience, the ability to sample gourmet wine and food, a peek back in time to the Old West, or a sports adventure in the mountains, you'll find it in this exquisitely diverse part of the Golden State.

Northern California History

The state of California is a mighty big place. Its Pacific Ocean shoreline alone is 1,264 miles long and stretches so far from north to south that it easily serves as home for everything from towering redwood forests to flat deserts of shifting sands. The geographic differences are so imposing that even native Californians distinguish one place from another by its topography. Perhaps the best-known example is the area just outside of Los Angeles, colloquially called "the Valley."

Northern California is no different, with regions named Pacific Coast and Sierra Nevada, the latter thanks to the mountain range that sprawls down the middle of the state like a backbone gone slightly askew. But the section of California known as "northern" is more of a mental division than a geographic one, a line drawn by lifestyle.

Los Angeles, with its flashy movie stars and Jimmy Choo shoe stores, creates the tone for the southern part of the Golden State, while San Francisco, with its environmentally conscious thinkers and Birkenstock outlets, sets the pace for life in the north. Yes, those are stereotypes, but as with most stereotypes, they're rooted in reality. Folks who call northern California home tend to be a bit more, well, granola. They're more one with the earth than their fellow Californians to the south.

Even within that generalized description, life in northern California is varied—just as it has been since the days of the 1848 gold rush that flooded the Sierra Nevada with white settlers from all directions.

≡ FAST FACT

During the first two years of the gold rush in the mid-1800s, northern California's premier city of San Francisco exploded from about 500 residents to well more than 25,000. Today nearly 750,000 people live inside the city limits, making San Francisco the second most densely populated city in the United States.

The Gold Rush

The day that brought northern California its first wave of settlers was January 24, 1848. That's when James Marshall, a foreman for Sutter's Mill near the present-day town of Colona, found pieces of shiny metal in the flume that led away from the mill's water wheel.

Those pieces turned out to be gold, and within two months, rumors had spread all the way to San Francisco that there were fortunes to be made in the wilds of California. A San Francisco newspaper soon printed the fact that there was gold in the region, and by that summer—less than six months after Marshall's discovery— newspapers on the East Coast were reporting that a gold rush was on in California.

 **TRAVEL TIP**

Many families try their hands at panning for gold during a northern California vacation. Keep in mind that you can do this on a small or large scale. Some tour companies even have guides in period dress to re-create not just the experience of panning, but panning as it was back in the key gold rush year of 1849.

Some 300,000 people relocated to northern California during this time, by way of boat, railroad, and covered wagon. The prospectors came from as far away as Europe, Asia, Latin America, and Australia. These "forty-niners," as they were known (from the year they came looking to dig up their own personal fortunes), were northern California's first major group of immigrants. Towns sprang up like daffodils on an April morning, as did churches, schools, and other foundations of civilization as we know it today. Railroads and farms began to spread, constituting the beginning of other industries that are still a major part of the area and its tourism industry. By the end of 1849, California was a state.

Other Areas Emerge

As folks flooded in, and as the clamor settled down, it was hard not to notice the area's stunning natural beauty. All around were pristine woods, beaches, lakes, rivers, and mountains, begging for hearty souls to set up homes and businesses and create towns that would last for years. Many of the most beautiful areas were, thankfully, preserved for future generations to enjoy, just as the earliest settlers did. Today, these protected natural gems stretch from Redwood National Park in California's far northwestern corner to Yosemite and Kings Canyon national parks, in the southeastern part of the northern California divide.

In between these gorgeous natural wonders, settlers discovered soil rich for planting everything from olives to almonds to grapevines. Napa County—known worldwide for its production of fine wines—actually started out as a place where people grew grain and fruit and raised cattle. Silver mining, too, took hold in this part of northern California while everyone else was a little farther to the east looking for gold.

Just south of Napa, near the budding town of San Francisco, settlers discovered the opportunities that awaited them in San Francisco Bay. European explorers had been poking around in the bay since the 1700s, but it wasn't until the mid-1800s, the great gold rush, and the Mexican-American War that the United States took control of this vast Pacific port. Not only was San Francisco Bay an incredible asset in terms of shipping and transportation, but it was a breeding ground for Dungeness crab, Pacific halibut, and salmon—northern California delicacies that are still much in demand today, from tourists and locals alike.

≡FAST FACT

Dungeness crab is widely considered a San Francisco–area treat, but the crabs actually are harvested as far north as Alaska's Aleutian Islands. They take their name not from California, but from the town of Dungeness in the state of Washington, where a festival is held each October in their honor.

Each of these areas has developed distinguishing characteristics that set them apart. You don't think of wine when someone says "Yosemite," you don't think of rock climbing when you hear "Napa Valley," and you certainly don't think of hill-climbing streetcars when anyone utters the name of a city other than San Francisco.

That's why, to plan your ideal vacation, you need to break the region into smaller areas and understand what type of activities each tends to offer.

Lay of the Land

Much of this book is organized by geographic zone to help you understand the typical vacation activities you'll find in different parts of the broader region. Sometimes, the zones are cities, as is the case with major hubs like San Francisco and Sacramento; sometimes, they're counties, like world-famous Napa and Sonoma; and sometimes, they're topographical, like the North Coast or Gold Country, where cities and counties tend to blend into a broader swath of general life-style and tourist attractions.

In general, this book covers the following regions:

- San Francisco within the city limits
- San Francisco Bay area
- Sacramento, the capital of California
- Wine Country, primarily Napa and Sonoma counties
- North Coast
- Central Valley
- South Coast
- Northern Mountains
- Sierra Nevada
- Gold Country
- Lake Tahoe, which crosses the California border into Nevada

As you can see by looking at the map in this chapter, most of these regions are defined by natural boundaries such as mountains and oceans. It really is the lay of the land that determines where you are and what opportunities you can expect to find in much of northern California.

Getting Here

One of the nice things about northern California is that getting to your destination can be as mesmerizing and beautiful an experience as the destination itself. Certainly, the region is easily accessible by major international airports, but if you have the time and inclination, consider visiting by train, car, camper, or boat. The scenery is gorgeous from literally any direction, and the more of it you and your family see along the way, the better your vacation memories will be.

By Airplane

There are five international airports located in northern California—San Francisco, Sacramento, San Jose, Fresno-Yosemite, and Oakland—plus Reno-Tahoe International Airport located across the state border in Nevada. The San Francisco hub is by far the biggest, with some 16 million passengers climbing onboard jets and shuttles there each year. Oakland is the second-busiest with 7 million, Sacramento and San Jose are close behind with 5 million each (the same amount as Reno-Tahoe in Nevada), and Fresno-Yosemite has just over 1 million.

≡FAST FACT

For some people, San Francisco International Airport is a destination unto itself. The aviation library and museum housed on-site are available for rent if you want to hold a private party for up to 250 guests. Catered fine dining and special parking passes can be part of your package deal, so guests don't have to schlep from economy lots to the food court.

United Airlines has its hub at San Francisco's airport, and dozens of other airlines also offer service in and out. Commuter and light rail lines connect from the airport to downtown San Francisco and a few other areas, and of course there are easily accessible car rentals, bus transfers, and other private transportation pickups to get you to any part of northern California you would like to visit.

By Train

Amtrak has multiple routes operating within the region. The Capitol Corridor line runs from San Jose through Oakland and Sacramento up to Auburn, toward the northeastern corner of the state. The San Joaquin line services Oakland, Sacramento, and Stockton, traveling all the way to Fresno. The Pacific Surfliner route begins in San Luis Obispo and heads south to Santa Barbara, eventually crossing into southern California and stopping at Los Angeles and San Diego.

If you're coming to California from another state, you can connect with Amtrak trains that head to northern California from multiple U.S. cities. The California Zephyr line runs from Chicago, Illinois, west through Denver, Colorado, and ends in San Francisco. The Coast Starlight line starts in Seattle, Washington, and heads south along California's length toward its final destination in Los Angeles.

 TRAVEL TIP

Some Amtrak trains are outfitted with a limited number of bicycle racks. You can use them on a first-come, first-served basis, or you can call ahead and reserve a space for your family's two-wheeled luggage. There is generally a $5 to $10 fee for reserving a bike rack space, depending on how far you're traveling.

By Bus

Greyhound offers countless routes and itineraries from big and small U.S. cities alike into various destinations within northern California. The region's major cities, including San Francisco, have terminals, as do a good number of the less-populated destinations such as Red Bluff and Arcada.

There's also a San Francisco-based company called Green Tortoise that offers short and long bus tours all around California and into Nevada. Some routes travel California's legendary Pacific Coast Highway while others head out toward the desert and Yosemite National Park.

By Car or Camper

Roadways and campsites are a huge part of the experience. Anyone driving to northern California will find plenty of roadside motels and hotels, and families arriving by camper will find more than 100 RV parks scattered around the landscape.

You might think that RV parks and campsites are limited to scenic areas like national parks and forests, but that's not the case. The city of San Jose has at least four RV parks, the tony towns of Monterey and Carmel have RV parks, and there are additional parks across the Nevada border in the Lake Tahoe area.

 RAINY DAY FUN

Some RV parks and campsites, like Yosemite Pines in Groveland, have indoor activities to keep the kids busy on days when nature fails to cooperate with your outdoor plans. The recreation room at Yosemite Pines includes Ping-Pong, air hockey, Foosball tables, and more.

By Boat

You might look at a map, see the size of San Francisco Bay, and think that northern California is a major boating destination. That's not the case, primarily because there are so few natural harbors in between San Francisco and points to the north and south. Families with weekend-cruise-style boats often find it difficult to navigate the long distances between, say, Seattle or San Diego and San Francisco Bay.

However, many private marinas along San Francisco Bay will happily offer you a transient slip for your boat for a few nights, a few weeks, or the entire summer season. The city maintains the San Francisco Marina Yacht Harbor, which is less than two miles from the Golden Gate Bridge and composed of two harbors called East and West.

Bigger boats—well, cruise ships, actually—visit San Francisco regularly. Some of the cruise lines that have routes starting, stopping, or visiting the city include Princess, Royal Caribbean, Celebrity, Norwegian Cruise Line, P&O, and Radisson Seven Seas. Of those lines, Princess typically has the most ships based on the West Coast, so your odds are pretty good of finding an available Princess itinerary that includes San Francisco.

 TRAVEL TIP

The San Francisco harbormaster puts out a newsletter with up-to-date information about slips, amenities, and more in the San Francisco Marina Yacht Harbor area. You can download the newsletter for free online by going to the Web site *www.sfgov.org*.

Weather and Seasonal Concerns

Determining the best time of year to visit really depends on what types of activities you and your family plan to enjoy. Some regions offer fabulous hiking all summer long followed by extensive snowmobiling come wintertime. The larger cities like San Francisco and San Jose have ongoing events year-round. You do have to be careful about driving through mountainous areas during winter months when snowfall can make roadways impassable, but aside from that, any time of year can be a good time to visit many parts of northern California.

In general, northern California has a Mediterranean climate, meaning warm to hot summers, cold and snowy winters, and pleasant spring and autumn seasons. In San Francisco, temperatures tend to be in the mid-50s Fahrenheit in January, in the low-70s Fahrenheit in June, and in the low-60s come November.

Some areas draw big crowds during certain times of the year. Napa and Sonoma counties, for instance, have year-round events but are busiest with tourists during the summer months. The same is true for places like Yosemite National Park, where many families visit while children are on summer vacation. Places like Mount Shasta are busy year-round, but the slopes fill up when there's fresh snowfall during the winter months.

Depending on what you want to do and where you want to go, the most popular times of year are—as you might expect—also going to be the most expensive in terms of food, lodging, and activities.

Typical Prices in Popular Areas

Make no mistake about it: California is an expensive place to live, visit, and even travel through. Northern California is no exception. The median family income in San Francisco is just shy of $68,000, the third-highest for any large city in the United States. Folks need to earn a lot of money to live in this part of California, as everything seems to cost just a bit more than anywhere else.

Prices for lodging, rental cars, fuel, food, and the like are difficult to pin down in a book, but the following sections will explain what kinds of prices you'll typically find during the prime seasons in traditional vacation hot spots like San Francisco, Wine Country, and Yosemite National Park.

Prices in San Francisco

When you think about vacationing in San Francisco, expect to pay rates that are on par with other major U.S. cities such as New York, Chicago, and Miami. July and August are typically the most tourist-packed with the fewest deals available, but even during the height of winter in December and January, you'll have to find a discount package in order to make a dent in the typically sky-high rates.

 TRAVEL TIP

If you're planning to visit San Francisco during a weekend, try to make it one when the Giants or the 49ers are playing out of town. Hotels book up fast, leaving nothing but premium-price rooms when the teams play on their home fields.

The top-rated hotels in San Francisco are operated by the Ritz-Carlton corporation and can average as much as $500 a night during the prime vacation months each summer. Four-star options can be found at about half that rate at chains including Hilton, Hyatt, and Marriott. Most are within walking distance of popular downtown attractions.

If you're willing to stay by the international airport, outside the city limits in a place like Oakland, or outside the cityscape altogether, you can usually find rooms for less than $200 a night. Sometimes, with a good deal and a little luck in your planning, you can find a three-star hotel room in the $150-per-night range.

When choosing a hotel in San Francisco, you can often save money by basing your decision as much on location as on amenities. For instance, if you're incorporating a cruise ship visit into your vacation plans, you'll need a hotel near Fisherman's Wharf instead of downtown—at an average savings of several hundred dollars a night.

You can also save money if you plan your hotel stay as part of a package deal, either by using a Web site company such as *www .expedia.com* or by choosing a package that's offered by the city of San Francisco itself. The official Web site *www.onlyinsanfrancisco .com* promotes package deals on everything from shopping to San Francisco Bay cruising to urban adventures that include electric car rentals.

Prices in Wine Country

There are a lot of places to find good wine in northern California, but Napa and Sonoma are the most popular counties, known the world over as California Wine Country and particularly noted for the Chardonnays they produce.

You can visit Wine Country any time of year, but summer tends to be the most hectic, with county fairs and wine festivals jamming the streets and hotels. Fall is actually the busiest season in Napa and Sonoma counties because it's when the wine grapes are harvested and crushed. Watching the vintners in action can be akin to fine theater, and many wine-lovers enjoy the show as much as tasting the wines themselves.

 **RAINY DAY FUN**

If you want to learn about winemaking, consider visiting Napa and Sonoma counties during the winter. The crowds die down, the tasting rooms are less packed with people, and the winery workers will have more time to answer your questions and help you understand the subtleties of the varietals they produce.

Lodging in Wine Country is typically of the bed-and-breakfast or cottage variety, with inns that range from basic, which charge less than $150 a night, to antique-filled, which cost $400 a night. There are budget motels and spa retreats alike, and you can also find familiar brand names such as Best Western, Travelodge, and Marriott.

Consider, though, that inns serving food will also typically serve wine, or at least let you carry it in—which is part of the Wine Country experience you're there to enjoy. That extra $30 a night for a nicer room may make up for your not needing a taxicab or rental car to take you back and forth from eateries to bed night after night during your vacation stay.

 RAINY DAY FUN

If you choose to stay overnight in your mobile camper at the Napa Valley Expo, you can take the whole family to the Bingo Emporium, where games are held every night of the week some 350 days a year. Games are run by local nonprofits and benefit groups like high school bands and children's sports teams.

There's also the option of RV or tent camping in this area—and it can save you a great deal of money. The town of Napa has two such parks, and you can also find places to stay in Calistoga and Helena.

The Web site *www.napavalley.com* offers links to these and more, showing prices as low as $35 a night for RV sites with full hookups.

Prices in Yosemite National Park

Yosemite National Park is open year-round, though heavy snow-fall can lead to road closings from November until as late as May or June as cleanup continues. The summertime is just as beautiful as the winter, though most of the waterfalls are fed by natural snowmelt, so some will tend to slow to a trickle or even dry up altogether come August. The best months to see waterfalls are May and June, which also happens to be when a lot of the wildflowers bloom—before the hazy, hot, and thunderstorm-marred days of deep summer.

You can stay inside the park in anything from a basic tent to a luxury room at the Ahwahnee. Both campgrounds and top-dollar rooms tend to book up fastest from April through September. Rooms at the Ahwahnee start around $400 a night and reach $1,000 a night for suites. At the other end of the price spectrum are places like the Housekeeping Camp, which offers outdoor camping units (three walls and a curtain) with bunk beds and a campfire for as little as $76 per night—and that's for up to four people in a single unit, not a per-person rate.

Outlying Options for Budget-Conscious Travelers

It's hard to pinpoint which outlying areas are the best for budget-conscious travelers for the simple reason that so much of northern California is made up of outlying areas. Charming little towns and out-of-the-way camping grounds are the norm, not the exception, outside of the major tourist areas like San Francisco, Napa, and Yosemite. That's good if you'll be traveling on a tight budget, but bad if you're looking for an easy fix for your vacation-planning purposes. You will have to research each chapter to look for the outlying area that best suits you. With that caveat in mind, here's a look at a couple of off-the-beaten-track locations that tend to be more budget-friendly than the hot spots.

Arcata

Arcata is in the northwestern corner of California, well-positioned for anyone who wants to visit Redwood National Forest or take a drive down the scenic Pacific Coast Highway. The highest temperatures of the year tend to be in the low-60s during the summer months, and thermometers dip down into the 40s each winter.

The hotels include budget chains such as Best Western, Howard Johnson, Super 8, and Comfort Inn. Rates can be as high as $150 a night, but there are deals close to the $75-a-night range, even during the summer. Nearby camping and RV sites have rates as low as $29 a night.

Chico

Chico is in the Sacramento Valley, about ninety miles north of California's capital city of Sacramento. Chico has a historic downtown that dates to the mid-1800s and is home to Bidwell Park, which, at 3,670 acres, is one of the largest municipal parks in the entire United States. The city hosts a major air show every August, an arts celebration each October, and self-guided tours of the charming city streets all year round.

 RAINY DAY FUN

Looking for a museum to tour with the kids on a cloudy day in Chico? How about the National Yo-Yo Museum, home to the world's largest yo-yo, which weighs in at a whopping 256 pounds. If you visit in October, you can also attend the national yo-yo contest.

Chico has hotels, motels, bed and breakfasts, and nearby RV parks alike. There are brand-name chains like Best Western, Marriott, and Days Inn, and even during the dog days of August, you can find rooms from $40 to $100 a night. RV site rates can be less than $25 a night, and tent-only camping spots are sometimes as low as $10 or $12.

San Francisco

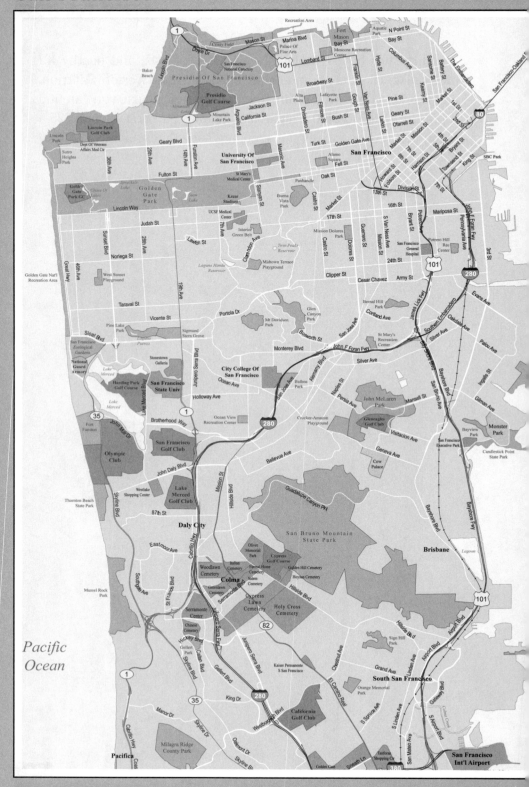

CHAPTER 2

San Francisco

NORTHERN CALIFORNIA'S best-known metropolis was once known as the "City of Flags"—a fitting moniker given the diversity of people who make up San Francisco's population. All those different cultures have swirled together to create a unique cosmopolitan experience, with everything from streetcar rides to Chinatown parades. Even the city's darkest historical corners, including Alcatraz prison, are now popular tourist destinations that you can enjoy with the entire family.

The City's History

San Francisco is surrounded by water on three sides. The Pacific Ocean, San Francisco Bay, and the Golden Gate Strait make up the city's western, eastern, and northern borders—so it should be no surprise that much of the city's history has to do with the sea, rivers, and estuaries. Even today, the area's great bodies of water make themselves known in the fog for which the city is known. July and August, the prime tourism months, are actually also the peak times of year for fog in San Francisco.

It was ever thus, most likely, from the days when the area's first settlers arrived as clans who wandered across the Bering Strait from Asia a good 20,000 years ago. Those first residents set up villages that survived until the 1500s, when European explorers started poking the bows of their great ships into San Francisco Bay. Great Britain's legendary Sir Francis Drake arrived in 1579, though historians still argue about whether he made it into San Francisco proper. Spanish explorer Gaspar de Portolá is credited with making the first recorded entrance into San Francisco Bay in 1769, nearly two full centuries after Drake's visit.

As settlers on the East Coast prepared to launch the American Revolution, the Spanish began colonizing what would become modern-day San Francisco. Mexico also had a hand in settling the area and controlled it for several years. The city was still coming into its own when the United States annexed California in 1846.

≡ FAST FACT

Spanish settlers originally called the San Francisco area Yerba Buena, an alternate form of *hierba buena*, which means "good herb" in Spanish. The herb in question, often called Oregon tea today, is used in making drinks and natural medicines. It's abundant in and around San Francisco, which is why the city went by that name until 1847.

The gold rush brought San Francisco widespread attention. Most of the prospectors and fortune hunters were men, which gave early San Francisco a male-to-female ratio of about ten to one—a helpful tidbit that helps to explain the evolution of the tawdry Barbary Coast section of the city. Many businessmen also emigrated from distant places, bringing with them a banking structure and lending capabilities that helped San Francisco continue to emerge into the 1850s. The transcontinental railroad followed, shipping businesses set themselves up along the waterfronts, and there wasn't a town that could rival San Francisco any closer than Chicago, Illinois. Indeed, the city seemed poised for unstoppable growth—right up until 1906 and its first major environmental disaster.

Great Earthquake of 1906

San Francisco sits atop the San Andreas earthquake fault line. Most residents did not know this until 5:14 A.M. on April 18, 1906, when the earth opened up and roared to the tune of 8.25 on the Richter scale—a force so strong it's estimated to occur no more than once a year on the entire planet. Gas and water mains exploded beneath the city's streets, hospitals and civic buildings crumbled, and fire sprang up like out-of-control fireworks, eventually burning through what was left of the downtown area for the better part of a week.

 RAINY DAY FUN

If you want to learn about the San Francisco earthquake, just go to the Virtual Museum of the City of San Francisco at *www .sfmuseum.org*. There, you can view photographs, read eyewitness accounts, and even see the desperate mayor's orders to "instantly kill anyone caught looting or committing any other serious crimes."

San Francisco became a virtual tent city after that, but its residents did not give up easily. In fact, the city was in good enough shape to host the World's Fair in 1915. The Golden Gate Bridge went up in the 1930s, and an orderly pace of life continued to take root well into the 1960s.

Summer of Love

Social change, as you might call it, grew out of the neighborhoods in San Francisco's Haight-Ashbury district in 1967. That was the year of the "summer of love," when Grateful Dead fans, psychedelic drug users, and hippies from the counterculture first came into the public awareness. Across San Francisco Bay in Berkeley, free speech pioneers became more outspoken, joined by Vietnam War protestors and members of the fledgling Black Panther Party.

The counterculture movement continues today in San Francisco, which is well known for its liberal bent. But big business is never too far beneath the surface, as quickly became apparent during the 1990s with the dot-com boom.

Rise of Silicon Valley

The Silicon Valley, as it were, is just south of San Francisco proper, but many of the people who made the high-tech region such a powerful economic force are commuters who live or play in the city. The area is generally believed to be the epicenter of the dot-com Internet boom of the mid-1990s, when real estate prices in San Francisco jumped sky high. The effects of those property gains are still felt today, which is why hotel rooms in the city are so much more expensive than in other similar-sized cities around the world. The good news is that you can usually find WiFi pretty much anywhere you choose to sleep, eat, or just grab a cup of coffee.

Still, as big as the technology sector is, it is dwarfed by San Francisco's tourism economy. The city typically draws the third-highest number of foreign tourists in all of America each year, injecting billions of dollars into the economy, thanks to a widespread desire to ride on streetcars, eat Rice-A-Roni, and cross the Golden Gate Bridge.

Must-See, Must-Do

You could spend a lifetime in San Francisco and still not be able to enjoy everything the city has to offer. But if you have only a week, there are definitely a handful of must-see, must-do treats that should be on your family's list.

Traverse the Golden Gate Bridge

The Golden Gate Bridge is one of the most recognizable landmarks in the world, and any trip to San Francisco should include at least a glimpse of the famous structure. When it was built in 1937, it was the world's largest suspension bridge. It's now the second-largest in the United States, after New York's Verrazano-Narrows Bridge.

After you've taken your fill of photographs from afar, check out the Golden Gate Bridge up close and in person. You can drive across by paying a $5 toll, but if you really want to enjoy the scenic views, take the free route and walk along the sidewalk. It's a two-mile hike each way, and parking is available at both ends of the bridge. The sidewalks are open from 6 A.M. to 6 P.M.

≡FAST FACT

What color is the Golden Gate Bridge? If you said red—well, guess again. The bridge is actually a shade called "international orange," which consulting architect Irving Morrow chose in part to make the bridge more visible in San Francisco's notorious fog. A team of close to forty painters work on periodic maintenance to ensure the bridge maintains its photogenic appeal.

Take a Cable Car Ride

If you've ever seen a Rice-A-Roni commercial, then you're familiar with San Francisco's famous cable car system. The bus-like vehicles still make their way along train track–like rails that are built right into the hilly city streets. The infrastructure that makes cable cars work has itself become an icon, as it is the world's last remaining manually operated cable car system in permanent operation.

Cable cars actually date back to well before the 1906 earthquake, which, as you might imagine, decimated the public transportation system along with pretty much everything else. The system was rebuilt, but never with the same gusto it had in the early days, since electric and then gas-fueled cars soon overtook cable cars in terms of speed, cost, and comfort. Today, there are three cable car routes still in operation, with the main two ferrying tourists from the Union Square area to Fisherman's Wharf.

Cable car rides cost $5 per person, but if you plan to ride all day, consider getting the $10 daylong pass. If you're older than 65, you can ride for just $1 before 7 A.M. or after 9 P.M.

Visit the Coit Tower

Coit Tower is not as well known as, say, New York City's Empire State Building, Chicago's Sears Tower, or Seattle's Space Needle. But the principle is the same: This is where you go if you want a spectacular 360-degree view of San Francisco and all the land and water beyond the city limits.

The tower stands 210 feet and gets a bit more of a height bump from the fact that it is built atop Telegraph Hill in Pioneer Park. From the top on a clear day, you can see the Golden Gate Bridge, Alcatraz prison, Pier 39, Treasure Island, and more.

Inside the Art Deco tower, there are some pretty terrific views, too—of murals by twenty-six different artists. You can see most of the murals free of charge. However, if you don't want to take the stairs up to the top of the tower, you'll have to pay the $3.75 elevator fee (kids between 6 and 12 pay $1.50).

 TRAVEL TIP

Because Coit Tower is at the top of a hill, parking can be limited, especially during peak tourism months like July and August. If you are in good health, leave the rental car at the hotel and use a good pair of sneakers to get up the hill.

Other Places to Visit

The Golden Gate Bridge, streetcars, and Coit Tower are just a few of the places you'll want to see during your family vacation to San Francisco. Check out a few of the areas downtown, not to mention the Golden Gate Recreation Area, Alcatraz Island, and cultural spots like the Fillmore.

Touring Downtown

Touring downtown San Francisco is just like touring any other major city—you need to keep your wits about you, keep your cash hidden, and keep your family together. There's no need for alarm. This city is safe enough to remain popular with tourists year-round, but keep in mind that tourists tend to draw pickpockets and unscrupulous sellers of everything from $5 ice cream cones to bus tours that don't go anywhere. Work with reputable operators, and use common sense to avoid becoming a victim.

Downtown San Francisco has many sections, including a Financial District and a Civic Center. Most tourists aren't interested in trading stocks or talking with government representatives, though, so the rest of this section will focus on four areas that you may want to check out: Fisherman's Wharf, Chinatown, Union Square, and the Alamo Square Historic District in the Western Addition section.

Fisherman's Wharf

Many tourists go straight from the airport to the Fisherman's Wharf section of downtown, where you can get fresh Dungeness crab with a side of clam chowder served in a sourdough bread bowl. In fact, Fisherman's Wharf is well known for its food, but there's a lot more to the area that you can enjoy if you take some time to look around.

 TRAVEL TIP

Fisherman's Wharf is always bustling with tourists and locals alike, but if you want to see the area at its most impressive, visit during the Fourth of July holiday for fireworks or during Fleet Week in October, when you can catch some of the best overhead views of fighter pilots speeding across the sky in fantastic formations.

The wharf area extends from Pier 39 to Aquatic Park, which abuts the National Maritime Museum of San Francisco and the grounds of Fort Mason. The wharf also includes Pier 41, which is the base for ferries to Angel Island and Alcatraz, and the Cannery Shopping Center and Ghirardelli Square, which are filled with store owners ready to help you lighten the load of souvenir money in your pocketbook. There's no longer a thriving working waterfront here, as most of the landscape has been overrun by shops, amusement areas, and quirky establishments like the Wax Museum at Fisherman's Wharf and the Ripley's Believe It or Not Museum. Pier 39 is a shopping extravaganza, with local enterprises mixing in among the national chains such as the Disney Store and the NFL Shop. Places to spend a little less coin on Pier 39 include the San Francisco Carousel, which is just $2 per ride, and the docks overlooking nearby rocks, where you and the kids can watch sea lions play for free. If you decide on the latter, consider going *after* you eat. The smell of sea lion poop just may ruin your appetite.

 RAINY DAY FUN

Aquarium of the Bay is right next to Pier 39 and has a 300-foot see-through tube that you can walk through while watching sharks and other animals swim all around you. There's also a program called "Aqua Tots" specially designed for 2- to 5-year-old kids who want to learn in interactive style about the animals that live in San Francisco Bay.

Right next to the Aquatic Park section of Fisherman's Wharf, you'll find the National Maritime Museum of San Francisco and the Hyde Street Pier Historic Ships, where you can climb aboard an 1886 schooner, an old passenger ferry, a 1915 steam schooner, and more.

The ships are often called a floating national park because they're so impressive. The 301-foot *Balclutha*, for instance, is a three-masted vessel built to carry goods all over the world. She entered service in 1886 after being built near Glasgow, Scotland, and was found to be so reliable on the ocean's waters that she ended up carrying freight around South America's Cape Horn seventeen times. She even appeared in the 1962 movie *Mutiny on the Bounty.*

 TRAVEL TIP

If you want to get the most bang for your buck, consider buying a Fisherman's Wharf Pass. It's $61 for adults and $38 for children ages five to eleven, and it gets you into multiple area attractions plus a city tour and a one-hour cruise around San Francisco Bay. You can review the details at *www.wharfpass.com.*

Chinatown

San Francisco's Chinatown is so big it has its own Web site: *www .sanfranciscochinatown.com.* Unlike the Chinatowns in some other major metropolitan cities, this one is much more than a row of Chinese restaurants. The area boasts the largest number of Chinese residents outside of China today, and it is marked by a spectacular Asian gate that was bestowed on San Francisco in 1969 by the Republic of China itself.

Cultural sites are the big deal here, including the Chinese Historical Society of America and the Pacific Heritage Museum. They may not appeal as much to the kids as the Ripley's Believe It or Not Museum at Fisherman's Wharf, but they're treasures of multiculturalism. On the lighter side, you can also enjoy the sights of local life, including shop owners bustling at daybreak and games of checkers in Portsmouth Square every afternoon.

No matter what you do, don't settle for imitation Chinese food. There are some fabulous, authentic restaurants in this section of San Francisco, and there are stores dedicated to helping you take authentic cuisine back home; everything from souvenir woks to specialty teas are on sale.

Union Square

Interestingly, if you're standing on Union Square, you're standing on the roof of the world's first underground parking structure. That may be hard to believe when you see all the street performers atop pedestals and the sculptures made of light, but it's true. One of San Francisco's main cultural and shopping centers is a lid on a parking garage.

Union Square Park underwent a $25 million renovation and restoration in 2002, when it became a site fit to host the Macy's Christmas tree each year. The streets that run adjacent to the square are brimming with fine antiques shops, theaters featuring traveling Broadway and off-Broadway shows, and a building designed by Frank Lloyd Wright.

 RAINY DAY FUN

The Xanadu Gallery is inside San Francisco's only Frank Lloyd Wright building. The folk art it showcases is interesting, to be sure, but so is the building, which has a Guggenheim-style two-story spiral staircase. The interior is worth a look, even if folk art isn't your thing.

There's shopping galore all around Union Square, including high-end outlets such as Saks Fifth Avenue and Tiffany and Co. Boutique-style stores feature designers such as Yves Saint Laurent, Christian Dior, and Armani. Also worthy of note is the Williams-Sonoma flagship store, boasting some 19,000 square feet of merchandise for your home—plus cooking classes if you can't figure out why you might need a deviled egg tray or a crepe-making machine.

Alamo Square Historic District

Alamo Square is a residential neighborhood inside the Western Addition section of the city. This place is about as opposite as you can get from the tourist-friendly hustle and bustle of Fisherman's Wharf or Union Square. It's filled with Victorian homes and mansions that are among the city's most photographed icons.

≡ **FAST FACT**

If you watched the television sitcom *Full House*, you'll recognize Alamo Square from the show's opening credits. Alamo Square Park is the place where the Olsen twins romped with their three "fathers," and you can do the same with your children—and even your dog, too, if you've brought her along on your San Francisco adventure.

Golden Gate National Recreation Area

The Golden Gate National Recreation Area is one of the most visited national parks in the United States, drawing some 13 million visitors each year with its extensive hiking trails, comfortable campsites, and spectacular views. Interestingly, the park extends well beyond the borders of San Francisco and is made up of multiple areas that are not always adjacent. To get an idea of just how expansive the park is, check out the free downloadable map from the National Park Service at *www.nps.gov*. You'll soon see that if exploring the entirety of the park is your vacation goal, you're most likely going to need a lifelong vacation. The main parts of the park that are inside the city limits include the Fort Point National Historic Site and the Presidio of San Francisco.

Fort Point National Historic Site

Fort Point was once known as the Gibraltar of the West Coast for its duty in protecting San Francisco both before and after the U.S. Civil War. Its construction dates back to the mid-1850s and the gold rush, when it was planned to stand as a formidable deterrent to any nation or rogue group that might have designs on attacking the newly annexed state of California (or the gold believed to be in its mountainsides).

Construction of the Golden Gate Bridge nearly meant the end for Fort Point, which was almost demolished to make way for the new structure. Luckily, the fort was maintained for its historic value, and it became a National Historic Site in 1970. Some of the family-friendly activities at Fort Point include watching a cannon-loading demonstration (year-round) or a pier crabbing demonstration (March through October).

Presidio of San Francisco

The Presidio served as an army post for more than 200 years. The grounds include a national cemetery, a historic airfield, forests, vistas, and of course terrific views of the water all around the city. There are eleven miles of hiking trails and fourteen miles of paved roads for bicyclists to enjoy. There's also a golf course, tennis courts, a bowling alley, and athletic fields on the grounds.

Especially good for children is the visitor center's self-guided tour, Kids on Trails, which leads you through a hiking path that's good for littler legs and helps explain the region's ecology to your wee ones along the way. Guided tours are also available, many of them including educational discussions about the Presidio's military past.

Alcatraz Island

The Golden Gate National Recreation Area also includes Alcatraz Island, a name that conjures up images of infamous inmates such as Al Capone and George "Machine Gun" Kelly, two of the more noted inmates to be housed there during the 1930s. No prisoners ever escaped from "the Rock," though thirty-four inmates did try. In the most violent escape attempt, in 1946, two guards were killed.

During the early years of Alcatraz, the warden maintained a strict policy of silence that was said to be slowly driving some of the inmates insane. There was also a place called the Strip Cell; there was no sink or toilet, only a hole in the ground that got "flushed" at the guards' discretion. Inmates were placed into this hole naked and given limited quantities of food. When the solid steel outer door closed, the inmates were left in complete darkness.

Despite its horrifying realities, Alcatraz prison has become legendary in the public imagination thanks to its appearances in many popular movies. The better-known titles include *Birdman of Alcatraz* with Burt Lancaster, *Escape from Alcatraz* with Clint Eastwood, *Murder in the First* with Kevin Bacon, *The Rock* with Sean Connery, and *X-Men: The Last Stand*, where it hosts the final battle between Magneto's Brotherhood of Mutants and Professor Xavier's X-Men.

 TRAVEL TIP

Trips to Alcatraz Island frequently sell out—sometimes more than a week in advance during the height of the summer tourist season. You can buy tickets online as much as sixty days before your visit by going to *www.alcatrazcruises.com*, which also has sections on Fisherman's Wharf and other popular attractions.

The federal penitentiary has been closed to visitors for some time, but you can take self-guided tours, including a cell house audio tour that's included in the price of your ferry ticket from the mainland. The ferry ride can be as interesting as Alcatraz Island, with the boat circling the Rock and including a narrated history about the island and prison.

The Fillmore and Other Cultural Spots

If San Francisco's psychedelic '60s era is more your scene, then consider heading down to the corner of Fillmore Street and Geary Boulevard, where you'll find The Fillmore—which led the counterculture revolution by hosting such acts as The Grateful Dead, The Who, Jimi

Hendrix, Steppenwolf, Creedence Clearwater Revival, Jefferson Airplane, Cream, Led Zeppelin, The Doors, and Janis Joplin.

Though the original members of those groups no longer play at The Fillmore, there are shows almost every night—and you can still help yourself to a large tub of free apples waiting for concert-goers by the door. To see who is playing and reserve advance tickets, go to the Web site *www.livenation.com.*

The Roxie New College Film Center

Founded in 1909, the Roxie is the oldest continually operating cinema in San Francisco—and it also has a reputation as one of the most provocative, risk-taking cinemas in the entire country. It has more screenings of documentaries each year than any other American movie theater, hosts multiple film festivals, and recently began serving as a classroom for the New College's media studies department.

≡FAST FACT

Despite the erudite status the Roxie holds today, its history includes serving as a pornography theater during the late 1960s. Community leaders in San Francisco's Mission District bought and remodeled the theater in 1976, and it has gone on to host Jewish, Arab, Indian, and other kinds of high-end film festivals.

A schedule of upcoming films is available at the Roxie's official Web site, *www.roxie.com.*

Yerba Buena Center for the Arts

If you prefer your experimental art to be within the walls of a museum, consider a stop at the Yerba Buena Center for the Arts in San Francisco's SoMa district (South of Market Street). It's a complex that highlights experimental, marginalized, and emerging artists and features everything from paintings to sculptures to films. Most of the works on display are created by artists who are still living, and San Francisco Bay artists get special attention.

About 250,000 people a year visit YBCA, as it's known among the locals, and corporate sponsors include Citibank and United Airlines—so you know there's something beyond quirky craziness going on within the facility's grounds. Check out current and upcoming exhibits at the center's Web site, *www.ybca.org.*

Lodging and Restaurants

There is no shortage of places to stay or eat in San Francisco. Here are some suggestions you might want to consider. Each suggestion is marked by one, two, or three dollar signs.

For lodging:

$ = a room costs less than $100

$$ = a room costs from $101 to $200

$$$ = a room costs more than $200

For restaurants:

$ = entrées cost less than $15

$$ = entrées cost from $16 to $30

$$$ = entrées cost more than $30

Lodging
Cathedral Hill Hotel
1101 Van Ness Avenue

(415) 776-8200

www.cathedralhillhotel.com

$$

Fairmont San Francisco
950 Mason Street

(415) 772-5000

www.fairmont.com

$$$

Grand Hyatt San Francisco
345 Stockton Street
(415) 398-1234
www.hyatt.com
$$$

Hilton San Francisco
333 O'Farrell Street
(415) 771-1400
www.hilton.com
$$

Holiday Inn Express Hotel & Suites
550 North Point Street
(415) 409-4600
www.ichotelsgroup.com
$$

Holiday Inn—Golden Gateway
1500 Van Ness Avenue
(888) 465-4329
www.goldengatewayhotel.com
$$

Hotel Nikko San Francisco
222 Mason Street
(415) 394-1111
www.hotelnikkosf.com
$$$

Hyatt at Fisherman's Wharf
555 North Point
(415) 563-1234
www.hyatt.com
$$$

InterContinental Mark Hopkins
1 Nob Hill
(415) 392-3434
www.ichotelsgroup.com
$$$

Marriott San Francisco
55 Fourth Street
(415) 896-1600
www.marriott.com
$$

Omni San Francisco Hotel
500 California Street
(415) 677-9494
www.omnihotels.com
$$$

Parc 55 Hotel
55 Cyril Magnin Street
(800) 595-0507
www.parc55hotel.com
$$$

San Francisco Clift
495 Geary Street
(415) 775-4700
www.clifthotel.com
$$$

The Stanford Court
905 California Street
(415) 989-3500
www.marriott.com
$$$

Westin–St. Francis Hotel
335 Powell Street
(415) 397-7000
www.starwoodhotels.com
$$$

Restaurants

A16
2355 Chestnut Street
(415) 771-2216
www.a16sf.com
$$

Asia SF
201 Ninth Street
(415) 255-2742
www.asiasf.com
$$$

Boulevard Restaurant
1 Mission Street
(415) 543-6084
www.boulevardrestaurant.com
$$

The Cheesecake Factory
251 Geary Street, 8th Floor
(415) 391-4444
www.thecheesecakefactory.com
$$

Delfina
3621 18th Street
(415) 552-4055
www.delfinasf.com
$$

Farallon
450 Post Street
(415) 956-6969
www.farallonrestaurant.com
$$$

First Crush Restaurant and Bar
101 Cyril Magnin
(415) 982-7874
www.firstcrush.com
$$

Fleur de Lys
777 Sutter Street
 (415) 673-7779
www.fleurdelyssf.com
$$$

Harris' Restaurant
2100 Van Ness Ave.
(415) 673-1888
www.harrisrestaurant.com
$$$

House of Nanking
919 Kearny Street
(415) 421-1429
$

House of Prime Rib
1906 Van Ness Avenue
(415) 885-4605
www.houseofprimerib.ypguides.net
$$$

Max's Opera Cafe
601 Van Ness Avenue
(415) 771-7300
www.maxsworld.com
$$

Restaurant Gary Danko
800 North Point
(415) 749-2060
www.garydanko.com
$$$

Scoma's
Pier 47 No. 1
(415) 771-4383
www.scomas.com
$$

The Slanted Door
1 Ferry Building No. 3
(415) 861-8032
www.slanteddoor.com
$$

CHAPTER 3

San Francisco Bay Area

SAN FRANCISCO MAY BE THE BIGGEST CITY on San Francisco Bay, but it's certainly not the only one—nor is it the only place near the water where you can find memorable family fun. From the Point Reyes National Seashore on the north side of the water to the city of San Jose to the south, there is a great deal to see and do in the San Francisco Bay area. In a day's time, you can go from serious cultural institutions to an NFL football game to a Humming Toadfish Festival of costumed kazoo players.

Regional Overview

The San Francisco Bay area is somewhat sprawling in terms of geography. It includes areas all around the bay, which adjoins San Pablo Bay to the north. West of San Pablo Bay are places like the Point Reyes National Seashore, which, while not technically connected to San Francisco Bay, is still considered part of the greater bay area. The same is true of the city of San Jose, which is well southeast of San Francisco Bay but is a major community in the region.

The three main cities in the San Francisco Bay Area are San Jose, Oakland, and Sausalito. Oakland is probably the best known to tourists because it's the home of the National Football League's Oakland Raiders, which have won three Super Bowls and sent seventeen team members to the NFL's Hall of Fame, including coach John Madden, known today for his video games and play-by-play analysis on television. That's not to say that San Jose or Sausalito are any less interesting than Oakland, of course. They just aren't towns that most people see on television every Sunday afternoon while they tailgate and indulge in bratwursts.

You could spend a few hours or a few days in any of the San Francisco Bay area's major towns and hot spots, depending on what kind of activities you and your family enjoy.

San Jose

San Jose is the third-largest city in California, with even more residents than San Francisco. It started out as a farming community and then boomed after World War II, becoming home to countless high-tech workers and their families during the dot-com days of the 1980s. Even today, its unofficial nickname is the capital of Silicon Valley. It is consistently ranked as one of the safest large cities in the United States. San Jose is a "short" city, with a permanent restriction on the heights of buildings because the city itself lies in the flight path of nearby Mineta San José International Airport.

≡FAST FACT

San Jose, which is Spanish for Saint Joseph, is the most commonplace name in the world. Northern California's San Jose is the largest city by this name, with just shy of 1 million residents, but you can also find towns called San Jose in Argentina, Belize, Colombia, Costa Rica, Guatemala, Mexico, Panama, Paraguay, the Philippines, and Uruguay.

National Hockey League fans will know the city from its San Jose Sharks, who play at the HP Pavilion at San Jose—more commonly called the Shark Tank. But culture abounds in this city, too, from an opera house to a youth theater company. If you want to plan a day out of the sun in northern California, San Jose is a good bet. There are a lot of indoor offerings for all tastes—and plenty of places that cater to kids as well as adults.

Getting Around

You may have seen photographs of historic streetcars riding around the streets of San Jose, but don't count on them unless you plan to visit during a holiday, which is the only time they run from the San Jose History Museum. Your best bet for public transportation in San Jose is the bus system run by VTA—the Valley Transportation Authority. It has schedules, maps, and fares on its Web site at *www.vta.org.*

There is an extensive freeway system in San Jose, so driving a car here won't be much worse than doing so in any other major U.S. city. Just be prepared to have to jostle or pay for parking.

HP Pavilion at San Jose

The HP Pavilion is best known as the home of the San Jose Sharks, but the site also hosts as many as 180 other events every year. The $162 million entertainment complex has close to 20,000 spectator seats, making it a venue for top acts from around the world.

Check out the schedule of upcoming events at the official Web site, *www.hppsj.com.* Look for everything from singers such as Justin Timberlake and Jennifer Lopez to ice shows and, of course, sporting events.

 TRAVEL TIP

While the HP Pavilion has nearly 20,000 spectator seats, it has only 1,500 parking spaces on-site. You can either jockey for spots in the nearby lots, or take public transit trains to the San Jose Diridon Station, which is across the street from the arena. When Sharks games run late, train service runs late as well. Valley Transit Authority buses also service the San Jose Diridon Station.

Children's Discovery Museum

The Children's Discovery Museum is a big purple building, which should tell you right away that this is no ordinary museum experience. It opened in 1990 and expanded in 1997, offering interactive exhibits that have garnered many awards. It is one of *Child* magazine's ten best children's museums.

In the Wonder Cabinet area alone, you'll find a crawlspace devoted to language development, a magical forest meant to encourage literacy, a hands-on art studio, a dress-up area meant for dramatic play, and an area filled with blocks to help with cognitive development. Then there's Bubbalogna, where kids learn about physics by playing with bubbles. There's also an on-site theater for when your little ones need a few minutes to sit down and recharge. The museum's official Web site, *www.cdm.org*, lists many more exhibits and provides links to parent resources that you can use with your children at home.

Tech Museum of Innovation

Much like the Children's Discovery Museum, the Tech Museum of Innovation is a hands-on adventure. Its goal is to "inspire the innovator in everyone," with gallery themes that focus on innovation, the Internet, the human body, and exploration. There's also an IMAX theater, and you can purchase combination tickets that will get you into both the museum and the theater.

Exhibits change regularly, but you can expect to encounter sections like Green by Design, which teaches you about renewable resources and how you can make them a part of your life. You can also design your own microchip and get a portrait made by a 3-D laser scanner. One of the great things about the Tech Museum is that you can sample its offerings before you even get there. There are special online exhibits in addition to general information available at *www.thetech.org*.

San Jose Museum of Art

The San Jose Museum of Art is more of a traditional space than the Children's and Tech museums, with major traveling exhibitions and a permanent collection that features paintings, sculptures, photographs, drawings, installations, and new media. There is a particular focus on West Coast artists. For families, a good bet is the museum's Art Education Programs for children and teens. Some of the programs are open only to school groups, but you can request a spot for individual kids by contacting the museum through its Web site, *www.sjmusart.org*.

Oakland

If you're looking for a sunshine-filled spot, look no farther than Oakland, which averages sunshine three-quarters of the time. Perhaps the weather is what has drawn so many people from different backgrounds to the city, where you can hear some 150 languages spoken at any given hour. Ethnic tensions divided the city during the 1980s, and by the 1990s Oakland had become known as the home of rap superstars such as MC Hammer and Tupac Shakur. You also might remember the city from its 1996 school board decision to recognize Ebonics as an ethnolect, or form of ethnic speech.

The downtown area is being revitalized in terms of tourism. Particularly in the Lake Merritt waterfront area, there are lovely sights and activities for the entire family to enjoy. Still, Oakland typically ranks high in terms of crime among U.S. cities. As in any major metropolitan area, you need to be careful.

===FAST FACT

You can't travel to Oakland by commercial liner, although the city is the largest seaport on San Francisco Bay. Oakland was one of the first seaports to update its infrastructure to allow the loading of cargo containers from ships onto either trucks or trains, thus cementing its future as one of the three dominant seaports on the entire West Coast.

Getting Around

The Bay Area Rapid Transit system, or BART, services the city of Oakland with routes that run straight from the international airport in San Francisco. Schedules, routes, and fees are available online at *www.bart.gov*. There is also a public bus service called AC Transit, or Alameda–Contra Costa Transit District. Its Web site for schedules, routes, and fares is *www.actransit.org*.

Lake Merritt, Children's Fairyland, and Jack London Square

Lake Merritt isn't actually a lake. It's a tidal lagoon named for Dr. Samuel Merritt, who lived on the shore, served as mayor, and worked to redirect sewage elsewhere so the lagoon could be enjoyed by locals and visitors alike. Today, the lagoon is a hub of activity for children and adults.

In 1950, Children's Fairyland was constructed as the first theme park in the United States for families with young children. It's still open today, a ten-acre maze of small rides, animals, costumed characters, and a puppet theater. The spot is a speck compared to places like Disneyland; then again, admission is only $6. The park is open year-round, though it closes on some weekdays during the colder months. You can view the official calendar online at *www .fairyland.org*.

Jack London Square, another area of Lake Merritt, is an old warehouse district that has been overtaken and rejuvenated by shops, restaurants, and entertainment. It hosts farmers' markets and artisans' markets, where you can buy everything from local produce to handmade jewelry. Permanent merchants include a movie theater, a jazz club, and chain hotels like Best Western. You can see a complete list of retailers, plus a calendar of upcoming events at the square, online at the official Web site, *www.jacklondonsquare.com*.

Oakland Zoo

The Oakland Zoo was established in 1922 and moved in 1936 to its current home, a 525-acre site in the Knowland Park section of the city. It is home to more than 440 native and exotic animal species, as well as a train, a sky ride, and a section of children's rides.

===FAST FACT

Don't expect just your garden-variety lions, tigers, and bears at the Oakland Zoo. Some of the more exotic species you might encounter include the laughing kookaburra, the white-faced whistling duck, the dromedary camel, the island flying fox, the white-handed gibbon, the bearded dragon, the common chuck-walla, the Gila monster, and the Taiwan beauty snake.

One of the more interesting family programs the zoo offers is its Family Sundown Safari overnight stays. The regular program accepts children six or older, while the Junior Sundown Safari program is for children as young as three. The programs include a twilight tour after the zoo closes to regular guests, plus a campout in the wild with some of the animals (probably not the lions). Go to the zoo's Web site, *www.oaklandzoo.org*, for available family campout dates and general information.

Oakland Museum of California

The Oakland Museum of California is on Lake Merritt and is actually three museums housed under a single roof. It is designed to help visitors understand the Golden State's environment, history, art, and people. It's a beautiful space in and of itself, with sculpture gardens and ponds making up a good deal of its three-level design. Permanent exhibitions include "Walk Across California," which lets you walk through the state's ecosystem and view some 2,500 natural specimens along the way.

Admission is $8 for adults and $5 for students; children younger than six enter for free. Learn more about upcoming events and exhibitions at *www.museumca.org*.

TRAVEL TIP

You can save a few bucks if you visit the Oakland Museum of California on a second Sunday, when it offers free admission for visitors of all ages. On the downside, Sundays are the shortest days of the week in terms of opening hours; entry begins at noon and the museum closes at 5 P.M. The museum is open from 10 A.M. till 5 P.M. Wednesdays through Saturdays but is closed on Mondays and Tuesdays.

McAfee Coliseum and Oracle Arena

In addition to being the home of the NFL's Oakland Raiders, McAfee Coliseum and Oracle Arena also host games for MLB's Oakland A's and the NBA's Golden State Warriors. If you want to get tickets to any home games, you will need to go to the individual team Web sites:

- Oakland Raiders, *www.raiders.com*
- Oakland A's, *http://oakland.athletics.mlb.com*
- Golden State Warriors, *www.nba.com/warriors*

The coliseum and arena also host touring shows and concerts, some of which are suitable for families. Noteworthy recent examples include Disney ice shows and the Hannah Montana tour. You can view a complete list of upcoming events at *www.coliseum.com*, or you can usually purchase tickets directly through Ticketmaster, *www.ticketmaster.com*.

Chinatown

Chinatown in Oakland is more of a general Asian-American neighborhood that is home to Chinese as well as Japanese, Korean, Vietnamese, Thai, and Filipino residents and businesses. Its center is at Eighth and Webster streets, within walking distance of the

Oakland Museum of California, and the whole of the district comprises sixteen blocks. While this Chinatown is smaller than San Francisco's, it is also less touristy and is considered more authentic by many people who visit its shops and restaurants.

Some of the main events held each year include Chinese New Year in late January or early February, the Dragon Boat Race in mid-August, the StreetFest at the end of August, and the Moon Festival in mid- to late September. For information about these events, go to:

- Dragon Boat Race, *www.edragons.org*
- StreetFest, *www.oaklandchinatownstreetfest.com*
- Chinese New Year and Moon Festival, *www.oaklandchina townchamber.org*

If you aren't visiting Chinatown during one of these annual events, you can still wander through the open-air markets that sell everything from live fish to ceramics handcrafted overseas. You can also take a look around the Oakland Asian Cultural Center, which has exhibits, events, and even one-day classes in crafts such as fruit and vegetable carving. For details and hours, check out the center's official Web site at *www.oacc.cc*.

Chabot Space and Science Center

As you might guess based on its name, the Chabot Space and Science Center includes an observatory, a planetarium, exhibits, and a natural park that are designed to teach visitors about planet Earth and the greater universe that surrounds it. There are classes, lectures, shows, and interactive exhibits that offer an array of science and technology-based educational experiences.

One of the more interesting offerings is the Challenger Learning Center, which lets you take part in a simulated space mission. You can be a mission controller or an astronaut, all the while using math, science, and communication skills to solve problems along the ride.

JUST FOR PARENTS

Okay, okay, so kids of all ages can attend the Telescope Maker's Workshop, but with the finished product likely to cost a couple hundred dollars in materials, the odds are you won't want your littlest ones playing with the moving parts. The workshop is available every Friday at the Chabot Science Center from 7 P.M. until 10 P.M., and it's open to anyone.

Another interesting choice is the Tien Megadome Theater, a seventy-foot dome screen that shows films about dinosaurs, the human body, and more. For current exhibits, movies, and general information, go to the museum's Web site at *www.chabotspace.org*.

Sausalito

Sausalito is well known for its communities of houseboats, which took over the abandoned shipyards after World War II and thrived until the 1970s, when waterfront developers retook the area. You might catch a glimpse of some of the remaining houseboats if you choose to visit Sausalito during a ferry ride from San Francisco or as you walk along the waterfront checking out the various shops and restaurants.

If ever you were looking for an eclectic place to explore, Sausalito is the town for you. That's especially true in the summertime, when the drone of the local humming toadfish gets so loud that the locals celebrate it by dressing up in costumes and playing kazoos.

Getting Around

The easiest way to get to Sausalito is on the Blue & Gold Fleet ferry service that runs from San Francisco. Separate fall and summer schedules are posted online at *www.blueandgoldfleet.com*, where you'll also find rates and availability. Once you land in Sausalito, you can enjoy many of the town's offerings on foot. It's also practical to drive to Sausalito.

Sausalito Art Festival

The annual, open-air Sausalito Art Festival draws more people to the city than any other event. It has been held every Labor Day weekend since 1952 and now lures around 50,000 visitors who are interested in contemporary works of art. More than 20,000 works are typically on display, along with three stages' worth of entertainment, gourmet food and wine, and beautiful views of the historic waterfront.

 TRAVEL TIP

If you plan to take the ferry from San Francisco during the Labor Day art festival, consider buying tickets online in advance at *www.blueandgoldfleet.com*. Spots on the ferry fill up quickly. You can also take a bus; check out Golden Gate Transit, *www.goldengatetransit.org*.

Lest you think the Sausalito Art Festival is just for adults, there are specific activities for children, who can attend the festival for free through age five, and for just $5 from ages six through twelve. You can learn more at the festival's official Web site, *www.sausalitoartfestival .org*.

Bay Area Discovery Museum

The family-friendly Bay Area Discovery Museum has won countless accolades and awards. *Parents* magazine dubbed it a must-see museum, and *North Bay Bohemian* named it a best place to inspire your kids in both 2005 and 2006. Exhibits are specifically designed for children in the six-month to eight-year age range, and nursing is allowed anywhere inside or outside of the museum. Admission is $8.50 for adults and $7.50 for children.

Permanent exhibitions include Lookout Cove, a two-and-a-half-acre outdoor exploration area where kids can climb onboard a fishing boat or hike a family-friendly trail. There are two art studios on site—one for children younger than five and the other for older kids—that offer everything from painting to ceramics. There's also a performing arts theater where you and your children can watch puppets, dancers, storytellers, and circus acts.

 RAINY DAY FUN

The Bay Area Discovery Museum has daily drop-in programs that include demonstrations and hands-on activities for kids. Some of the programs include boat building, ornament making, marionette making, and collage. For a list of dates, go to the museum's Web site at *www.baykidsmuseum.org.*

Even if you can't make it to the Bay Area Discovery Museum during your vacation, you can still download some of its learning opportunities from its Web site, *www.baykidsmuseum.org.* There's a special section for homeschoolers, as well.

Bay Model Visitor Center

It's not every day that you think of the U.S. Army Corps of Engineers as a tourism organization, but in the San Francisco Bay Area, the group administers the Bay Model Visitor Center—a working hydraulic model of the bay and the Sacramento–San Joaquin River delta system. It is capable of simulating tides and currents, encompassing an area of about an acre and a half.

Many technical groups and scientific experts tour the center to gain a better understanding of the local ecosystem, but you can also take versions of the tours that are accessible to people with all levels of education. Your kids can even become junior rangers by using a booklet that is downloadable from the Web site, *www.spn.usace.army.mil/bmvc.*

≡FAST FACT

The U.S. military used the Bay Model as a working laboratory from 1954 until 2000, when high-speed computers became capable of performing the same kinds of experiments that engineers and scientists used to do at the model itself. Some of the theories that were tested at the facility include how to collect and store fresh water and how to keep the environment clean for future generations.

Point Reyes National Seashore

If your family enjoys outdoor exploration rather than museums, head straight for the Point Reyes National Seashore. It comprises some 65,000 acres that are administered by the National Park Service, offering everything from hiking and camping to ranger-guided programs that the whole family can enjoy.

Depending on the time of year, you'll have an interesting choice of animals and more to watch in the wilderness:

- From January through April, you can see the gray whales migrating along the coastline.
- From December through March, you can watch the elephant seals breed in a large colony.
- From March through May, and again from August through December, you can see various species of migrating birds.
- From March through June, you can see what the park service calls harbor seal pupping, which means the young ones are learning their way around the water.
- From April through May, you can enjoy the peak flower season.

Two major manmade annual events also take place at Point Reyes National Seashore: the Big Time Festival in July and the Sand Sculpture Contest in September. The Big Time Festival focuses on Native American culture and history, while the Sand Sculpture Contest offers prizes in various age divisions.

 TRAVEL TIP

If you're looking for an authentic backcountry camping experience, then Point Reyes National Seashore is a good place to go. Its campsites—which take reservations and fill up fast—are accessible only by foot, bicycle, horseback, or kayak. If you want to park a car or an RV, you'll have to stay at a campsite outside the park itself. Learn more about the available sites and rates at *www.nps.gov*.

For those families who just prefer to wander, 147 miles of trails are great for hiking, bicycle riding, and horseback riding. Seven of the trails take less than an hour to traverse, so even the littlest of legs won't get too tired. For more serious hikers, there are six trails that take from three to six hours to complete.

Don Edwards San Francisco Bay National Wildlife Refuge

This national wildlife refuge spans some 30,000 acres that are beloved by bird-watchers, who flock to see about 280 different species flying overhead and nesting each year. During the spring and fall migration seasons, there are literally millions of shorebirds and waterfowl here. The site is named for former U.S. Representative Don Edwards, a Democrat who worked to protect the wetlands in South San Francisco Bay.

There is a visitor center on site as well as an Environmental Education Center, which is meant to be a classroom and hosts school field trips and weekend interpretive programs for the public. Some of the programs include guided nature walks and tours led by naturalists and rangers, but you can also explore the refuge's trails with a map from the visitor center. If you bring your kayak or canoe, you can use one of the public launch ramps.

 JUST FOR PARENTS

Waterfowl hunting is allowed at the Don Edwards San Francisco Bay National Wildlife Refuge from mid-October until mid-January. Most of the hunting areas are accessible only by boat, and you will need a special-use permit before you start shooting. Details about hunting-accessible areas, as well as links for permits, are available at the refuge's Web site, *www.fws.gov/desfbay*.

Check the refuge's Web site, *www.fws.gov/desfbay*, for information about upcoming programs. Some examples of programs include "ABCs of Raptors," "Exploring Owls," and "Marsh Mud Mania."

Silicon Valley

Many, many people who visit northern California stop at the local gas stations to ask, "Which way to Silicon Valley?"

The truth is, you aren't going to find Silicon Valley on a map. It's an idea, a region of techno-thinkers, if you will, more than a destination with geographic borders. The closest you're likely to come to experiencing the Silicon Valley lifestyle is a visit to the Tech Museum of Innovation in San Jose, or a drive past the vast Googleplex campus. The Googleplex is probably northern California's best-known institutional monument to all things Internet, but it's not open for tours (unless you learn the secret code for making it to the top of the searchable rankings). Even so, the Silicon Valley set have built a couple of museums that pay homage to the technological revolution that made the World Wide Web the force it is today.

Computer History Museum

The Computer History Museum is about a fifteen-minute drive west of San Jose in the town of Mountain View. Its motto is "Where Computing Lives," and it lives up to that slogan with exhibits about the creation of computers, silicon chips, the Internet, and more. It has been in its "first phase" opening state since 2003, with plans to expand its existing 9,000-square-foot space into even more galleries.

In addition to seeing "pre-computer computers," you can enjoy rotating lectures on computing's past, present, and future. Hours are Wednesday, Friday, and Sunday from 1 P.M. to 4 P.M., and Saturday from 11 A.M. till 5 P.M. More information is available at the appropriately accessible Web site *www.computerhistory.org*.

Tech Museum of Innovation

The Tech Museum of Innovation in San Jose focuses not just on how technology works, but also on how it affects people's lives. There are many interactive exhibits in the 132,000-square-foot facility, including ones focusing on space and the human body. For more information, go to *www.thetech.org*.

Lodging and Restaurants

There is no shortage of places to stay or eat in the San Francisco Bay Area. Here are some suggestions you might want to consider. Each suggestion is marked by one, two, or three dollar signs.

For lodging:
$ = a room costs less than $100
$$ = a room costs from $101to $200
$$$ = a room costs more than $200

For restaurants:
$ = entrées cost less than $15

$$ = entrées cost from $16 to $30

$$$ = entrées cost more than $30

Lodging

SAN JOSE

Fairmont San Jose
170 South Market Street
(408) 998-1900
www.fairmont.com
$$$

Hotel De Anza
233 West Santa Clara Street
(408) 286-1000
www.hoteldeanza.com
$$

Hotel Montgomery
211 South First Street
(408) 282-8800
www.jdvhotels.com
$$$

Hotel Valencia
355 Santana Row
(408) 551-0010
www.sanjose.hotelvalencia.com
$$$

San Jose Marriott
301 South Market Street
(408) 280-1300
www.sanjosemarriott.com
$$$

OAKLAND
Executive Inn & Suites
1755 Embarcadero
(800) 346-6331
www.executiveinnoakland.com
$$

Jack London Inn
444 Embarcadero West
(800) 549-8780
www.jacklondoninn.com
$

Oakland Marriott City Center
1001 Broadway
(510) 835-3466
www.marriott.com
$$$

The Washington Inn
495 Tenth Street
(510) 452-1776
www.thewashingtoninn.com
$$

Waterfront Plaza
10 Washington Street
(510) 836-3800
www.jdvhotels.com
$$$

SAUSALITO
Casa Madrona
801 Bridgeway Avenue
(800) 288-0502

www.casamadrona.com
$$$

Gables Inn Sausalito
62 Princess Street
(415) 289-1100
www.gablesinnsausalito.com
$$$

Hotel Sausalito
16 El Portal, Sausalito
(888) 442-0700
www.hotelsausalito.com
$$

The Inn above Tide
30 El Portal
(800) 893-8433
www.innabovetide.com
$$$

TIBURON
The Lodge at Tiburon
1651 Tiburon Boulevard
(415) 435-3133
www.thelodgeattiburon.com
$$

Restaurants

SAN JOSE
Arcadia
100 West San Carlos Street
(408) 278-4555
www.michaelmina.net
$$–$$$

Blowfish Sushi
355 Santana Row
(408) 345-3848
www.blowfishsushi.com
$$$

Habana Cuba
238 Race Street
(408) 998-2822
www.998cuba.com
$$

Left Bank
377 Santana Row
(408) 984-3500
www.leftbank.com
$$

Original Joe's Italian Restaurant
301 South First Street
(888) 841-7030
www.originaljoes.com
$$

OAKLAND
BayWolf Restaurant
3853 Piedmont Avenue
(510) 655-6004
www.baywolf.com
$$

Citron
5484 College Avenue
(510) 653-5484
www.citronrestaurant.com
$$

Le Cheval
1007 Clay Street
(510) 763-8495
www.lecheval.com
$–$$

Oliveto Café & Restaurant
5655 College Avenue
(510) 547-5356
www.oliveto.com
$$

Yoshi's Japanese
510 Embarcadero West
(510) 238-9200
www.yoshis.com
$–$$

SAUSALITO
Horizons
558 Bridgeway
(415) 331-3232
www.horizonssausalito.com
$$

Poggio
777 Bridgeway
(415) 332-7771
www.poggiotrattoria.com
$$

Scoma's Sausalito
588 Bridgeway
(415) 332-9551
www.scomassausalito.com
$$–$$$

The Spinnaker
100 Spinnaker Drive
(415) 332-1500
www.thespinnaker.com
$$

MUIR BEACH
The Pelican Inn
10 Pacific Way
(415) 383-6000
www.pelicaninn.com
$$

CHAPTER 4

Smart Spots to See

NORTHERN CALIFORNIA INSTITUTIONS such as Stanford University and Fresno State aren't typically promoted for vacationers in the same way as Yosemite National Park and Napa Valley, but if your kids are older—or particularly brainy—then university campuses can be really smart spots to visit during a family vacation. Not only do these institutions have lectures, displays, concerts, athletics, and other events on their schedules, but they also can pique the interest of high school students and help them to see learning as a path to cool colleges.

Why Visit Universities?

If you're the parent of a high school sophomore or junior, then you're probably already thinking about planning road trips to the colleges and universities of your child's choice. Visiting campuses is important both for you and for your children, in part so that you can make sure your son or daughter is going to be someplace safe and in keeping with your values, and in part to whet your teenager's appetite for wanting to live and study away from home for the first time.

Northern California has an abundance of state and private universities—not to mention world-renowned libraries and museums on various campuses—that can make excellent destinations as part of your family's broader vacation plan. Whether you have a couple of older kids or just one with a few younger children following close behind, a day at the University of California at Berkeley or the California Maritime Academy can be an interesting way to work education into your vacation mix.

 TRAVEL TIP

If your child has certain educational interests but isn't sure which northern California school might be a good fit, then visit the Web site *www.californiacolleges.edu* before you visit any colleges. The site helps prospective students identify their educational areas of interest and then matches those interests to the programs offered by leading universities in the Golden State.

Proper tours of college campuses are one option—and usually must be scheduled in advance of your arrival—but there are also plenty of events taking place on northern California campuses that can be fun for your family whether your child is interested in attending a particular university or not. This chapter takes a look at some of the larger campuses in the region, as well as on- and off-campus museums and institutions that might be of interest to children of all ages.

University of California at Berkeley

The University of California at Berkeley is a 178-acre oasis in the middle of San Francisco's busy suburbs, about a half hour's drive from San Francisco International Airport. It has long been known for its liberal bent, as is much of the broader San Francisco area. UC Berkeley (as the locals call it) has also long been well respected for the quality of its libraries, which draw researchers from all over the world.

Organized tours include free walking tours, fee-based electric cart tours, and reservation-only group tours. The university's museums house some eighty different collections, including six separate natural history museums focusing on everything from botany to paleontology. There are also regularly scheduled theater and musical performances, plus intercollegiate sporting events ranging from football to water polo.

Getting to UC Berkeley

As with many college campuses nowadays, parking is pretty tough to find at Berkeley. The college recommends public transportation, in particular buses and trains.

- The Bay Area Rapid Transit system, or BART, operates trains from several locations including San Francisco International Airport. The Berkeley BART station is a mile and a half from the campus. You can get additional information and schedules at *www.bart.gov.*
- The AC Transit system provides bus service to several stops that are within walking distance of the UC Berkeley campus. University administrators recommend the following lines: 65, 52, 51, 43, 40, 15, 9, F, and U. You can view maps and get more information at *www.actransit.org.*

Once you're in the city of Berkeley, you can make the campus part of a day's touring. The city has a lot to offer beyond the world-renowned university's gates, everything from tours of the Scharffen Berger Chocolate Maker (*www.artisanconfection.com*) to the Adventure Playground (*www.ci.berkeley.ca.us*) at Berkeley Marina, where the rides are free for kids as long as they're accompanied by adults.

 JUST FOR PARENTS

After a day of touring the UC Berkeley campus with the kids, consider a stop at Takara Sake USA. It's a brewery that houses a contemporary, Japanese-style sake-tasting room in keeping with the brewery's name, which is Japanese for "treasure from the rice paddy." Tastings are free and the room is open daily from noon until 6 P.M. Learn more at the brewery's Web site, *www.takarasake.com.*

Organized Tours

Students from UC Berkeley give free tours for groups of ten or fewer people every day, seven days a week. No reservations are required. Monday through Saturday, the tours begin at 10 A.M., and on Sundays, the tours begin at 1 P.M. Weekday tours leave from the Visitor Center at University Hall, while weekend tours depart from Sather Tower in the middle of the UC Berkeley Campus. Group tours leave more frequently, but they require reservations and cost $50 for up to thirty-five people, $70 for up to fifty people, $90 for up to seventy people, and $110 for up to 100 people.

Electric cart tours of the campus are another option if you prefer not to walk and are willing to pay the $50 fee. The tours take an hour, and each cart holds as many as five people. You must make a reservation at least two weeks in advance, and the cart tours run only during certain weeks of each semester. For upcoming dates and departure schedules, go to the UC Berkeley Web site, *www.berkeley.edu*.

Museums and Cultural Events

UC Berkeley has tons of museums, performances, and libraries where you can find interesting speakers and exhibits. A few in particular might be worth checking out during a family vacation, since kids generally have a hard time saying no to things like dinosaurs and music concerts.

University of California Museum of Paleontology

The Museum of Paleontology is primarily a research facility, but the public does have free access to some pretty cool fossil exhibits during any hours when the Valley Life Sciences building is open. Typically, that means Monday through Thursday from 8 A.M. till 10 P.M., Friday from 8 A.M. till 5 P.M., Saturday from 10 A.M. till 5 P.M., and Sunday from 1 P.M. till 10 P.M. Some of the exhibits include a life-size *Tyrannosaurus rex* and the skull of a *Triceratops horridus*—which will capture the imaginations of any children who have ever read a dinosaur book or seen a movie such as *Jurassic Park*.

Berkeley Art Museum and Pacific Film Archive

This is one of the largest university art museums in the United States, containing the largest collection of Japanese films outside the nation of Japan as well as films from every movie-making country in the world. The museum's galleries are open every day except for Monday and Tuesday. Admission is $8 for adults, $5 for students between thirteen and seventeen years old, and free for kids younger than twelve. Theater tickets are an additional expense; adults are charged $9.50 and children seventeen and younger are charged $6.50. The museum exhibits and film offerings rotate frequently, so your best bet is to check the museum's Web site before visiting. It's at *www.bampfa.berkeley.edu*.

Cal Performances

Cal Performances is responsible for bringing dance, music, and theater shows to the UC Berkeley campus. Expect to see new acts as well as names you may recognize from worldwide tours such as the Joffrey Ballet, cellist Yo-Yo Ma, author Garrison Keillor, singer Arlo Guthrie, and saxophonist Sonny Rollins. There are four venues for performances: Zellerbach Auditorium, Zellerbach Playhouse, Hearst Greek Theatre, and Wheeler Auditorium. To view a schedule of upcoming shows at each location or to order tickets online, go to *www.calperfs.berkeley.edu*.

RAINY DAY FUN

For an exciting afternoon of sports at a reasonable price, you can't do better than the Golden Bears' women's basketball team. The program has produced two Olympians, including one who took home a gold medal. Family ticket packages are available, giving you general admission for two adults and three children for $25 (and an extra $1 for each additional child). Single-game tickets for each season typically go on sale around mid-November.

Sporting Events

Berkeley is a member of the PAC-10 Conference for intercollegiate sports. The site *calbears.ctsv.com* is the official home of most of the university's teams, known as the California Golden Bears. Tickets are available through the Web site for pretty much any sport you can think of, from men's football and basketball to women's gymnastics and soccer. If you're interested in water polo, swimming, or diving events, there is a separate Web site for information: *www.calaquatics.com*.

Stanford University

Stanford University is about forty miles southeast of San Francisco and twenty miles northwest of San Jose. The closest major city to this private university is Palo Alto, part of the high-tech corridor in northern California. That helps to make clear Stanford's reputation for programs in business, engineering, and science.

Known as "the farm," the campus offers five different kinds of organized tours, both on foot and in golf carts. You'll also find the Cantor Arts Center on the campus, live theater and musical productions, and the nearby Hanna House, a Frank Lloyd Wright design that was restored and opened for tours in 1999 after it was damaged in a severe earthquake. The Stanford Cardinal teams compete at everything from lacrosse to rowing.

Getting to Stanford

As with the University of California at Berkeley, Stanford University has extremely limited parking on-site. If you absolutely must drive to the campus, you will need to get a "special event" daily permit or park in one of the metered spaces that accept cash or credit cards. If you want to get a permit in advance via the Internet, go to *www.stanford.edu*.

Public transportation is much easier. There are several ways to get close to the campus:

- BART train system
- Caltrain commuter rail service

- Santa Clara Valley Transportation Authority (VTA) buses
- SamTrans buses, which connect to San Francisco International Airport
- Altamont Commuter Express (ACE) trains
- Dumbarton Express trains
- AC Transit service, which runs a special Line U Stanford Express route on weekdays

If you're not sure which mode of transit is best from your starting point, go to the helpful planning Web site *www.transit.511.org.*

Once you're at your chosen line's closest stop to the Stanford campus, you can make use of the university's free shuttle bus system, the Marguerite Shuttle. It runs year-round Monday through Friday, and it offers evening and weekend service from September through June (when school is typically in session). For schedules and stops, go to *transportation.stanford.edu.*

 TRAVEL TIP

If you plan to visit the city of Palo Alto in addition to the Stanford University campus, your best bet is to park your car in the city and use the city's Free Shuttle, a bus service with two separate lines to get you around town. The Palo Alto Free Shuttle connects to the university's Marguerite shuttle line at the Palo Alto Transit Center, so you can get to and from the campus for free without having to worry about parking.

Organized Tours

Guided walking tours of the Stanford campus are offered nearly year-round, twice a day, seven days a week. They depart at 11 A.M. and 3:15 P.M. The tours are free and no reservations are required as long as you have fewer than ten people in your group. If you have ten people, you need to make reservations for a private tour; prices start at $60 per tour for up to twenty people.

If you prefer to walk instead of ride, you can take a golf cart tour of the campus. Tours leave at 1 P.M. daily almost year-round, and the $5-per-person fee is waived for anyone who is mobility impaired, as well as for that person's companion. You can also tour the residence halls at Stanford each Monday and Friday beginning at noon. Reservations are required, and you have to have a prospective student with you to secure a space. For additional tour information and reservations, go to the university's Web site, *www.stanford.edu.*

Museums and Cultural Events

Stanford hosts a lot of one-night-only events featuring everything from lectures to concerts. There are seminars about subjects such as clean energy as well as faculty readings of books and other works. For an up-to-date list of events taking place during your planned travel dates, go to *events.stanford.edu.* There also are several major campus centers that feature the arts as well as architecture. Three of those that might interest your family the most are Stanford Lively Arts, the Cantor Arts Center, and Hanna House.

 JUST FOR PARENTS

Stanford Lively Arts has many productions that are open to children and adults alike, but some performances are specifically noted as being suitable for adults only. In addition, the box office requests that you notify them about children who will be attending when you purchase your ticket so they can help you make the best possible seat selection depending on the child's age and level of attentiveness during longer performances.

Stanford Lively Arts

Lively Arts brings three or four dozen performing artists to the Stanford campus each year. You can see everything from jazz pianists to dance troupes at five venues: Dinkelspiel Auditorium, Frost Amphitheater, Memorial Auditorium, Memorial Church, and Pigott Theater. Some recent noteworthy offerings included "An Evening with Spike Lee," the Jazz at Lincoln Center Orchestra with Wynton Marsalis, and Roseanne Cash. There are graphics depicting each theater and its seating sections at the Web site *livelyarts.stanford.edu*, where you also can purchase tickets before your visit and view a schedule of upcoming events.

Cantor Center for Visual Arts

There are twenty-seven galleries at the Cantor Center, some of them featuring works by world-famous artists such as Jasper Johns and Georgia O'Keeffe. You can see the largest collection of Rodin bronze sculptures outside of Paris, take a tour with a museum docent, or sit in on gallery lectures.

Admission is free, and the museum is open Wednesday through Sunday, including Easter Sunday and the Fourth of July holiday. You can view lists of special seminars, lectures, and changing exhibitions at *museum.stanford.edu*. The Web site also includes a list of upcoming films as well as classes specifically designed for children.

Hanna House

The Frank Lloyd Wright-designed Hanna House is located just off campus and served for years as the home of the university's provosts. It was designed in the 1930s for Paul Hanna, a university professor who needed a home for his family of five. Today, Hanna House is a National Historic Landmark with tours available by appointment on the first and third Sunday or the second and fourth Thursday of each month. Tours take an hour, you must wear soft-soled shoes, and children younger than twelve are not allowed to attend. The cost is $10 per person, plus $5 for parking. Learn more at *www.stanford.edu*.

≡≡≡**FAST FACT**

Unlike most colleges and universities, Stanford does not have an official mascot. The Stanford Cardinal is a reference to the school color of red. There is a tree on the school's logo, which is an "S," but the tree is a redwood that is also part of the city of Palo Alto's logo. According to the university, the tree is not a mascot but instead is a member of the band. There's no word on what instrument the redwood plays.

Sporting Events

The Stanford Cardinal teams have their own Web site, *gostan ford.cstv.com*, where you can learn about individual sports, check upcoming game schedules, and purchase tickets online. Whether it's fencing or field hockey, baseball or golf, you'll find it here.

Sacramento State

Sacramento State is one of the largest campuses in the entire California State University system. Currently, the campus comprises some 300 acres. There's an initiative under way to add a new Science and Space Center with a planetarium, as well as new athletics facilities, by 2010.

Interestingly, though the university sits in the state capital city, political science is not one of the most popular undergraduate programs. Instead, many of the students attending Sacramento State choose to study education, business, computer technology, criminal justice, psychology, or communications. Individual, group, and self-guided tours are available. While cultural events do take place on campus, they are not as well promoted as athletics, which are a main draw.

Getting to Sacramento State

The university recommends driving, with entrances at either the north or south end of the campus. Sacramento State is easily accessible from Highway 50 or Highway 80, and you can find detailed directions posted at the college's official Web site, *www .csus.edu*. Parking costs $2.75, and daily permits are available at kiosks in the parking lots. You'll also find parking information at the booths located at both entrances to the campus.

Organized Tours

Individuals and families with no more than five people are eligible for free, one-hour guided tours of the campus. Tours are available weekdays, leaving at 9 A.M. and 1 P.M. The college tries to limit each group to twenty-five people, so reservations are required—and you are asked to bring your confirmation with you. To fill out the reservation form online and print out your confirmation receipt, go to the page for future students at *www.csus.edu* and click on "tours." Group tours are also available through the online reservation system, which takes requests for weekday slots between 9 A.M. and 4 P.M. These tours are specifically recommended for prospective students.

 TRAVEL TIP

If you're visiting Sacramento State with younger children, the college suggests that you take a self-guided tour. There are downloadable maps on the Web site and at the information desk on campus at Sacramento Hall. Individual and group tours are geared toward prospective students, so younger children's legs may not be able to keep up with the pace.

Sporting Events

Sacramento State is a Division I school, and most teams compete in the Big Sky Conference. Football is an exception; Sacramento State competes at the Division 1-AA level. Historically, Sacramento State has been a dominant force in women's sports, winning national championships in golf, volleyball, and softball. Of late, the men's divisions of tennis, golf, and track and field have taken home conference championships.

You can find upcoming schedules, team information, and ticket information at the Web site, *www.hornetsports.com*. If your kids want to participate in the action, you'll also find links to youth camps in soccer, tennis, and more. Some of the camps last just a few days, possibly coinciding with your vacation plans.

California Maritime Academy

Cal Maritime, as it's known around campus, is the only degree-granting maritime academy on the West Coast. It's located in the city of Vallejo, just south of the Napa wine region. Its hands-on learning facilities include the nearly 500-foot-long training ship *Golden Bear*, affectionately known as "Square Bear" because of its hulking profile.

Cal Maritime offers a limited number of specialized bachelor's degrees, including:

- Business administration
- Facilities engineering technology
- Global studies and maritime affairs
- Marine engineering technology
- Marine transportation
- Mechanical engineering

While the Cal Maritime campus is not known for its arts or athletic events, it does have tours that include a walk onboard the *Golden Bear*—something no other northern California campus offers.

Getting to the California Maritime Academy

Cal Maritime is not far off Interstate 80, and visitors are welcome to park on campus. There are also several public transportation options, all of which run into the city of Vallejo and some of which get closer to the campus than others. For most visitors, especially those coming from San Francisco, the best—and most interesting—transit option is the Blue & Gold Fleet's ferry service, which stops right in Vallejo about two miles from the Cal Maritime campus. You'll have to call a cab or drive from there. Directions and parking information are online at *www.csum.edu.*

Organized Tours

All tours are on a reservation-based system, with an online form that you must fill out in advance so that the university can comply with federal security regulations regarding tours of the T.S. *Golden Bear.* In addition to filling out the online form for each member of your party, you also must bring photo identification with you in order to take the full tour including the training ship, which is on campus eight months a year and on mission at sea from May through August.

 TRAVEL TIP

The training ship *Golden Bear* is not accessible to people who use wheelchairs or are severely mobility impaired. To get on and off the ship, you have to walk from a pier down a sloping gangway with handrails. There also are several steep staircases onboard that are not suitable for mobility-impaired people or small children.

The guided tours are available Monday through Friday at 10:30 A.M., beginning at Cal Maritime's Office of Admission. Tours do not operate during holidays or academic breaks, which are listed on the online calendar at *www.csum.edu.*

Fresno State

California State University at Fresno has a 388-acre main campus on the northeast edge of the city of Fresno. Fresno State's business school is frequently ranked as one of the best in the western United States. There's also a 1,011-acre farm for students, which makes sense given that the San Joaquin Valley is a substantial agricultural region.

The Department of Physics has its own planetarium, which includes a seventy-four-seat theater and shows that are open to the public. There are also a large convention and concert hall on campus and an art gallery.

Getting to Fresno State

If you plan to visit Fresno State from San Francisco, consider staying overnight. The drive will take three to four hours each way. Driving is recommended over public transportation from places like San Francisco and San Jose, and there are downloadable maps for you to print out from the university's official Web site, *www.csufresno.edu*. From San Francisco, the bulk of your drive will be on Interstate 580 (about forty-five miles) and Highway 99 (nearly 110 miles).

Organized Tours

Whether you want to take an individual or a family tour of the Fresno State campus, you will need to make reservations online at least two weeks in advance. Tours are offered Monday through Friday beginning at 10 A.M. or 1 P.M. Individual tours leave from the Smittcamp Alumni House, and group tours depart from the Joyal Administration Building. There is no posted fee for either type of tour, and Saturday tours may be available by request.

If one of your children is a prospective Fresno State student, you can also request an additional tour of any given academic departments. Again, you must reserve your guide in advance. You can do so online at *www.gotofresnostate.com*.

Museums and Cultural Events

The biggest hot spot in town is the Save Mart Center, which can hold as many as 18,000 people. Fresno State's basketball teams play here, but during most of the year the venue is used for concerts and events. The Downing Planetarium is smaller but just as interesting.

Save Mart Center

Save Mart Supermarkets paid some $40 million to have its name on this center for two decades. Pepsi paid about the same amount for exclusive rights to beverage distribution inside, so don't even think about ordering a Coke or a Sprite.

Save Mart Center's size attracts big name talent such as Elton John, The Rolling Stones, and Madonna. In addition to concerts, the center is home to the Fresno State Bulldog basketball teams and the Fresno Falcons, a minor league ice hockey team affiliated with the National Hockey League's San Jose Sharks.

 RAINY DAY FUN

If your vacation happens to coincide with one of your children's birthdays, you can arrange for a birthday party during a Fresno Falcon game at the Save Mart Center. Packages include ten tickets, birthday pucks, a goodie bag, a T-shirt, a birthday card from the team, and a center-ice celebration during intermission. Details are at www.pumpitupparty.com.

Downing Planetarium

The Downing Planetarium is just north of the Fresno State Science Building. It opened in 2000 and now offers public shows on Friday nights and Saturday afternoons. Expect to see titles such as *Destination: Pluto* and *Stella: Adventures of a Black Hole.*

If you plan to visit with a group, you'll need to make a reservation through the planetarium's Web site, *www.downing-planetarium.org.* Individual tickets can be purchased on-site and cost $5 per adult or $2.50 for children between the ages of three and eighteen. Parking is free in campus lots O and P, which you can view on a downloadable map at the same Web site. Reservations are not required, but they are suggested. The planetarium will hold your family's tickets at the door until ten minutes before any scheduled showtime.

Sporting Events

Fresno State's athletic teams are called the Bulldogs, and they compete in the NCAA's Division I league. All the university's squads are featured on the official Web site *gobulldogs.cstv.com*, where you can find events schedules, links to purchase tickets, and tips on how to become part of the "Red Wave" that supports all of Fresno State's student athletes.

Lodging and Restaurants

There is no shortage of places to eat or stay in northern California. Here are some suggestions you might want to consider. Each suggestion is marked by one, two, or three dollar signs.

For lodging:
$ = a room costs less than $100
$$ = a room costs from $101 $200
$$$ = a room costs more than $200

For restaurants:
$ = entrées cost less than $15
$$ = entrées cost from $16 to $30
$$$ = entrées cost more than $30

Lodging

BERKELEY
Claremont Resort & Spa
41 Tunnel Road
(510) 843-3000
www.claremontresort.com
$$$

Doubletree Hotel & Executive Meeting Center Berkeley Marina
200 Marina Boulevard
(510) 548-7920
http://doubletree1.hilton.com
$$

EMERYVILLE
Woodfin Suites
5800 Shellmound
(888) 433-9042
www.woodfinsuitehotels.com
$$–$$$

PALO ALTO
Garden Court
520 Cowper Street
(650) 322-9000
www.gardencourt.com
$$$

Sheraton Palo Alto Hotel
625 El Camino Real
(650) 328-2800
www.starwoodhotels.com
$$$

The Westin Palo Alto
675 El Camino Real
(650) 321-4422
www.starwoodhotels.com
$$$

SACRAMENTO
Doubletree Hotel Sacramento
2001 Point West Way
(916) 929-8855
www.doubletree1.hilton.com
$$

Holiday Inn Sacramento
300 J Street
(916) 446-0100
www.sacramentohi.com
$$

Red Lion Hotel
1401 Arden Way
(916) 922-8041
www.redlion.rdln.com
$

VALLEJO
Best Western Inn & Suites at Discovery Kingdom
1596 Fairgrounds Drive
(707) 554-9655
www.bestwestern.com
$

Quality Inn Vallejo
44 Admiral Callaghan Lane
(866) 643-1061
www.qualityinn-vallejo.com
$

Ramada Inn Vallejo
1000 Admiral Callaghan Lane
(707) 643-2700
www.ramadainnvallejo.com
$

FRESNO
ExtendedStay America—Fresno North
7135 North Fresno Street
(559) 438-7105

www.extendedstayamerica.com
$

La Quinta Inn Fresno Yosemite
2926 Tulare
(559) 442-1110
www.lq.com
$

Piccadilly Inn—University Hotel
4961 North Cedar
(559) 224-2400
www.piccadillyinn.com
$$

Restaurants

BERKELEY
Adagia
2700 Bancroft Way
(510) 647-2300
www.adagiarestaurant.com
$$

Berkeley Thai House
2511 Channing Way
(510) 841-8424
www.berkeleythaihouse.com
$

Herbivore: The Earthly Grill
2451 Shattuck
(510) 665-1675
www.herbivorerestaurant.com
$

PALO ALTO
Evvia Esiatorio
420 Emerson Street
(650) 326-0983
www.evvia.net
$$

Tamarine Restaurant
546 University Avenue
(650) 325-8500
www.tamarinerestaurant.com
$$

Zibibbo
430 Kipling Street
(650) 328-6722
www.zibibborestaurant.com
$$

SACRAMENTO
Biba
2801 Capitol Avenue
(916) 455-2422
www.biba-restaurant.com
$$

Frank Fat's
806 L Street
(916) 442-7092
www.fatsrestaurants.com
$$

Tapa the World
2115 J Street
(916) 442-4353

www.tapatheworld.com
$

VALLEJO
Black Angus Steakhouse
124 Plaza Drive
(707) 647-0595
www.blackangus.com
$$

Zio Fraedo's
23 Harbor Way
(707) 642-8984
www.ziofraedos.com
$

FRESNO
Cracked Pepper
389 East Shaw Avenue, No. 102
(559) 222-9119
http://restauranteur.com/crackedpepper
$$

Senses World Cuisine
1110 North Van Ness Avenue
(559) 445-1957
www.sensescuisine.com
$

Tahoe Joe's Famous Steakhouse
7006 North Cedar Avenue
(559) 323-8592
www.tahoejoes.com
$$

CHAPTER 5

Wine Country 101

NORTHERN CALIFORNIA'S WINE COUNTRY has helped make the region a world-renowned destination. From gorgeous sprawling vineyards to gourmet restaurants and charming inns, Wine Country is a place that satisfies all five senses. This chapter will introduce you to the basics of all that Wine Country has to offer—including how to taste wine without looking like a beginner—and offers some tips on traveling with children and making smart purchases to ship back home.

Northern California's Wine History

Franciscan missionaries first planted vineyards in Napa and Sonoma counties—the heart of what is now known as California Wine Country. This was in the late 1700s, long before California became part of the United States. The missions were secularized in the early 1830s but continued to plant only the Mission grape. These grapes were used to make the bulk of Napa Valley wines until well into the 1870s. It was then, after the California gold rush and immigration surge had ended, that the Zinfandel grape began to show up in Napa and Sonoma fields.

A Growing Industry

German and Italian immigrants brought their winemaking techniques to the area as the population continued to grow. They brought new grapes and growing methods, which they adapted to the terrain in Napa and Sonoma. By the 1890s, northern California's vineyards began to settle into the patterns that would make them the power-houses they are today.

≡ **FAST FACT**

Chinese immigrants built much of Wine Country's stone fences and wineries, but most were forced to leave California altogether in the 1890s because of racial prejudices. Many of their jobs were taken by Italian immigrants, who brought that nation's winemaking culture with them.

Well into the 1960s, most of the wine produced in the region was destined to become part of blends and generic brands. But World War II veterans and exchange students returned to the United States from their tours abroad, bringing with them the European culture's love of wine as a sophisticated part of life. Napa County wineries began to produce Chardonnays that could stand up to these awak-ened palates, and by the 1970s even the French champagne com-pany Moët & Chandon had fallen under northern California's spell, buying vineyards to make its cork-popping fineries for Americans from locally grown grapes. Two Napa Valley wines beat the competi-tion at a major wine tasting in Paris in 1976; from that day, California Wine Country was known the world over as a destination for lovers of the finest wines grown anywhere.

Modern-Day Wine Country

Today, Napa and Sonoma counties hold year-round festivals and events to keep the region's magic alive in the minds of tourists, and wine-growing itself has become revered beyond regular Wine Coun-try borders. You can sample whites and reds alike in places like Mon-terey and Carmel at vineyards that continue to vie with their northern neighbors for the world's attention.

TRAVEL TIP

If you want to sample northern California wines but aren't too keen on going from one winery tour to the next, consider visiting the area in July, when the Napa County Fair takes place in the town of Calistoga. You can find local vintners offering their wares in between tours of agricultural expositions and rides on carnival attractions.

In fact, if you want to take in a bit more of the landscape while you sample Chardonnays and Pinot Noirs, you also can do your tasting on the go by taking advantage of the Napa Valley Wine Train. It offers round-trip luncheon and dinner rides departing from downtown Napa, stopping at a couple of wineries along the way.

 RAINY DAY FUN

Children are welcome on the Napa Valley Wine Train, though its operators suggest that toddlers younger than three might have a hard time "relaxing" for the several hours that the luncheon and dinner rides require. You can turn your time aboard into a fun train ride for a train ride's sake, skipping the wineries altogether if you so choose.

The Napa Valley Wine Train has been operating since 1989, but its tracks were actually laid back in 1864 as a way to get tourists from San Francisco to the Napa County town of Calistoga. Thus, as you're sampling fine local wines and cuisines on board, you are simultaneously enjoying a bit of tourism as it was back in the days of the first visitors to this storied region. The train's Web site is *www.winetrain.com*.

Traveling with Children in Wine Country

There's no use in trying to pretend differently: Northern California's Wine Country is tailor-made for adults more so than families. Wine tasting is obviously a grown-up pursuit, and it's the rare child who can appreciate the quality of a well-prepared foie gras.

Having said that, there's enough for children to do in and around Wine Country that you shouldn't feel like you have to skip the region altogether during your northern California vacation. A handful of wineries offer kid-friendly activities, and there are things to do close by that can help you split each day between parent and child pursuits.

At the Wineries

The tasting rooms at wineries aren't always off-limits to children, but the main activity going on inside those rooms is sampling alcohol, which most certainly is off-limits to anyone not of the legal drinking age. While most wine-tasting rooms are perfectly civil places full of connoisseurs and curious types, you will find the occasional drunk who makes a racket and spews vocabulary that you wouldn't want your twelve-year-old to hear.

Tasting rooms aside, the wineries themselves are often pretty interesting places, and tours of the facilities are usually open to adults and kids alike. Many children will enjoy learning how wine is made from grapes, perhaps even tasting a locally grown grape to see how bitter it is compared to the sweet green ones at the school cafeteria. If you happen to visit Wine Country during the harvest season, your kids will delight in watching the grapes get crushed to smithereens.

Some wineries have attractions that kids can enjoy, too, such as the gondolas that climb 300 feet toward the sky at Sterling Vineyards in Calistoga and the fountains where children can play with racing sailboats at Niebaum-Coppola Estate in Rutherford. If you have a few wineries in mind for your own tasting plans, call them ahead of your visit and ask what, if any, child-friendly activities they offer on-site.

Outside the Wineries

If you want to introduce your kids to the idea of wine without cruising from vineyard to vineyard, stop off in the town of Napa at the COPIA American Center for Food, Wine, and the Arts. It's a fascinating place for children of all ages, and it includes a kids' garden where your children can get their hands dirty learning about how food is grown. Children twelve and younger get in free, and students of any age pay just $4 with a school identification card. Note, though, that children sixteen and younger must be accompanied by an adult at all times.

You can also skip the wine of Wine Country altogether and take in a kid-friendly museum tour. The Charles M. Schulz Museum in Santa Rosa pays homage to the cartoonist who brought Charlie Brown and Snoopy to life. There are instruction books, tables, and supplies for kids who want to try their own hand at cartooning, and there are classes that last from a single afternoon to an entire week or longer if you have a budding young artist in your family.

 RAINY DAY FUN

Some of the kids' classes at the Charles M. Schulz Museum in Santa Rosa include "The Science of Peanuts," in which children do experiments to learn how high Charlie Brown's kite can fly, and "It's a Joe Cool Summer," in which kids can decorate a dog dish à la Snoopy to take home to their favorite Fido. Learn more at *www.schulzmuseum.org*.

Another good option for family fun outside the vineyards is Mrs. Grossman's Sticker Factory in Petaluma, where they print more than 15,000 miles' worth of stickers every year. The hour-long tours are by reservation only, and they include a chance to decorate a keepsake postcard using stickers fresh from the factory floor. Speaking of which, part of the tour itself is on the factory floor, so children younger than five are required to hold an adult's hand at all times. Check out additional details at *www.mrsgrossmans.com*.

Grapes to Know

A dozen different grapes are grown in northern California Wine Country: six red and six white. Some wines are bottled using only single styles of grape, while other wines are made from blending different kinds of grapes.

The Whites

The six styles of white-wine grape that you're likely to encounter are (in alphabetical order):

- Chardonnay
- Marsanne
- Pinot Blanc
- Riesling
- Sauvignon Blanc
- Viognier

Chardonnay is grown all over the world, including France, Italy, Australia, and New Zealand. It has become an incredibly popular varietal in recent years, so much so that "wine snobs" sometimes refer to themselves as people who drink ABC—anything but Chardonnay. Don't let this deter you from sampling Chardonnays in northern California, which produces some of the finest bottles in the world today. Pinot Blanc is often mistaken for Chardonnay, and sometimes vintners go out of their way to bottle it in a way that mimics the tastes of popular Chardonnays. Sauvignon Blancs have an entirely different taste and are sometimes called Fumé Blancs to distinguish California wines for marketing purposes.

Riesling grapes grown in northern California are typically destined to become dessert wines, and they taste different than the Rieslings you might know from vineyards in Germany, where the grape is very popular.

Marsanne is a less-popular varietal that's often used in blends. Viognier is also a little-known grape, one that California planters have embraced even as growers in France—the grape's homeland—have increasingly shied away from it.

The Reds

The six styles of red-wine grape that you're likely to encounter are (in alphabetical order):

- Cabernet Franc
- Cabernet Sauvignon
- Merlot
- Pinot Noir
- Sangiovese
- Zinfandel

Most of the red-grape varietals you'll find in northern California vineyards can stand on their own as popular wines. Merlot and Cabernet Sauvignon are perhaps the best known, with Zinfandels, Pinot Noirs, and Sangioveses following close behind. Cabernet Franc is mostly grown for use in blends with Cabernet Sauvignon or Merlot. For that matter, some northern California wineries blend all three grapes to create more complex tastes. In general, Cabernet Sauvignons tend to be the heaviest of the red wines. If you want to ease your taste buds in, start with Merlot, Sangiovese, and Pinot Noir.

A Typical Tasting Experience

Don't be nervous if your upcoming vacation is going to include your first experience at a wine tasting. Many, many, many people who tour the wineries in Napa and Sonoma counties are first-time wine tasters, and the vineyard staffs are highly accustomed to helping beginners make their way through the experience. Just go with the flow (or the pour, as it were) and you'll be just fine.

The first thing you'll have to do after making your way into a winery's tasting room is decide which package you want to buy. Packages include wine "flights," a term used to describe anywhere from three to several dozen wine samples that you can taste at a time. Some flights include only reds, some include only whites, and some include a mix. There is no right or wrong way to choose a flight. It's just a matter of how many wines you want to taste at any given winery.

Usually, the vineyard staff member will pour one or two wines for you at a time, even if you've purchased a flight of eight or ten wines altogether. There is often good reason behind this method, perhaps allowing you to compare two Sauvignon Blancs side by side before moving on to compare a couple of Chardonnays. Again, there is no right or wrong way to sample the wines in your flight. Just move at your own pace and enjoy any details the server can offer to help you understand why one wine tastes different from the next.

 TRAVEL TIP

After a full day of wine tasting, you may not be in any condition to drive yourself back to the hotel. Plan ahead for this possibility by prearranging a taxicab or car service, or by taking advantage of a bus or train tour that will get you safely to your home away from home after a long day of tasting wines.

Typically, your tasting will include a sheet the winery gives you to keep track of which wines you like the best. Don't be shy about crossing off wines that don't suit your fancy. When the tasting is over, you can look through your list of favorites and purchase them by the bottle or by the case—or you can thank the winery staff for their time and leave with all your money still in your wallet.

CHAPTER 6

Napa County

GRAPES HAVE BEEN GROWING in Napa County since long before there were vintners, but the Native Americans who first called the area home never did figure out how to bottle the good stuff for mass distribution. That began in the 1830s in what is today known as the town of Yountville, around which some 400 wineries eventually sprang up. They flourish from the city of Napa north to the town of Calistoga—comprising one of the world's best-known regions for lovers of Chardonnay and Cabernet, and as well as other varietals that grow in its "microclimates," including Pinot Noir, Merlot, and Sauvignon Blanc.

Napa Basics

A man named George Calvert Yount (for whom the modern town of Yountville is named) is said to be the first white settler ever to plant a vineyard in this region, back in 1836. That's more than ten years before Napa became a county, one of the original few in California when the state joined the union in 1849. And it wasn't until more than a century after that, when a Stag's Leap offering took home the top prize at the Paris Wine Tasting of 1976, that Napa County began to enjoy the worldwide reputation it has today for producing fine wines under dozens of labels. Today it is certainly the best-known wine-growing area in the United States, and it is regularly discussed in the same breath as the most famous wine regions of France, Italy, and beyond.

Napa County's only city also goes by the name of Napa, but the city is not where most of the wineries are located. They're to the north, many along Route 29 as it passes through the towns of Yountville, Rutherford, St. Helena, and Calistoga. A good number of wineries are off this main route to the east and west, but you can certainly follow the main route to enough wineries to fill a week's worth of tasting time, including some well-known operations such as Robert Mondavi.

≡FAST FACT

According to the Napa Valley Vintners Association, each five-ounce glass of wine is made from a little more than a half-pound of grapes. You might think that every square inch of county land is planted with vines to keep production at the highest possible level, but it's not. In fact, less than 10 percent of Napa County is planted vineyards—and there's almost no land left that's suitable for grape growing.

Note that north of Yountville, Route 29 changes from a freeway into a two-way highway—one jam-packed with tourist traffic during the high season every summer. Getting around can be a challenge to your patience, but luckily, cars are not your only option for seeing the Napa Valley sights.

Getting Around

The big thing to remember when planning your trip to Napa County is that by all odds, you're going to get drunk. At least a little bit drunk, anyway.

Yes, there is a custom of spitting wines out instead of swallowing them during tastings, but few people have the willpower or even the desire to do that—and thus most people are feeling a pretty good buzz by the time they decide to leave the Napa Valley area each afternoon. This reality can lead to some pretty dangerous congestion on the local roads, something to try to avoid if at all possible.

You can see Napa Valley by car, of course, but it's just one among many options for touring. If your family or group tends to be on the heavy-drinking side, then you might consider using a tour service or taking the Napa Wine Train to avoid getting behind the wheel at all.

By Car

Perhaps ironically, Napa Valley is one of the best-laid-out routes for drivers. A single highway, Route 29, runs the length of the 35-mile county from south to north. You can drive north along the highway until midday, then turn around and drive back on your way to dinner.

 TRAVEL TIP

Most adults find that touring three to four wineries a day is a maximum number, especially if you plan to operate a car. When planning your itinerary, select wineries in advance and stick to your schedule—and make your midday visit to a winery that offers lunch as well as wine tastings.

There's also a route known as the Silverado Trail (*www .silveradotrail.com*), which passes through 35 wineries along the eastern side of Napa County—far from the typically congested Route 29. Lest you think this route "misses" some of the biggest label names the county has to offer, consider that the Silverado Trail includes both Stag's Leap and William Hill.

By Shuttle or Bus

You have several choices of shuttle bus operators in Napa County, some operating along fixed routes from places like Yountville and St. Helena, and others offering private charters. There's also a trolley that runs through the city of Napa.

The VINE System

The Napa County Transportation and Planning Agency operates the VINE, a fixed-route bus system that includes the Yountville and St. Helena shuttles, as well as the Napa city trolley. The service operates seven days a week with the exception of New Year's Day, Memorial Day, Independence Day, Labor Day, Thanksgiving, and Christmas.

Rates depend on which routes you choose and whether you decide to transfer between one route and the next, but the system can take you from towns south of the city of Napa north to Calistoga at the top of the county. Times of operation are as follows:

- Until 9:25 P.M. on weekdays
- Until 8:40 P.M. on Saturdays
- Until 7 P.M. on Sundays

Maps and additional information are available online at *www.nctpa.net.*

California Wine Tours

With hubs in both Napa and Sonoma counties, the California Wine Tours company offers everything from Lincoln Town Cars to full-size motor coaches and mini-buses. The company prides itself on having knowledgeable drivers—referred to as guides—and can help you arrange itineraries that include off-the-beaten-path wineries where public buses don't go.

Rates start at $50 per hour, so a full day of wine tasting is going to run about $300 (or as much as $1,800 for a 28-person limo bus). Learn more at *www.californiawinetours.com.*

By Bicycle

Drunken bicycle riding isn't ideal, but the odds are that if you crash on a bike, you'll do damage only to yourself. Mountain bikes are best for Napa Valley's hilly terrain; expect to put a little muscle into the effort of getting around.

Napa Valley Bike Tours

If you want to ride from winery to winery on two wheels, you can work with companies like Napa Valley Bike Tours (*www.napavalley biketours.com*), which is based in Yountville and offers prearranged itineraries as well as rentals for simply getting around.

An example of a prearranged itinerary is the company's "Bike in the Vineyards" tour, which takes you on mountain bikes through Bouchaine Vineyards all morning, followed by lunch on a hilltop and tastings at McKenzie-Mueller Vineyards, Acacia Winery, or Domaine Carneros. Other itineraries combine bicycling with hot-air balloon rides or kayak tours.

If you rent two or more bicycles for a day, the company will drop them off at your hotel in the morning and pick them up the following day. Rates start at $30 a day, and kids' bikes are available starting at $20 a day. Discounts apply if you rent for a few days in a row.

Bicycling Resources

The Napa County Transportation and Planning Agency produces a color-coded map that tells you which routes are the best for biking, which have the heaviest traffic, which have actual bicycle lanes, and so on. The map also provides distances from popular stopping points, as well as notations where uphill climbs can become difficult for anyone a wee bit out of shape. You can download the map from the agency's Web site, *www.nctpa.net*.

By Foot

Outside Napa Valley's city and towns, "walking" is better described as "hiking" since the mountainous terrain that is oh-so-good for grape growing is sloped quite steeply in many places. Walking from winery to winery is possible once you get to a cluster of vineyards, but usually walking from town to a group of wineries is more of a hike. Frankly, in most circumstances, you'll do better taking a shuttle bus or bicycle to get from winery to winery than hoofing it.

By Boat

Napa Valley wineries are of course inland, which means you can't actually get to them by boat. However, you can get to the region by way of a private or group cruise that offers excursions to wineries, an option that can be a nice alternative to sitting in traffic jams as you make your way by car from San Francisco.

CruiseWest

CruiseWest offers two Wine Country itineraries that run round-trip from San Francisco to Napa and Sonoma counties. "Culture of the Vine" is a four-day cruise that includes an expert wine speaker. The cruises are typically available during the months of September and October, with prices starting at $1,300 per person. The 257-foot ship *Spirit of Yorktown* carries 138 guests. "Vintner's Choice" gives you a bit more time for exploring, with five days onboard the *Spirit of Yorktown* on selected dates in September and October. Rates for that itinerary start at $1,950 per person. Learn more at *www.cruisewest .com*.

Club Nautique

For a more intimate boating experience, you might work with Club Nautique, a sailing and powerboating school that has two locations on San Francisco Bay: at Alameda and Sausalito. Itineraries can be arranged with licensed skippers who can get you within walking distance of the Napa Wine Train. Of course, since Club Nautique's main focus is on learning to sail, you can combine your cruise with instruction on operating a sailboat or a trawler motoryacht. Details are online at *www.clubnautique.net*.

Napa Wine Train

The Napa Wine Train's depot is in the city of Napa, and its route runs straight up the county virtually parallel to Route 29. There are lunch tours, dinner tours, winery tours, murder-mystery tours—pretty much everything you can imagine.

 RAINY DAY FUN

You don't have to step off the Napa Wine Train to enjoy scenic views of the county or the best local foods and wines. There's even a three-course luncheon ride called the "Gourmet Express" that has an onboard day-care car where kids younger than twelve can ride for free while the adults in your group enjoy everything from roasted beef tenderloin to pan-seared salmon.

Most of the train's round-trip routes from Napa run about three hours long. There are dining and lounge cars onboard, so you won't be stuck at a dinner table the entire trip. Some of the itineraries include stops and private tastings at the Grgich Hills Winery or the Domaine Chandon facility. Rates for adults run from about $30 to $50, depending on the itinerary and package plan you select. For more information, go to the Napa Wine Train's official Web site at *www.winetrain.com*.

Main Towns

There is one city—Napa—plus the three main towns of St. Helena, Yountville, and Calistoga in Napa County. There are smaller towns along the county's length, too, including Rutherford and Oakville, but most visitors look to the city or the bigger towns for accommodations, dining options, and transportation access.

Napa

The city of Napa is at the base of the county, the first major hub you'll encounter if you're coming north from San Francisco. It is home to bed and breakfasts, inns, full-scale resorts—pretty much any type (and price range) of accommodations you might require. There are also a good number of restaurants, spas, and antiques shops, plus three separate golf courses, some of which have on-site condominiums with kitchens. The city of Napa is also where the Napa Wine Train starts and ends its round-trip tours of the county.

 TRAVEL TIP

Want to get a bird's-eye view of the landscape around Napa before beginning your tours on the ground? Check out the offerings at Balloons Above the Valley (*www.balloonrides.com*), which takes you 1,000 to 3,000 feet above the wineries in a hot air balloon. Prices start at $190 per adult and $145 for children twelve and younger, and guides meet you right at the Napa General Store on Main Street downtown.

One of the most popular stops in downtown Napa is COPIA: the American Center for Food, Wine, and the Arts. It's a nonprofit center that explores wine, its relationship to food, and its significance in culture. There are wine tastings, courses in food and wine pairings, garden tours, and food classes that discuss everything from different kinds of tomatoes to Thanksgiving vegetable recipes. The on-site restaurant, Julia's Kitchen, is inspired by famous chef Julia Child and prepares meals infused with ingredients from the COPIA gardens. Learn more about all that COPIA offers at *www .copia.org*.

In downtown Napa you might also want to enjoy a show at the Napa Valley Opera House, shop for specialty foods at NapaStyle, and rummage for collectibles at the half-dozen antiques stores. For a complete listing of all the local shops, places to stay, restaurants to sample, and more, go to *www.napavalley.com.*

St. Helena

St. Helena, a town of about 6,000 people, is located in the northern part of Napa County, between Calistoga to the north and Yountville to the south. The best-known winery near the town is Beringer, which has been producing wine at the same site since the mid-1800s. There also are a half-dozen or so artists' galleries in town, plus various restaurants, antiques stores, and other quaint shops.

One of the biggest draws is the Greystone campus of the Culinary Institute of America. There, just as at the college's Upstate New York campus, you can take cooking classes or enjoy a multicourse meal produced and served by the celebrity chefs of tomorrow at the Wine Spectator Greystone Restaurant on campus. Oftentimes, the menu will include wine pairings that highlight the best of the region's offerings. Plan in advance—you'll need to make reservations before you arrive if you want a table. Learn more at *www.ciachef.edu.*

Yountville

Yountville is located between the city of Napa and the town of St. Helena, and it's home to the Napa Valley Museum, where exhibits focus on everything from fine arts to natural science. One of the permanent exhibits is "California Wine: The Science of an Art," which gives you an interactive introduction to the process of winemaking. Admission is $4.50 for adults, $2.50 for children between the ages of seven and seventeen, and free for children ages six and younger. The museum is open from 10 A.M. till 5 P.M. every day except Tuesday, when it is closed. Learn more at *www.napavalleymuseum.org.*

Also in Yountville, you'll find the V Marketplace, a festival-style center that houses upscale and gourmet shops, restaurants, a wine-tasting cellar, cobblestone walkways, and gardens designed specifically to entice picnickers. Seasonal events are a big draw here, including the annual April flower showcase, the Father's Day auto show, and the chamber music festival held in August. For details about stores and upcoming events, go to *www.vmarketplace.com*.

 RAINY DAY FUN

The Lincoln Theater in Yountville hosts everything from string quartets to ballet productions to performances by comics like Paula Poundstone. It's Napa Valley's premier performing arts venue, having recently undergone a $20 million renovation in time to celebrate its fiftieth anniversary. For upcoming shows and ticket information, check out *www.lincolntheater.com*.

Calistoga

Calistoga is the town at the top of Napa County, the northernmost outpost of civilization, if you will, along Route 29. The locals do take their preservation of civilization quite seriously; fast-food franchises are banned in an effort to keep the town much as it has been for nearly two centuries. The town is known for its hot spring spas, more than a half-dozen of which offer mud baths for individuals, couples, and groups. There's also an Old Faithful Geyser here, not as big as the one in Wyoming's Yellowstone National Park, but still worth a look if you're enchanted by the sight of water spewing forth from the earth.

 TRAVEL TIP

If you're pregnant, you may want to skip the overland tours at Safari West in Calistoga. The paths are quite bumpy, which is why the facility also recommends forgoing the tour if your children are younger than three. Also leave any food behind, as it can attract wild animals.

There are only four wineries in Calistoga proper, with most of the Napa Valley vintners located to the town's south. There is, however, something here that no other Napa town offers: Safari West, a 400-acre wildlife preserve that is home to everything from giraffes to zebras and cheetahs. Open-air Jeep tours are conducted year-round, with prices ranging from $62 for adults to $28 for children between the ages of three and twelve. Details are online at *www.safariwest.com*.

Popular Wineries

It's impossible for anyone to tell you which are the "best" wineries in Napa County, as wine is as much about personal taste as it is about bottling techniques and blends of grapes. Having said that, there are a few brand names you are likely to recognize in Napa, and it's always fun to visit at least a few of the more popular vintners just so you can tell your friends back home that you stood on the same ground where their grapes are grown. To that end, here's a look at a handful of wineries whose offerings you've likely tried in the past— and whose in-house tastings may surprise you with some options that you can't find in your local wine shop back home.

Robert Mondavi

The Robert Mondavi Winery is perhaps the best-known in Napa Valley, and it offers a tour that is a good first stop because it includes information about the wine-making process that will help you understand what you sample at additional wineries in the area. The winery is open daily from 10 A.M. until 5 P.M. with the exception of four days each year: Easter, Thanksgiving, Christmas, and New Year's Day.

There are more than a dozen kinds of tastings and tours here, so even if you don't care about the wine-making process, you can enjoy a guided or educational tasting that incorporates cheeses, lunches, and dinners. There are even wine-tasting classes that last about two hours and help give you an idea of how to tell one wine from the next.

≡ **FAST FACT**

Every year in late June and throughout July, the Robert Mondavi Winery hosts a summer festival that includes fireworks and live music. Some big-name acts tend to perform, with kickoff night usually headlined by the Preservation Hall Jazz Band. Throughout the month-long event, you can expect to see well-known performers such as Los Lobos and Herbie Hancock. Learn more at *www.robertmondaviwinery.com.*

Stag's Leap

Located on the Silverado Trail near Yountville in the Stags Leap District is Stag's Leap Wine Cellars—not to be confused with the nearby Stags' Leap Winery, which is a bit fussier about the apostrophe in its name and keeps its doors closed to visitors. It's the Stag's Leap Wine Cellars that you want to visit for tours and tastings, with two levels of tastings available daily: $15 for the four wines of the day, or $40 for a sampling of premier estate wines.

You might recall from earlier in this chapter that it was Stag's Leap that put Napa Valley on the world's wine map during the 1976 tasting in Paris with a Cabernet Sauvignon that threw the French back on their bouquet-boasting heels. Cabs are still what you'll find among the reds produced here, along with an occasional merlot. If you're a white-wine drinker, look to sample Chardonnays and Sauvignon Blancs.

Beringer

Beringer, founded in 1876, is the longest continually operating winery in Napa County, located just north of St. Helena on Route 29. You might be surprised to learn that today the winery is owned by a division of the Foster's Group, best known for its American television commercials that pronounce: "Foster's. Australian for beer."

A half-dozen tours are available at Beringer, ranging from a look around the historic grounds to a semi-private tasting in the cellar.

Prices range from $10 to $35 per person, and the tours and tastings are available daily from 10 A.M. until 6 P.M. during the high season, or until 5 P.M. during the winter months. The winery is closed on Thanksgiving, Christmas, and New Year's Day.

RAINY DAY FUN

Ever tried to sort out which cheeses go best with which wines? The Beringer winery's "Wine and Cheese Pairing Seminar" will straighten you out during an hour-long presentation that includes four different types of fromage. You must make reservations at least forty-eight hours in advance, so go online to *www.beringer .com* to reserve one of the ten seats in the class for the day you plan to visit.

Domaine Chandon

Don't call it champagne—that has to come from France. What they make at Domaine Chandon, west of Yountville, is called sparkling wine. You probably know it by the name "Brut" on the gold label.

What you may not know is that the Domaine Chandon winery was the first to open a restaurant in Wine Country, back in 1977. It's called *étoile* (no need to uppercase; this is, after all, not the Champagne region), and it offers lunches, dinners, and a seven-course tasting menu that pairs foods with Chandon wines. You'll find everything from sashimi to veal tenderloin on the tasting menu, and there are two separate tasting options if you want to return for a second day to sample another seven of the vintner's offerings.

The winery is open daily from 10 A.M. until 6 P.M. except for Thanksgiving, Christmas Eve, Christmas Day, and New Year's Day. The restaurant is open every day except Christmas if you want to sneak in a tasting of your own during dinner. Learn more—or make much-recommended dinner reservations—at *www.chandon.com*.

Labels to Learn

So far, this chapter has highlighted wineries whose labels you're likely to recognize. There are literally hundreds of other wineries that you can explore in Napa Valley, and certainly there aren't enough pages to devote to each one of them here. Instead, here's a look at a few labels you might want to learn, from wineries that continue to receive good ratings from wine lovers around the globe.

Trefethen

Trefethen Vineyards is the first winery you'll come to if you head north along Route 29 from Napa city. The wines of choice here (as at so many of Napa Valley's wineries) are Chardonnay and Cabernet Sauvignon, though Trefethen also produces good-quality Merlot and Rieslings.

There are tours of the winery itself—which is a National Historic Landmark—as well as both reserve tastings ($20 per person) and estate tastings ($10 per person). It's hard to find a grander setting for a wine tasting than Trefethen's wine library, where you can sink back into a leather club chair and perhaps uncork a bottle of whichever of the day's offerings you like best. For details, go to *www .trefethenfamilyvineyards.com*.

Grgich Hills

Tours are by appointment only at the Grgich Hills Cellar near Rutherford, but there are daily tastings of everything from the winery's continually good Chardonnay to its lesser-known Fumé Blancs and Zinfandels. The folks are friendly here—and they'll even let you kick off your shoes and stomp grapes with them during harvest time in September and October. On Fridays, you can taste wines straight from the barrel, before they're ready to be bottled. The experience is included in the regular $5 tasting fee.

Hours at Grgich Hills are 9:30 A.M. until 4:30 P.M. daily, except for Easter, Thanksgiving, Christmas Day, and New Year's Day, when the winery is closed. Learn more at *www.grgich.com*.

Caymus

Tasting is by appointment only at Caymus Vineyards, which is east of Rutherford on Route 128. But it's worth the effort to sign up and head over—especially if you're a fan of Cabernet Sauvignon. That's what they have been producing the most of in recent years, though the vineyard still has a nice following from a white blend called Caymus Conundrum that spiked in price a few years ago following a sharp increase in demand. You can't register for a tasting online. Instead, you have to call (707) 967-3010.

Lodging and Restaurants

There is no shortage of places to stay or eat in Napa County. Here are some suggestions you might want to consider. Each suggestion is marked by one, two, or three dollar signs.

For lodging:
$ = a room costs less than $100
$$ = a room costs from $101 to $200
$$$ = a room costs more than $200

For restaurants:
$ = entrées cost less than $15
$$ = entrées cost from $16 to $30
$$$ = entrées cost more than $30

Lodging

NAPA
Best Western Elm House Inn
800 California Boulevard
(707) 255-1831
www.bestwestern.com
$$

Chateau Hotel and Conference Center
4195 Solano Avenue
(707) 253-9300
www.napavalleychateauhotel.com
$$

Hilton Garden Inn
3585 Solano Avenue
(707) 252-0444
www.hiltongardeninn.com
$$–$$$

John Muir Inn
1998 Trower Avenue
(707) 257-7220
www.toc.com/johnmuirinn
$$

Napa Valley Marriott Hotel & Spa
3425 Solano Avenue
(707) 253-8600
www.marriott.com
$$$

ST. HELENA
El Bonita Motel
195 Main Street
(800) 541-3284
www.elbonita.com
$$–$$$

Harvest Inn
1 Main Street
(800) 950-8466
www.harvestinn.com
$$$

The Inn at Southbridge
1020 Main Street
(707) 967-9400
www.slh.com
$$$

YOUNTVILLE
Napa Valley Lodge
2230 Madison Street
(888) 455-2468
www.napavalleylodge.com
$$$

CALISTOGA
Calistoga Inn
1250 Lincoln Avenue
(707) 942-4101
www.calistogainn.com
$–$$

Dr. Wilkinson's Hot Springs Resort
1507 Lincoln Avenue
(707) 942-4102
www.drwilkinson.com
$$–$$$

EuroSpa & Inn
1202 Pine Street
(707) 942-6829
www.eurospa.com
$$–$$$

Lodge at Calistoga
1865 Lincoln Avenue
(800) 652-5130
www.thelodgeatcalistoga.com
$$

RUTHERFORD
Rancho Caymus Inn
1140 Rutherford Road
(800) 845-1777
www.ranchocaymus.com
$$$

Restaurants

NAPA
Bayleaf Restaurant
2025 Monticello Avenue
(707) 257-9720
www.bayleafnapa.com
$–$$

Celadon
500 Main Street
(707) 254-9690
www.celadonnapa.com
$–$$

The Grill at Silverado
1600 Atlas Peak Road
(707) 257-5400
www.silveradoresort.com
$$

Julia's Kitchen
500 First Street
(707) 265-5700
www.juliaskitchen.org
$$

Piccolino's Italian Cafe
1385 Napa Town Center
(707) 251-0100
www.piccolinoscafe.com
$–$$

Royal Oak at the Silverado Resort
1600 Atlas Peak Road
(707) 257-5400
www.silveradoresort.com
$$

Siena at Meritage Resort
875 Bordeaux Way
(707) 251-1950
www.themeritageresort.com
$$

Solbar at Solage Calistoga
755 Silverado Trail
(707) 226-0800
www.solagecalistoga.com
$–$$

Zinsvalley Restaurant
3253 Browns Valley Road
(707) 224-0695
www.zinsvalley.com
$–$$

ST. HELENA
Cindy's Backstreet Kitchen
1327 Railroad Avenue
(707) 963-1200
www.cindysbackstreetkitchen.com
$

Meadowood Napa Valley
900 Meadowood Lane
(707) 963-3646
www.meadowood.com
$$$

Wine Spectator Greystone Restaurant
2555 Main Street
(707) 967-1010
www.ciachef.edu
$$

YOUNTVILLE
Domaine Chandon's etoile
1 California Drive
(707) 944-2892
www.chandon.com
$$$

CALISTOGA
Bosko's Trattoria
1364 Lincoln Avenue
(707) 942-9088
www.boskos.com
$

Brannan's Grill
1374 Lincoln Avenue
(707) 942-2233
www.brannansgrill.com
$–$$

CHAPTER 7

Sonoma County

SONOMA MARKS THE SOUTHWESTERN EDGE of California's best-known Wine Country, sharing a border with Napa County to the east. Napa may still be a bit better known, but Sonoma is no slouch in the wine-making department—besting the actual tonnage of grapes harvested in Napa by some 30 percent at last count. Sonoma also has made a name for itself among the culinary elite thanks to its olive oils. You can enjoy Sonoma County as part of a broader experience in the wine region or focus your entire tasting adventure here alone.

Sonoma Basics

Sonoma County has two distinct regions, at least in terms of wine-making. There's the Sonoma Valley to the south, including the large town of Sonoma, as well as the smaller towns of Glen Ellen and Kenwood, and then there's the Russian River region to the north, including the towns of Santa Rosa and Healdsburg.

You'll find wineries in both the northern and southern parts of the county. Because the terrain changes from one place to the next, you may be surprised at how wines made from the same grapes can taste dramatically different even if they're grown just a few miles apart.

The name *Sonoma* translates from Native American as "valley of the moon," a moniker made popular throughout the United States in 1913 when novelist Jack London published *The Valley of the Moon*.

He had a ranch in Glen Ellen and no doubt lived many of the scenes he described in the book, which is about a couple who leave the city for Sonoma country and the farming life. Today, Sonoma County is still affectionately called "the valley of the moon."

≡ FAST FACT

There are some 250 wineries in Sonoma County, which has seventy-six miles of Pacific Ocean coastline along its western side. Despite the ocean's pronounced effect on the area's climate, it's not the only water that affects the local vintners. Many rely on the Russian River and its tributaries, which help grapes grow along the mountains and plains alike.

Wine has been made in Sonoma County since 1812, when Russian immigrants planted the first recorded grapes. By the 1920s there were more than 200 wineries in operation, but only fifty of them survived Prohibition. Today, the numbers are back up—and the quality of Sonoma bottling continues to rise, as well.

 ## RAINY DAY FUN

Growers who offer both wine and olive products often have tasting rooms and shops that can keep you busy (and your belly happy) for hours. One example is Viansa, which calls itself a "winery and Italian marketplace." Its gourmet foods include everything from pesto to dessert sauces, not to mention gourmet gift baskets and a cookbook from their chefs. Learn more at www.viansa.com.

There are also some fifty olive oil producers in Sonoma County, a good number of them divisions of wineries or vineyards, and others standalone operations making everything from the bottled stuff used in cooking to tapenades for spreading atop fresh bread. Some of the merchants who grow olives offer tours and tastings that are similar to those you'll find at wineries, complete with $25 bottles of the good stuff to take home.

Getting Around

As with Napa County, Sonoma County has one main route that runs from its southern end to its northern border. That's Route 12 in the valley, connecting in Santa Rosa to Route 101, which continues north through the Russian River region to Healdsburg.

In the valley, most of the wineries are right along the main high-way, though of course some are a short drive away along connecting country roads. Up toward Healdsburg, you'll have to leave the main highway to get to the bulk of the wineries, which are located on routes along the Russian River, such as Westside and River roads.

By Car

If your primary purpose in visiting this part of Northern California is to sample its many fine wines, be careful not to get behind the wheel if you have been indulging in the tastings. Drunken driving is a recipe for disaster in a place like Sonoma County, where virtually every driver on the road during the peak summer tourist months will have imbibed at least a bit before getting behind the wheel. Avoid accidents by selecting a designated driver or by leaving the car behind and using another form of transportation to the wineries. Yes, the driving is easy in Sonoma County, but only if you're sober.

By Bus

Sonoma County Transit operates the buses in this part of northern California. You can check out routes and even order a bus pass online at *www.sctransit.com*, including passes for "zone" use that give you discounted access to the towns you think you might visit (as opposed to the entire transit system). The most expensive one-way fare is $3.10, and a thirty-one-day adult pass is $55. In terms of pure economics, buses are well worth considering in Sonoma County.

Routes are a different story. They'll get you from main area to main area, but all that money you saved by taking the bus might have to be spent on taxis to get you from the bus stop to the actual wineries. Some of the available daily bus routes include:

- Russian River area to Santa Rosa
- Santa Rosa to Sonoma Valley
- Petaluma to Santa Rosa

Bicycles are allowed on some of the buses, and some of the bus stops have bike racks. Check out the Sonoma County Transit Web site for more detailed information.

By Hired Car

As you might imagine, there's a good business to be done in ferrying wine lovers from vintner to vintner. Plenty of car and limousine services are available, including some that offer Wine Country packages.

Wine & Roses Limousine Service

As this company's name suggests, its drivers bring wine and roses (as well as fine chocolates) to your driving experience. Its fleet of Lincoln Town Cars, Escalade Limousines, Rolls-Royces, and more can be rented by the hour or by the day. The company's Sonoma Wine Tour package includes croissants to line your belly on the way up to Wine Country, as well as snacks to help keep you going throughout the day. Learn more at *www.wineandroseslimo.com*.

Preferred Limousine

This company offers Sonoma County wine tours that can begin or end at any hotel in the greater San Francisco Bay area. Tours typically include at least four of the county's wineries as well as a stop for lunch around midday—and you can customize the itinerary if there are specific wineries you would most like to see. Expect to pay at least $300 for six hours. For a specific price quote, go online to *www.preferred-limo.com*.

Elite Limousine Service

The people who run this car service claim to be wine aficionados themselves—which should serve you well when it comes time to decide exactly which wineries are worth a visit in Sonoma County depending on the day's traffic congestion. Standard tours are available, as are customized itineraries. Published rates start at $325 for a six-hour tour, and hourly rentals are also an option. Learn more at *www.elitelimo.net*.

By Bicycle

If you want to get around Sonoma County by bicycle, you'll have a good number of options. There are companies that allow you to rent bicycles by the hour, join a one-day or multiday tour, or organize a group tour to suit everyone in your family. Biking from the southern edge to the northern tip of Sonoma County is probably an impractical idea unless you're in training for the Olympics, but if you want to stay around a key town or two, bicycles can be a safe alternative to driving a car and an inexpensive alternative to renting a limousine with a driver.

 TRAVEL TIP

The Sonoma County Transportation Authority devotes an entire section of its Web site to downloadable PDF maps showing existing and proposed bicycle routes. There are maps that show the entire county, plus others that focus on cities such as Sonoma and Santa Rosa. The site also posts tips for riding bicycles in traffic. Check them out at *www.sctainfo.org*.

Wine Country Bikes

Based in Healdsburg in northern Sonoma County, this company offers all kinds of rentals and tours, including a Classic Winery option with a guide who covers some twenty-five miles and several winery stops with a picnic lunch. There are also multiday tours that include overnight stops at strategically situated bed and breakfasts or inns. The company's Web site, *www.winecountrybikes.com*, even has a section featuring the most-popular Sonoma bicycle routes if you want to plan your path in advance.

Getaway Adventures

This company, which has been in business since 1991, offers single- and multiday bicycle tours. You can focus specifically on Sonoma County or mix up your adventure with excursions across the border into Napa County. The Four-Day Multisport Wine Country tour, for instance, combines wineries in both counties with bicycling, hiking, and kayaking. Details are available online at *www.getaway adventures.com*.

Spoke Folk

Based in Healdsburg, this company is run by self-described "bike heads." If you're a serious rider, the Spoke Folk are probably your kind of people. You can rent bicycles by the hour, including tandems starting at $15 per hour or $50 for the day. You'll get a free map of the area with every rental or you can check out the company's recommended self-guided tours on its Web site, *www.spokefolk.com*.

On Foot

Walking from one end of Sonoma County to the other is a haul and a half, but if you want to see Wine Country on foot, you can opt to stroll from winery to winery in one location, such as the towns of Sonoma or Kenwood. Depending on your hotel's location, you may be able to get to at least a handful of wineries on foot. Of course, you can always skip the wineries altogether and just walk to a good restaurant in town that has a fantastic local wine list.

Main Towns

The cultural center of Sonoma County is the town of Sonoma, which is located at the base of the valley—the first major town you'll come to if you travel to the area from San Francisco. Traveling north from there, you'll find the good-sized towns of Glen Ellen, Kenwood, Santa Rosa, and Healdsburg—plus some smaller towns along the way that have charming and eclectic inns, restaurants, and shops.

Sonoma

Sonoma is built around an eight-acre central plaza, the largest of its kind in all of California and a beautiful place to simply wander and enjoy the fresh air. City Hall is worth a look during your meander around town; it is beautifully built from stone in Spanish style. There are of course more modern sights and shops here—this is, after all, the site of the first-ever Williams-Sonoma store back in 1956.

FAST FACT

The town of Sonoma revolted against the Mexican province of California in 1846, creating the Bear Flag Republic—which takes its name from the design on a flag that thirty-three men raised in Sonoma's town square as a sign of rebellion. The new republic lasted less than a month, but the bear flag became the basis for modern-day California's state flag. The original bear flag was designed by William Todd, whose aunt went on to marry Abraham Lincoln.

If you have time for only one town in Sonoma County, then Sonoma is a good choice. It has good lodging options plus a fair number of nearby wineries, including the popular Ravenswood facility. There are also attractions such as Sonoma State Historic Park where you can take a break from tasting and simply enjoy the gorgeous countryside.

A good resource for hotel options is *www.sonomavalley.com*, which is the official Web site of the Sonoma Valley Visitor's Bureau.

Sonoma State Historic Park

Interestingly, Sonoma State Historic Park is not a physical plot of land. Instead, it includes the following six historic sites located within the town of Sonoma:

- Mission San Francisco Solano
- Blue Wing Inn
- Sonoma Barracks
- Toscano Hotel
- La Casa Grande
- Lachryma Montis

Docent-led tours are available at some of the sites, though days and hours of operation vary. The sites are managed by the California State Parks department, which offers additional information online at *www.parks.ca.gov*.

Sonoma Valley Museum of Art

Located downtown on Broadway, the Sonoma Valley Museum of Art offers everything from permanent and rotating exhibits to artist-led discussions and music concerts. Local, national, and international artists are featured in the 3,000-square-foot facility, which has a maximum capacity of 225 people. Hours are 11 A.M. till 5 P.M. Wednesday through Sunday. Tickets start at $5 per person or $8 per family—with admission free for everyone on Sunday. Learn more at *www.svma.org*.

Infineon Raceway

If you want a little more zip in your tour, head to Infineon Raceway, which offers drag racing, motorcycle racing, and even a racing school if you want to sit behind the wheel of a go-fast car yourself. If you're a racecar fan, you'll recognize this course from the nationally televised NASCAR Nextel Cup, which it hosts.

Worth noting are the four campgrounds at Infineon Raceway, including plenty of spaces for RV parking. Ticket prices, an upcoming schedule of events, and additional information are available at *www.infineonraceway.com.*

Glen Ellen

During the last census this town had fewer than 1,000 residents— none of them as famous as Jack London, who lived in Glen Ellen from 1909 until 1916. The site of the ranch London built is now known as Jack London State Historic Park, and it's a nice diversion from winery tours if you need a breather during one of your daily itineraries. Glen Ellen is just five miles north of the town of Sonoma, located right on the main highway, Route 12.

Jack London State Historic Park

When Jack London himself lived here, he called the place "Beauty Ranch." It's certainly an inspirational setting, and London penned many books, stories, and letters here when he wasn't out working in the fields like the rest of Sonoma County's farmers. Imagine, the author of such well-regarded tomes as *The Call of the Wild* and *White Fang* out fretting over vines in the heat of summer.

 RAINY DAY FUN

If you can't appreciate the beauty of a sunny day at Jack London State Historic Park, maybe you can appreciate some of the author's socialist views. Pick up a copy of *The Iron Heel*, which many experts say influenced George Orwell's famous book *1984*. London wrote his book in 1908—making it remarkably predictive of the socialist regimes to come in Europe.

Hiking is the main activity that draws most people to the site, which also has some bicycle and horseback riding trails. Some hikes lead to picturesque views, while others lead to London's gravesite and the remains of Wolf House—London's dream home—which burned to the ground in 1913. There's also a picnic area on site if you want to pack a lunch. Learn more at *www.parks.ca.gov.*

Sonoma Valley Regional Park

If you're traveling with your family's favorite dog, then by all means plan a visit to Sonoma Valley Regional Park, which, in addition to 162 acres of human-ready trails, offers the Elizabeth Anne Perrone Dog Park. It's a fully fenced, one-acre site where dogs can mix, mingle, and even drink from their own fountain. Details are online at *www.sonoma-county.org.*

Kenwood

Kenwood doesn't have a recognizable town center; some folks would argue that it doesn't even really look like a town. The area is best known for its wineries and vineyards, most of which are strategically positioned along Route 12, the main highway, making them easy to visit one after the next.

Some of the wineries are so new and small that they don't have their own rooms for visitors to taste their latest offerings. Instead, these wineries all bring their best bottles to Family Wineries of Sonoma, a cooperative tasting room. Complete information is available online at *www.familywineries.com.* It's open daily from 11 A.M. till 6 P.M. and works with the following vintners:

- Deerfield Ranch Winery
- Mayo Family Winery
- Noel Wine Cellars
- Nelson Estate Winery
- Meredith Wine Cellars

Russian River Region

The Russian River region is basically synonymous with northern Sonoma County. It starts right around the town of Santa Rosa and works its way north to the town of Healdsburg, with most of the wineries located off the main Route 101 to the east, where the Russian River runs.

Santa Rosa

Santa Rosa is the largest city in Sonoma County, although because it's farther north than the town of Sonoma, it's not as well known to tourists. That's not to say there isn't plenty to do and see here, of course. In fact, the town has a free, downloadable visitor's guide available at *www.visitsantarosa.com*.

The Pacific Coast Air Museum pays tribute not just to nuts-and-bolts aircraft but also to the people who have flown them throughout history. In addition to on-site exhibits—including planes that you can walk through—the museum sponsors an air show every August featuring flybys performed by antique planes and modern-day aircraft alike. Details about the upcoming show's dates are available at *www.pacificcoastairmuseum.org*.

There are no fewer than six golf courses in Santa Rosa, about a third of the total number in all of Sonoma County. Some offer stay-and-play packages, making it easy to combine a golf getaway with a long weekend of winery tours. For a complete list of courses including links to individual club Web sites, go to *www.visitsantarosa.com*.

 TRAVEL TIP

If you love *Peanuts*—the kind you read, not the kind you eat—you can pay homage to the creator of Charlie, Linus, Lucy, and Snoopy at the Charles M. Schulz Museum in Santa Rosa. In addition to exhibits and a well-stocked gift shop, the museum has a theater with daily screenings of *Peanuts* animation, interviews with Schulz, and more. Learn more at *www .schulzmuseum.org*.

Healdsburg

One of the best things about the sleepy little town of Healdsburg is that several wineries have set up tasting rooms and shops amid the stores and restaurants of the downtown plaza. You don't even have to leave town to sample offerings from Gallo, Windsor, and Kendall-Jackson, to name a few. The Russian River runs right through the town, so if you're visiting during the warm weather months, you can also enjoy kayaking and canoeing. For a full list of vendors, go online to *www.healdsburg.com*.

Popular Wineries

Sonoma County, like its neighbor Napa County, has so many wineries that you can't possibly expect to visit them all. Also like Napa, Sonoma County has well-known brand names along with local favorites that may be new to you. Your best bet is to select three or four wineries a day, perhaps mixing and matching the best-known brands with labels you'd like to learn. To that end, here's a look at some of the wineries with a wide enough distribution that you may have sampled their wines in the past.

Kenwood

Sharing a name with its home town, Kenwood Vineyards is best known for its Sauvignon Blanc, Cabernet Sauvignon, and Zinfandel. The vineyard was established in 1970 and continues to offer free tastings of up to four of its wines per day. If you really want to immerse yourself in the local experience, sample one of Kenwood's Jack London labels, made from grapes grown in a vineyard formerly owned by the novelist. The winery is open from 10 A.M. until 4:30 P.M. daily. Learn more at *www.kenwoodvineyards.com*.

FAST FACT

Ever wonder how a vineyard like Kenwood can produce so much wine? Consider the fact that the winery has more than 125 stainless steel fermenting and upright oak tanks, along with some 14,000 French and American oak barrels. They must be doing something right with that equipment, too, as Kenwood wines consistently win 85- to 95-point ratings from top critics.

Ravenswood

Located right in Sonoma town itself, Ravenswood Winery is best known for its Zinfandel. In fact, its Web site brags about being a "Department of Zinformation"—giving you a peek at the lighthearted humor you'll find at this winery.

The Ravenswood motto—or battle cry, as they say—is "No Wimpy Wines," and the winery challenges you to show your own mental muscle by making your own blend of its California varietals to take home. There are tours and tastings of its regular and premium offerings, plus barbecues held from Memorial Day through Labor Day to help you keep your stomach good and padded. The winery opens at 10:30 A.M. daily. Learn more at *www.ravenswood-wine.com*.

Geyser Peak

Geyser Peak is way up north, upward of Healdsburg on the Sonoma County map, in what is known as the Alexander Valley. It's been a staple of wine making in the region since 1882, and today it's owned by the worldwide beverage conglomerate Jim Beam Brands. *The Wall Street Journal* calls its tasting room one of the best in Napa and Sonoma counties—quite an endorsement given the amount and breadth of competition. There's also a VIP tasting room that features the Reserve and Block Collection wines. Hours are 10 A.M. until 5 P.M. daily, and special events are promoted throughout the year. For details about what's happening during your visit, go to *www.geyserpeakwinery.com*.

TRAVEL TIP

Ever wanted to learn how to cure an olive? Participate in an event called Martini Madness? Taste new recipes made from the finest local olive oils? The Sonoma Valley Visitors Bureau conceived the annual Olive Festival to provide all that and more, which it's been doing since 2001. Event dates change from year to year, but you can get a look at what's coming up—not to mention some terrific, free olive-oriented recipes—at *www.sonomavalley.com.*

Benziger

Located near the town of Glen Ellen, the Benziger Family Winery has a tractor-pulled tram that you can take for a look around the vineyards while you rest your weary feet for a solid forty-five minutes. The tour includes a look at underground caves, plus, of course, a stop at the tasting room.

 TRAVEL TIP

The tram tour at Benziger departs several times a day depending on the season and demand—and seats fill up fast. Your best bet for ensuring that you get a ride is to contact the winery in advance at (888) 490-2739. They'll give you a tour schedule over the phone, though reservations for the $10 tickets typically are not accepted in advance.

You can skip the ride and go straight to the good stuff, which is available daily from 10 A.M. until 5 P.M. Be sure to try the varietals for which the winery is best known, including its Cabernet Sauvignon, Merlot, and Chardonnay. The winery's Web site is *www.benziger.com.*

Labels to Learn

Along with Sonoma County's more popular wineries, there are literally dozens of winemakers whose labels you might want to learn. Big production doesn't always mean the best taste, and you can find some delightful bottles to take home even at the smallest mom-and-pop operations in Sonoma County.

Valley of the Moon Winery

You know where the name came from, and now you can taste the wine that goes along with it. Located in Glen Ellen, this winery has been around since 1863, surviving multiple owners as well as Prohibition to become the longest-operating winery in the Glen Ellen area. The history remains, but the old buildings do not. They were torn down in the late 1990s to make way for a fancy new operation. Tastings and tours are available daily. For information about seasonal hours and events, go to *www.valleyofthemoonwinery.com*.

Kunde Estate Winery

This operation is in Kenwood, where a barn is the winery itself. If you think that's a little dated compared with newer and fancier facilities, just wait until you take a tour of the underground caves where Kunde ages its varietals in small oak barrels. It doesn't get much more old school than that. The tasting room is open daily from 10:30 A.M. until 4:30 P.M., with options for a $5 estate tasting or a $10 sample of reserve wines. Cave tours are only on Friday, Saturday, and Sunday, and they occur throughout the day, free of charge. Learn more at *www.kunde.com*.

Simi Winery

Located right in Healdsburg, the Simi Winery is a local leader in the art of helping visitors understand how to better pair food and wine. Simi is known for its Cabernet Sauvignon, Sauvignon Blanc, and Merlot varietals. Tastings and tours are available daily. Tours begin in a visitor's center that is paneled with wood from a 25,000-gallon barrel that once held wine in Simi's cellar. You can get a sneak peek (or a sneak taste, as it were) at some of the on-site chef's recipes by going to the Web site, *www.simiwinery.com*.

Carneros District Wineries

The Carneros District is just that, a district—one that overlaps the southern portions of both Napa and Sonoma counties. The wines you find here may call themselves Napa or Sonoma brands, but Carneros has, in fact, been a distinct viticulture area since 1983. There are fewer than a dozen wineries in the Carneros district. They all offer tastings and tours, some by appointment only. Here are the pertinent details:

- Artesa Winery, *www.artesawinery.com*
- Bouchaine Vineyards, *www.bouchaine.com*
- Cline Cellars, *www.clinecellars.com*
- Domaine Carneros, *www.domaine.com*
- Gloria Ferrer Champagne Caves, *www.gloriaferrer.com*
- Madonna Estate, *www.madonnaestate.com*
- Saintsbury Vineyard, *www.saintsbury.com*
- Schug Carneros Estate Winery, *www.schugwinery.com*
- Truchard Vineyards, *www.truchardvineyards.com*
- Viansa Winery & Italian Marketplace, *www.viansa.com*

Lodging and Restaurants

There is no shortage of places to stay or eat in this region. Here are some suggestions you might want to consider. Each suggestion is marked by one, two, or three dollar signs.

For lodging:
$ = a room costs less than $100
$$ = a room costs from $101 to $200
$$$ = a room costs more than $200

For restaurants:

$ = entrées cost less than $15

$$ = entrées cost from $16 to $30

$$$ = entrées cost more than $30

Lodging

SONOMA
El Pueblo Inn
896 West Napa Street

(800) 900-8844

www.elpuebloinn.com

$$

Fairmont Sonoma Mission Inn & Spa
18140 Sonoma Highway

(800) 862-4945

www.fairmont.com

$$$

Ledson Hotel & Harmony Lounge
480 First Street East

(707) 996-9779

www.ledsonhotel.com

$$$

Sonoma Creek Inn
239 Boyes Boulevard

(707) 939-9463

www.sonomacreekinn.com

$

Sonoma Hotel on the Plaza
110 West Spain Street

(707) 996-2996

www.sonomahotel.com

$$

BODEGA BAY
Bodega Bay Lodge & Spa
103 Coast Highway 1
(707) 875-3525
www.bodegabaylodge.com
$$$

PETALUMA
Quality Inn—Petaluma
5100 Montero Way
(707) 664-1155
www.qualityinn.com
$$

ROHNERT PARK
DoubleTree Hotel—Sonoma Wine Country
1 DoubleTree Drive
(707) 584-5466
www.dtsonoma.com
$$

Rodeway Inn
6288 Redwood Drive
(800) 591-9425
www.rodewayinn.com
$$

SANTA ROSA
Sandman Motel
3421 Cleveland Avenue
(707) 544-8570
www.sonoma.com
$

Vintners Inn
4350 Barnes Road
(707) 575-7350
www.vintnersinn.com
$$$

HEALDSBURG
Day Creek Inn—Best Western
198 Dry Creek Road
(707) 433-0300
www.bestwestern.com
$

Hotel Healdsburg
25 Matheson Street
(707) 431-2800
www.hotelhealdsburg.com
$$$

Les Mars Hotel
27 North Street
(707) 433-4211
www.lesmarshotel.com
$$$

SEBASTOPOL
The Sebastopol Inn
6751 Sebastopol Avenue
(800) 653-1082
www.sebastopolinn.com
$$

Restaurants

Sonoma
Depot Hotel Restaurant
241 First Street West
(800) 200-2980
www.depothotel.com
$–$$

El Dorado Hotel & Kitchen
405 First Street West
(707) 996-3030
www.eldoradosonoma.com
$$

Ramekins Cooking School
450 West Spain Street
(707) 933-0450
www.ramekins.com
$–$$

Saddles Steakhouse at MacArthur Place
29 East MacArthur Street
(707) 933-3191
www.macarthurplace.com
$$

Sante at the Fairmont Sonoma Mission Inn
18140 Sonoma Highway
(800) 862-4945
www.fairmont.com/sonoma
$$

GLEN ELLEN
Glen Ellen Inn Oyster Grill & Martini Bar
13670 Arnold Drive
(707) 996-6409
www.glenelly.com
$$

BODEGA BAY
Bay View Restaurant & Lounge
800 Coast Highway 1
(800) 541-7788
www.sonoma.com
$$

The Tides Wharf Restaurant & Bar
800 Coast Highway 1
(800) 541-7788
www.innatthetides.com
$$

PETALUMA
Running Rooster Sports Bar & Grill
2301 East Washington Street, Petaluma
(707) 778-1397
www.roosterrun.com
$

ROHNERT PARK
Latitude
5000 Roberts Lake Road
(707) 588-1800
www.latitudegrill.com
$–$$

VALLEY FORD
Rocker Oysterfeller's Kitchen + Saloon
14415 Highway 1
(707) 876-1983
www.rockeroysterfellers.com
$–$$

SANTA ROSA
Ca'Bianca
835 Second Street
(707) 542-5800
www.cabianca.com
$–$$

HEALDSBURG
Dry Creek Kitchen
317 Healdsburg Avenue
(707) 431-0330
www.drycreekvineyard.com
$–$$

GUERNEVILLE
Applewood Inn
13555 Highway 116
(800) 555-8509
www.applewoodinn.com
$$

La Buona Forchetta
13555 Highway 116
(707) 869-9093
www.sonoma.com
$–$$

CHAPTER 8

The North Coast

THE NORTH COAST SECTION of northern California has no exact borders, but for our purposes it starts on the western shores of Sonoma County, just north of San Francisco. It extends to California's border with Oregon; Crescent City is the last major Golden State outpost. You'll find Redwood National Park here, plus some great whale-watching spots and a handful of towns like Eureka and Arcata that offer more than their small size on the map might indicate.

Regional Overview

As with so much of California, the modern history of the North Coast region begins in the late 1840s with the gold rush. No, there weren't massive deposits of money-making ore amid the giant redwoods, but there certainly was plenty of room for pack stations where miners could find food and comfort before setting off again. Similar pack stations sprang up in other remote parts of the state like Yosemite.

Those first entrepreneurs who made their way up the North Coast of course saw a financial future in redwood logging, with seemingly endless forests of trees so big you could practically use a splinter as the beam for an entire house. The problem was getting them to a saw-mill, onto ships, and, later, onto the trains that transported goods to every market available. Some redwoods live longer than 2,000 years and grow nearly 400 feet tall—the size of a forty-story skyscraper in a modern city.

══FAST FACT

When people started flocking to California in the late 1840s, more than 2 million acres of the coastline was filled with redwood forests. Today, as logging efforts are all but completed in the area, the protected Redwood National and State Parks encompass just shy of 132,000 acres of the spectacular trees. What's left is considered a main tourism draw, and a few of the old logging roads are now touted as scenic drives.

Just as in other areas that drew settlers, there was a natural inclination to come together and form towns. Some eventually faded back into the natural landscape, but others have survived. In terms of touring the area, the places you'll want to know include Crescent City to the north, followed southward along the Pacific shoreline by Arcata, Eureka, Mendocino (including historic Fort Bragg), and the Sonoma County coastal area (including historic Fort Ross).

You don't necessarily have to think about each of these places as a must-see stop, but it will be helpful to think of them as waypoints if you plan to work your way from the top of the state down, back toward San Francisco.

Some locals consider the Sonoma County city of Santa Rosa to be part of the North Coast region, so you could combine a visit here with some of the other destinations you read about in Chapter 7. Sonoma County's wineries and fine restaurants, in fact, make a nice change of scenery after a few days of exploring the fog-filled redwood forests and watching for whales along the North Coast, and there is something to be said about easing back into civilization before returning to a metropolis like San Francisco to fly home.

TRAVEL TIP

Going straight up Highway 101, it's about 350 miles from San Francisco to Crescent City, the uppermost town in California's North Coast region. If you don't mind driving six to seven hours in a single day, you could fly into San Francisco, pick up a rental car, and drive to the top of the state before slowly working your way back south.

Crescent City

Here's a statistic that should tell you a great deal: Only about 7,500 people live in Crescent City, and it is the only incorporated city in the most northwestern California county. It's an outpost even today, much as it has been since gold miners started arriving in the late 1840s, and it is as much tied to nature as it was when the first settlers came.

The city is named for a crescent-shaped beach that is home to Crescent City Harbor, whose primary purpose is providing a home for commercial fishing boats that scour the Pacific waters for crab, salmon, tuna, and shrimp. There are a few pleasure boats in the harbor, but given the almost constantly foggy conditions and the lack of near-shore islands, most people would prefer to cruise around a place like San Francisco Bay than in the churning Pacific off Crescent City.

You may remember Crescent City from national news reports in 1964, when a 9.2-magnitude earthquake off the coast of Anchorage, Alaska, spawned a tsunami that slammed four giant waves into the town during just two hours. Some thirty city blocks were destroyed, including close to 300 buildings by some reports. It took years for the local people who decided to stay to rebuild.

Crescent City hasn't been hit with another major tsunami since, but there is an alert system in place that has been tested a few times by offshore earthquakes, most recently in late 2006. Highway 101 is the only main route in and out of town, so if you're the cautious type, make sure you know your proximity to it just in case a quake strikes during your visit.

The main reason most people visit Crescent City is that it is just north of Redwood National and State Parks, making it a good starting point if you want to get far to California's north and then work your way back down the state. You can, of course, visit the redwoods from the south, as well, starting in cities like Eureka and Arcata, but Crescent City is a good starting point if you want to see as much as possible of the forests' length along the coast.

 RAINY DAY FUN

Embrace the moisture in the air. That's the attitude that locals have in Crescent City, where the fog is thick enough—and fills enough of the sky—to sustain the giant redwoods that have lived there for centuries. Don't look for things to do here "if" it is damp outside. Instead, expect the weather to be uncooperative.

Redwood National and State Parks

You'll read quite a bit about touring the Redwood National and State Parks in Chapter 16, but suffice to say that if you find yourself in Crescent City and don't see any big trees, then you're just plain doing it wrong.

Trees are pretty much all anybody saw in this part of the North Coast for decades, as the first mills opened to support the logging business back in the early 1850s. More than a century and a half later, the redwoods are still the main draw, albeit today people come to enjoy instead of destroy what's left of the forests.

Battery Point Lighthouse

This part of northern California is awash in shipwrecks, including at least one American ship sunk during World War II. The rugged coastline itself makes it easy to see why a lighthouse is a key navigational aid, and the Battery Point Lighthouse served sailors well from the mid-1800s until it was decommissioned in 1953.

The light came back on in the early 1980s, when the lighthouse became a private aid to navigation as part of a restoration. It has been named a California Historical Landmark, one that you can tour along with the caretakers who run it and know it best.

It is located on a small islet just outside the harbor—across a land bridge that sometimes gets swamped by the tide. It is open from 10 A.M. to 4 P.M. Wednesday through Sunday, April through September, "weather permitting." If you don't know how to check a tide chart in the local newspaper, call first to make sure you won't get stuck out on the island should the tide roll in for the night. The number is (707) 464-3089. Additional information can be found at the official Web site, *www.lighthousefriends.com*.

Arcata

Arcata and Eureka are twin cities on Humboldt Bay. Arcata is on the northern coast of the bay, about eighty miles south of Crescent City and about 280 miles north of San Francisco along Highway 101.

═══FAST FACT

Arcata made national headlines in 1996, when it became the first city in the United States to elect a majority of members from the Green Party to its city council. The environmentally minded city is also a study in social progressivism, having banned the growth of genetically modified foods and passed a resolution that nullified the Patriot Act inside the city limits. The number of chain restaurants is also limited.

Arcata is a world apart from most other towns in the state, let alone the nation, in terms of its social bent. If you decide to drive here for a visit, try to do so in a hybrid car. That way, the locals might actually mistake you for one of their own. Think bongo drums, Hacky Sacks, and Grateful Dead fans, especially among the local college population. Not everyone who lives here is a postmodern hippie, but there are enough who call Arcata home to make you feel as if you've traveled back in time to the 1960s.

Aside from touring the shops and restaurants along the downtown plaza, there are two main spots that draw visitors to Arcata: the semi-pro baseball stadium and the local university's museum.

Humboldt Crabs

The Humboldt Crabs play at Arcata Ballpark, where 400 to 1,500 fans attend games on sunny summer days. The team has been a part of the local sports community since the mid-1940s, so you'll run into Arcata grandparents who can remember visiting the ballpark with their own grandparents back in the day.

Arcata Ballpark is just a block away from the town plaza, so if you're making a morning of seeing the shops and restaurants, then you can wander over in the afternoon for a game. Tickets are $6 for adults and $2 for children ages twelve and younger. You can get them online at *www.humboldtcrabs.com*, which also posts the season's schedule and a nifty downloadable video about the team's storied history.

Humboldt State University Natural History Museum

True to its location in Arcata, Humboldt State University is a campus known for its natural resources, science, and liberal arts programs. The college's Natural History Museum aims to inspire both students and visitors alike, with interactive exhibits and programs tailored for all ages, including toddlers who visit with adult supervision.

One of the museum's popular interactive exhibits lets you touch fossils, as well as a meteorite that's believed to be some 4.5 billion years old. Another exhibit includes a nearly 3-foot-long cast of a dinosaur skull that you can touch, including the teeth.

Museum hours are from 10 A.M. to 5 P.M. Tuesday through Saturday. Admission is $3 for adults and $2 for children. There's also a $10 family pass that's good for two adults and up to four children. Learn more at *www.humboldt.edu*.

 RAINY DAY FUN

The HSU Natural History Museum's "Saturday NatureKids" program is designed for children between the ages of four and eight. Topics range from "Wild, Wonderful Wolves" to "Give a Hoot for Owls," with prices for non-museum members running from $8 to $15 per session. There are hour-long sessions for younger kids, with two-hour sessions for older kids. Many of the sessions include a craft project such as making an owl mask.

Kinetic Sculpture Race

The big event that starts in Arcata's plaza every Memorial Day Weekend is a three-day, multicounty Kinetic Sculpture race—a competition to see who can build and use the fastest cross-country, human-powered vehicle over terrain that includes sand, water, and pavement.

The race has been held since the late 1960s and is covered over the local radio, just as an Olympic triathlon might be. For information about this year's event, go to the organizing committee's Web site, *www.kineticuniverse.com*.

Eureka

Eureka is just south of Arcata, almost right at the middle point of Humboldt Bay. It's not quite as politically quirky as its neighbor, and it offers a little more in terms of attractions—most of which are likely to appeal to your entire family. If you prefer to meander on your own instead of taking tours with other visitors, Eureka offers a waterfront boardwalk and a historic downtown area, both with shops and restaurants for you to explore.

The town is also the Humboldt County seat, big enough to support plenty of hotels, motels, and other lodging options. For a complete list, go to *http://redwoods.info*.

Humboldt Bay Maritime Museum

Founded in 1977, the Humboldt Bay Maritime Museum seeks to preserve the maritime history of California's entire North Coast. This is a classic-style museum with actual artifacts where newer institutions might have interactive exhibits. There's also a well-stocked library.

The museum also owns *Madaket*, which is operated by the Humboldt Bay Harbor Cruise company. If you want to come into Eureka the same way the first European settlers did, then your best bet is to travel by sea—or at least to pretend to travel by sea after parking your car and boarding *Madaket*, the last remaining local ferry from the early 1900s. It sails from June through September, offering narrated as well as cocktail cruises. Tickets are $15 for adults and $7.50 for children ages five and older.

Museum hours are 11 A.M. until 4 P.M. Tuesday through Saturday each summer. More information is available online at *www .humboldtbaymaritimemuseum.com*.

Morris Graves Museum of Art

The Morris Graves Museum of Art is inside the Eureka Carnegie Library building, which is more than a century old. The museum itself had its ribbon-cutting in 2000 and today includes seven galleries plus a sculpture garden and performance rotunda.

Exhibits rotate, and past exhibits have included everything from the art of children's book illustrators to small works benefits. Jazz shows also tend to be a part of the program at the museum. To see what's coming up during your visit, go to *www.humboldtarts.org*.

Discovery Museum

If a hands-on museum full of "smell labs" and "construction zones" sounds more like your family's speed, then head to the Discovery Museum in Old Town Eureka. It's a nonprofit institution designed specifically for children to explore the areas of science, technology, art, and culture.

This museum runs regular and special programs designed for families with younger children, including a jazz jubilee every March and a dropoff program on Tuesdays and Thursdays for kids between three and five years old. Learn more at *www.discovery-museum.org*.

Blue Ox Millworks

Blue Ox Millworks is keeping the lumber industry alive, using crafts-manship techniques of the 1800s to produce everything from doors to gutters. You can watch the craftsmen at work at the Historic Park, which has a blacksmith's shop, working antique tools, a ceramics studio, a boatbuilding shop, a print shop, and more. There are self-guided tours available Monday through Saturday for $7.50 per adult and $3.50 for children between six and twelve years old, or you can choose a guided tour that starts at $10 per person—though a ten-person minimum is required. There are also workshops where you can create ceramic tiles and forge nails. Learn more at *www.blueoxmill.com*.

 TRAVEL TIP

The busiest times of the year at Blue Ox Millworks are the first Saturday in May and the first weekend after Thanksgiving. That's when the millworks opens its doors to northern California craftsmen who want to share their knowledge with visitors from near and far—and perhaps make a sale on their recently cre-ated wares.

Sequoia Park Zoo

Eureka's Sequoia Park Zoo isn't exactly massive; in fact, it's one of the smallest institutions accredited by the Association of Zoos and Aquariums. Even still, it has lots of birds, bears, monkeys, snakes, and interesting species. There are no "big animals" such as elephants and lions; with only five acres of property, the zoo doesn't have a whole lot of room for them to move around.

The zoo is open during the summer from 10 A.M. until 7 P.M. Tuesday through Sunday. There is no admission fee, but suggested donations range from $1 to $3 depending on your age and your children's ages. More details are available online at *www.sequoiaparkzoo.net.*

Mendocino

Mendocino is a town in Mendocino County, just north of Sonoma County. Geographically speaking, it's just a hair out of desirable driving range for most San Francisco locals (about four hours away) who are looking for weekend getaways—which is good in terms of keeping it a quieter location for you to explore. Its proximity to Sonoma County also makes it a good place to combine a lower North Coast itinerary with a visit to Wine Country. You can experience a little bit of the best of both worlds: gastronomy and nature.

The town of Mendocino is not that much bigger than the book in your hands, with fewer than 1,000 residents as of the most recent census. It's an artsy place that considers itself part of a broader community up and down the coast, where several small towns exist side-by-side, collectively offering an interesting place to visit.

FAST FACT

Almost all of the episodes of the popular television series *Murder, She Wrote* were filmed in Mendocino. Dozens of local residents played background and small speaking roles, and actress Angela Lansbury was a familiar face on the town's streets from 1983 through 1995, when the final season was filmed. Her fictional home is a bed and breakfast called Blair House.

If you're not coming to the Mendocino area to visit local parks and hike or ride bicycles along the coast, then the odds are you'll be visiting for either water sports or a tour around historic Fort Bragg.

Fun on the Water

This isn't water-skiing territory, but it's heaven for swimmers and canoe and kayak lovers, at least during the warmer summer months. The Big River, which runs through the Mendocino Woodlands about ten miles from town, is the largest undeveloped, navigable estuary in northern California. The river boasts spectacular views of the forested canyon and its wildlife. Every once in a while, there's a swimming hole that looks like it's fresh off a postcard.

If you're interested in renting some gear and having it delivered (along with you) to the water, then get in touch with Catch-a-Canoe & Bicycles Too at *www.stanfordinn.com*. It's main competitor, near Fort Bragg, has gone out of business, so expect demand for kayaks to outstrip supply during the peak summer months.

Fort Bragg

You might associate the name *Fort Bragg* with the home of the U.S. military's paratrooper and special operations forces. That's not the same place as historic Fort Bragg, which is a town in Mendocino County. It's known for its outdoor offerings, such as whale watching, hiking, and kayaking, but it also has an interesting historic side that includes a couple of quirky institutions. One of them, the Triangle Tattoo and Museum, is dedicated to the display of tattoo artifacts.

There are also a couple of art galleries in town, some focusing on wildlife art and others on seascapes of the local surroundings. You can find opera and theater performances depending on the dates of your visit. Learn more at *www.fortbragg.com*.

Sonoma Coast

Closest to the San Francisco Bay area—and arguably not technically part of the North Coast region, but instead its gateway from the big city—is the Sonoma County coastline. It's a short strip, just seventeen miles long, but it packs a heck of a scenic wallop. Along the Sonoma Coast, you can take a meandering look at the local beaches or tour Fort Ross, a state historic park, depending on your family's mood.

The Beaches

Sonoma Coast's beaches are known for big rocks, big surf, and waves that literally swallow people right off the sand without warning. Forget your bathing suit and instead pack your running shoes and go for a walk or a jog a bit of the way up along the sand. These beaches are meant to be seen, not settled upon in a lawn chair for hours on end.

The Sonoma Coast beaches from Bodega Head to Vista Trail are actually all part of Sonoma Coast State Park—where again, the first thing they tell you on their Web site, *www.parks.ca.gov*, is that these beaches are not for swimming. Each section of beach is separated by rock bluffs or headlands, with distinct parking areas to help you navigate your way back home at the end of the afternoon.

There are seven beaches whose signs you might see. Each draws different people for different kinds of activities:

- **Bodega Head.** Popular with hikers, crabbers, and whale-watchers.
- **Goat Rock.** Picnic tables, restrooms, and a colony of sea lions.
- **Shell Beach.** Known for its tide pools
- **Duncan's Landing.** Notorious for large waves taking people caught unaware while walking along the rocks.
- **Portuguese Beach.** Sandy and known for surfing.
- **Schoolhouse Beach.** Popular with surfers.
- **Salmon Creek Beach.** Known for surfing and picnicking.

Fort Ross

Fort Ross State Historic Park has been around since 1812, when the Russian-American Company sent its Alaska fur trappers and traders in search of a southern outpost for gathering food and seeking shelter during the winter months. Today, one original structure still stands, along with five restored buildings, a visitor's center, a library, and a bookstore that contains the largest collection of Russian history in northern California.

===FAST FACT

The Russian-built Fort Ross was well prepared for attacks by Spanish or Native American warriors, but the fort's cannons never had to be fired in self-defense despite its sentry posts and well-armed gunnery blockhouses. A chapel was added a few years after the fort's initial construction.

The fort is located in the town of Jenner, at the southern end of Sonoma County. Hours are a half-hour before sunrise until a half-hour after sunrise each day, and the per-car entrance fee is $5. During the summer months, park personnel offer presentations about the local history and ruins. You can learn about what's coming up at *www.fortrossstatepark.org*.

King Range National Conservation Area

Known as the Lost Coast, the King Range National Conservation Area isn't as well known as the Sonoma Coast beaches, but it's worth a visit nonetheless. Its tallest mountain, King Peak, is more than 4,000 feet high—yet it's just three miles from the coast. It's hard to find that kind of juxtaposition anywhere in the world.

The conservation area extends for about thirty-five miles along the shore and includes some 64,000 protected acres. The landscape is so rugged that Highway 1 runs inland to go around it, but local roads can get you "inside" for a look at the really good stuff.

King Range offers six campsites, which a lot of campers love because they feel so remote in comparison to other campsites along the North Coast. This is true camping in a lot of ways. The biggest site has space for just thirteen trailers and tents, and most sites have no running water or hookups. When you see the phrase "pit toilets," you'll know the reality you can expect.

If you would like to visit without spending the night, there is a site that welcomes RVs. You can go to Mal Coombs Park within the conservation area. It has picnic tables, flush toilets, water, and even wheelchair accessibility. If you tow a boat, there is a launch ramp nearby, but it's privately operated and requires an additional fee.

 TRAVEL TIP

Be aware of your surroundings in the King Range National Conservation Area. Hunting is allowed from July through September, and bears aren't shy about checking out the campsites where tourists unwisely leave food containers open. Some black bears have been known to tear into backpacks and tents.

The best months to visit are May through September, with temperatures ranging from 60 to 80 degrees and a good number of bright, sunny days. During other times of the year, this is one of the wettest spots in the United States, averaging between 100 and 200 inches of rainfall annually—so be sure to bring layered clothing as well as rain gear. For directions and additional seasonal information, go to *www.blm.gov.*

Lodging and Restaurants

There is no shortage of places to stay or eat in this area. Here are some suggestions you might want to consider. Each suggestion is marked by one, two, or three dollar signs.

For lodging:
$ = a room costs less than $100
$$ = a room costs from $101 to $200
$$$ = a room costs more than $200

For restaurants:
$ = entrées cost less than $15
$$ = entrées cost from $16 to $30
$$$ = entrées cost more than $30

Lodging

CRESCENT CITY
America's Best Value Inn
440 Highway 101 North
(707) 464-4141
www.americasbestvalueinn.com
$

Best Western Northwoods Inn
655 Highway 101 South
(800) 485-0134
www.bwnorthwoodsinn.com
$–$$

Comfort Inn & Suites Redwood Coast
100 Walton Street
(707) 464-3885
www.comfortinn.com
$–$$

Crescent City Travelodge
353 L Street
(707) 464-6424
www.travelodge.com
$

Econo Lodge Crescent City
725 Highway 101 North
(707) 464-6106
www.econolodge.com
$

ARCATA
Howard Johnson Express Arcata
4700 Valley West Boulevard
(800) 804-8835
www.howardjohnson.com
$

Scottfield Executive Hotel
270 Fifth Street
(800) 804-6835
www.hotels.com
$$

The Ship's Inn
821 D Street
(707) 433-7583
www.shipsinn.net
$

EUREKA
Carter House Inns
301 L Street
(707) 444-8062
www.carterhouse.com
$$–$$$

Clarion Resort Eureka
2223 Fourth Street
(707) 422-3261
www.clarionhotel.com
$$

Econo Lodge
1630 Fourth Street
(707) 433-8041

www.econolodge.com
$

Quality Inn
1209 Fourth Street
(707) 433-1601
www.qualityinn.com
$

Red Lion Hotel Eureka
1929 Fourth Street
(707) 445-0844
www.redlion.com
$$

MENDOCINO
Agate Cove Inn
11201 North Lansing Street
(800) 527-3111
www.agatecove.com
$$–$$$

Restaurants

ARCATA
The Alibi
744 Ninth Street
(707) 822-3731
www.thealibi.com
$

Folie Douce
1551 G Street
(707) 822-1042
www.holyfolie.com
$$–$$$

Jambalaya Restaurant
915 H Street
(707) 822-4766
www.jambalaya-restaurant.com
$–$$

Round Table Pizza
600 F Street
(707) 822-3671
www.roundtablepizza.com
$–$$

Tomo Japanese Restaurant
2120 Fourth Street
(707) 822-1414
www.cafetomo.com
$$

Eureka
Restaurant 301
301 L Street
(707) 444-8062
www.carterhouse.com
$$

FORT BRAGG
Mendo Bistro
301 North Main Street
(707) 964-4974
www.mendobistro.com
$–$$

North Coast Brewing Company
455 North Main Street
(707) 964-2739

www.mendocino.com
$$–$$$

Rendezvous Inn & Restaurant
647 North Main Street
(707) 964-8142
www.rendezvousinn.com
$$–$$$

Silver's at the Wharf
32260 North Harbor Drive
(707) 964-4283
www.wharf-restaurant.com
$$–$$$

MENDOCINO
MacCallum House Inn & Restaurant
45020 Albion Street
(800) 609-0462
www.maccallumhouse.com
$$–$$$

Ravens Restaurant
Coast Highway and Comptche Ukiah Road
(800) 331-8884
www.ravensrestaurant.com
$$

LITTLE RIVER
Heritage House Inn
5200 North Highway 1
(800) 235-5885
www.heritagehouseinn.com
$$$

Sacramento Area

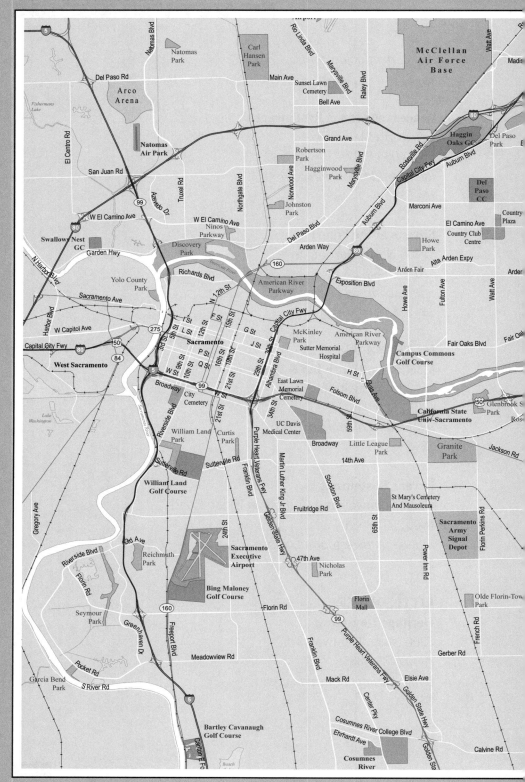

CHAPTER 9

Sacramento

SACRAMENTO IS A CITY UNLIKE ANY OTHER, a place where—in a single day—you can watch the Golden State's government in action, learn the history of automobiles, treat the family to an affordable Triple-A division baseball game, and walk the wooden sidewalks that used to serve as wandering spots for folks caught up in the gold rush of the late 1840s. The city has the charm of its distinct history as well as the conveniences and comforts you'd expect of a modern metropolis.

History of the State Capital

The city of Sacramento owes much of its history to John Sutter. Well, that's the name the kids learn in their schoolbooks today, anyway. The man's full name was Johann Augustus Sutter, a German-born entrepreneur who racked up so much debt in Switzerland that he was forced to immigrate to the area that is now California. When Sutter arrived in 1839, there were about 1,000 Europeans living in the region alongside some 30,000 Native Americans. Sutter had to become a citizen of Mexico, the area's ruling nation, in order to gain control of nearly 50,000 acres of agricultural land that would become Sutter's Fort.

California became part of the United States in 1847, and Sutter was outnumbered when U.S. troops took over his land for a short period. You might recall that James Marshall, a foreman at Sutter's Mill, found pieces of shiny metal in the flume that led away from the mill's water wheel in 1848. This was the first gold sighting in what would become the gold rush of 1849 in northern California. Tens of thousands of people would make their way west, trampling Sutter's precious agricultural land and destroying nearly everything in their quest to become wealthy overnight.

≡FAST FACT

When James Marshall, a New Jersey native, showed his first pieces of shiny metal to fellow workers at Sutter's Mill, they laughed at him and told him he was crazy for thinking that it was gold. Sutter himself determined that the original pieces Marshall brought him were indeed at least twenty-three carats after reading about the metal in his *Encyclopedia Americana*.

Sutter's son Augustus arrived in America from Switzerland at the same time as the gold rush, and Sutter bequeathed him a good deal of land. Augustus immediately set about turning it into a city that he wanted to call Sacramento, based on the name of the nearby Sacramento River. As more and more people descended on the area in search of gold, Sacramento became a metropolitan hub full of commercial and agricultural ventures. It was also the end of the line for various stagecoach routes, wagon trains, riverboats, the Pony Express, and the first transcontinental railroad.

From these Wild West roots grew the city that stands today, with nearly a half-million residents, Sacramento State University, the seat of the California state government (since 1854), the world-renowned *Sacramento Bee* newspaper, and the National Basketball Association's Sacramento Kings. The city is one of the most racially integrated metropolises in America; not quite half the residents are white, about 20 percent are Hispanic, about 15 percent are African-American, and another 15 percent are Asian. Gold hunting and agriculture have long since taken a back seat to government, which is the city's main employer today.

 TRAVEL TIP

If you're a fan of jazz, plan your trip to Sacramento to coincide with the Memorial Day weekend. Every year since 1973 the city has hosted the Sacramento Jazz Jubilee during the inaugural weekend of summer. Typically, there are at least thirty venues featuring more than 100 different bands playing everything from swing to zydeco to blues. Learn more at *www.sacjazz.com.*

That's not to say the people of Sacramento have forgotten the natural beauty that enchanted John Sutter so many years ago. While city residents are quite proud of their international city, they're just as proud of places like the 5,000-acre American River Parkway, preserved parkland that hosts picnickers, fishermen, and joggers alike. Just as Sutter and his son dreamed more than a century ago, the Sacramento area now offers virtually everything a person could want.

Getting to and Around Sacramento

Sacramento is a highly accessible city no matter how you prefer to travel. You can plan an entire weeklong vacation by coming into and out of Sacramento, or you can integrate a visit to the city into a broader itinerary, say stopping for a day or two as you make your way from San Francisco to the Lake Tahoe region.

By Air

The two-runway Sacramento airport was known as a metropolitan facility until 1996, when it officially became known as Sacramento International Airport. That was a bit of a nod toward the future, since the air traffic controllers didn't start helping international flights land in Sacramento until 2002.

Today, the following national airlines offer flights into and out of Sacramento:

- American Airlines
- Continental Airlines
- Delta Air Lines
- JetBlue Airways
- Southwest Airlines
- United Airlines
- U.S. Airways

The Sacramento airport is smaller than the ones in San Francisco and Los Angeles, so you may not be able to find a direct flight. Still, depending on your home base or future destination, the Sacramento airport now offers a great deal of flight options. There are some direct flights to Canada and Mexico, as well as to major cities on the East Coast.

By Train

Northern California's railway stations may not be as historic as, say, the grand *gares* in Paris, but the Amtrak depot in Sacramento is about as historic as train travel gets in Uncle Sam's book of memories. It was originally the last stop on the Southern Pacific Railroad line, which was one of the first to crisscross the young United States. There's a mural inside and its title—"Breaking Ground at Sacramento January 8, 1863, for the First Transcontinental Railroad"—tells quite a bit about this California city's connection to the days of railroad tycoons.

Amtrak is the service provider at the rail station nowadays, and you can get information on all of its lines at *www.amtrak.com*. Some forty trains depart daily, and you can also catch connections on light rail lines to the city's bus system.

 **RAINY DAY FUN**

If your kids are train buffs, consider riding the Amtrak Coast Starlight route to San Francisco, Oakland, or San Jose. Many of the original Southern Pacific Railroad trains ran these very same routes. Just make sure to build a few extra hours into your itinerary; locals call the line "Starlate" because it ran on time only 2 percent of the time from late 2005 until fall 2006.

By Car

Sacramento has four major highways: Interstate 5, Interstate 80, U.S. Highway 50, and U.S. Highway 99. Interstate 5 crosses the city from north to south and is a good choice if you want to continue on to Red Bluff or Mount Shasta during your vacation. Interstate 80 runs east to west through Sacramento, connecting it with San Francisco and Lake Tahoe. It also brushes close to the city of Napa, if the Wine Country is on your to-do list.

 TRAVEL TIP

In an effort to make the streets of Sacramento safer for pedestrians, the city has instituted several traffic-calming measures such as speed bumps, reduced speed limits, and pedestrian zones. If you choose to drive within the city limits and off the main highways, keep an eye out for these obstacles and be mindful of signs indicating oncoming barriers to traffic.

U.S. Highway 50 runs east from Sacramento and connects with local roads at the south shore of Lake Tahoe before running up along the lake's eastern shore. It's an alternative to Interstate 80, which runs just north of Lake Tahoe's northern shore before connecting to local roads. U.S. Highway 99 runs parallel to Interstate 5 south of Sacramento but then veers off toward the east. It's an option if you want a route from Sacramento to Yosemite, Kings Canyon, or Sequoia National Parks.

By Water

You can forget about airport security, late trains, and traffic obstructions altogether and instead get to Sacramento by water. The Delta River Cruise company offers a high-speed catamaran cruise from San Francisco to Sacramento. The trip takes about four hours and includes a narrator who talks about the region's history and landmarks—and it can be organized as part of a package deal that includes an Amtrak train ride back to San Francisco. For details, rates, and schedules, go to *www.deltarivercruise.com*.

Must-See, Must-Do

As with every major city in northern California, Sacramento has a handful of must-see, must-do landmarks and institutions. Walking through the Old Town and checking out the Capitol goings-on are on the list. For now, consider these options, which are some of the premier draws for tourists from all over the world.

Sutter's Fort

Now that you know the history of the Sacramento area, paying homage to Mr. Sutter himself is as good a way as any to begin your tour around the city. His compound isn't quite as big as it was back in the mid-1800s, but the main adobe house on the property has been restored and deemed a California State Historic Park. The only original building on the site, it is the place where James Marshall brought those first precious few pieces of gold to show his boss.

Today, there are guided tours as well as exhibits and special programs that explain details of the gold rush and the Overland Trail, an old pioneer route that a quarter-million immigrants traversed on stagecoaches and in wagon trains.

The park is open daily from 10 A.M. until 5 P.M. and is closed on major holidays including Thanksgiving, Christmas, and New Year's Day. For information about upcoming events or to inquire about tours, check out *www.parks.ca.gov*.

California State Railroad Museum

The railroad played such an integral part in flooding the Sacramento area with citizens, it seems only fitting that you and your family should pay homage to it at the California State Railroad Museum. It's located in Old Town Sacramento, and you'll find restored trains, rotating exhibits, and special events such as Halloween's "Spookomotive" train rides. Exhibits cover everything from the people who built and worked on the railroad to the exciting fascination that modern-day collectors have with model trains of the tiniest sizes. From April through September, restored steam-power trains depart on the hour, offering rides for the whole family.

FAST FACT

There are twenty-one restored locomotives and train cars at the California State Railroad Museum. You can see everything from 1800s Pullman sleeping cars to dining cars to a Railroad Post Office that you can actually step aboard. Some, like the diesel locomotive called Southern Pacific 8799, are the world's only surviving examples of their particular design.

The museum is open every day from 10 A.M. until 5 P.M., excluding major holidays such as Thanksgiving, Christmas, and New Year's Day. Adults pay $8 to enter, children ages six through seventeen pay $3, and kids five and younger can enter for free. Additional information is available online at *www.csrmf.org*.

Sports for the Whole Family

One of the great things about Sacramento is that you have terrific options for athletic entertainment whether you want to spend beaucoup bucks on top-notch sporting events or go the inexpensive route of a minor-league game. Since the big-brand team plays during the colder months while the smaller-budget roster takes the field from spring through fall, you have options for taking your family to a game year-round in this city.

Sacramento Kings

The NBA's Sacramento Kings have called Sacramento home since 1985. The team's first ten years in the city were inauspicious; they made the playoffs just once. New owners took over in 1997, and soon the Kings were winning division championships and playoff series. Up until 2007, the Sacramento Kings made the playoffs every single year for eight years straight.

They play at Arco Arena. It holds a little more than 17,000 people and hosts everything from ice shows to concert tours when the Kings are off-season or playing out of town. There's a seating chart diagram online at *www.arcoarena.com*, where you can also view upcoming game schedules and purchase tickets.

 TRAVEL TIP

You can save a few dollars when traveling with infants by bringing your own baby food into Arco Arena during game days. It's the only kind of outside food that's allowed inside. You and your older children will have to eat at the concession stands or at the upscale buffet served before games at the fourth-floor Skyline Restaurant.

You can get to the Sacramento Kings' official Web site through *www.nba.com*. It has a lot of nifty features, including downloadable videos of players practicing and talking, as well as podcasts for audio-only uses such as your iPod or MP3 player.

Sacramento Monarchs

The Sacramento Monarchs came into existence on October 20, 1996, when the WNBA was formed as the women's league counterpart to the NBA. The Monarchs play in the WNBA's Western Conference, competing against teams from Houston, Los Angeles, Minnesota, Phoenix, San Antonio, and Seattle. Since the league's inception, the Monarchs have won the overall title once, in 2005. The Monarchs were the runner-up as the best team in the nation in 2006.

Like the Sacramento Kings, the Monarchs play their games at Arco Arena. You can learn more about the team, view upcoming schedules, and buy tickets (which cost less than Kings' tickets) at the Monarchs' official Web site, which is accessible through *www .wnba.com*.

Sacramento River Cats

Even if you're a baseball fan, you may never have heard of the Sacramento River Cats. But you're likely to know who the Oakland A's are—and the River Cats are their Triple-A League affiliated team. You can pay big bucks for an Oakland A's game during your vacation or you can do less damage to your pocketbook at a River Cats game and get a glimpse of the A's future stars.

 TRAVEL TIP

Forget about trying to jostle for a good parking spot at the Sacramento River Cats' Raley Field. The team offers a shuttle that runs around the city collecting fans for every home game. Seats are just fifty cents per person, and the shuttle runs every five minutes. A map of downtown Sacramento, including each shuttle stop, is online at *www.rivercats.com*.

The River Cats have been in Sacramento since 2000. Year after year, the team leads its league in fan attendance numbers. That's in part because of its extremely high level of play, which in just eight seasons has garnered four division titles and two overall league championships. Some sixty River Cats players have gone on to compete for Major League Baseball teams.

Old Town

State government may be the key industry in Sacramento, but the place most tourists come to see is the Old Town—known as Old Sacramento or Old Sac for short. This section of the city is actually a State Historic Park as well as a National Landmark, comprising twenty-eight acres (about eight city blocks) of historic buildings and monuments. Most of the structures date to the 1850s, just after the great gold rush. You'll find wooden sidewalks, riverboats, and horse-drawn carriages filling in the backdrop today just as they did more than a century ago. You'll find the must-see California State Railroad Museum here, plus a few others that are well worth a visit for the whole family.

 RAINY DAY FUN

If it's too icky out to walk the streets of Old Sacramento, consider touring the area by covered boat. A couple of companies offer lunch and dinner cruises, as well as paddle-wheel tours. One riverboat, the *Delta King*, even does double-duty as a hotel and restaurant with dinner-theater productions. Learn more about your water-based options at *www.oldsacramento.com*.

Perhaps surprisingly, the parking situation in and around Old Sacramento is pretty good. There are metered spaces as well as daily lots, and a lot of the shops and restaurants will validate your ticket if you purchase a souvenir or a meal.

There are eleven museums in and around this district. You'll find five of the museums within the boundaries of Old Sacramento:

- California State Railroad Museum
- California Military Museum, which houses more than 30,000 military guns and other items
- Discovery Museum, which focuses on space, science, and technology
- Schoolhouse Museum, a living replica of a one-room schoolhouse
- Wells Fargo History Museum, which reproduces an agent's office in the days of the Pony Express

For families with children, your best bets are the railroad museum, the Discovery Museum, and the Schoolhouse Museum. You'll also find dozens of shops and restaurants in Old Sacramento, each offering something for even the pickiest people in your party.

Discovery Museum

This institution's formal name is the Sacramento Museum of History, Science, Space and Technology. It is the first northern California institution of its kind to be inducted into the Smithsonian Affiliate Museums program, which should tell you a great deal about the quality of the facility and its exhibits.

The two main draws at the Discovery Museum are the Gold Rush History Center and the Space and Science Center; they operate at two different sites but are within an accessible distance of each other. The Gold Rush History Center focuses on exactly what its name suggests. The Space and Science Center is also fairly self-explanatory; it includes a planetarium and a Challenger Learning Center.

There are drop-in arts and crafts programs during the weekends, plus special programs geared for children up to about the eighth grade. The museum's hours are 10 A.M. until 5 P.M. daily. Adult admission costs $5, tickets for teenagers cost $4, tickets for children ages four through twelve cost $3, and kids younger than four are admitted free. Learn more at the museum's Web site, *www.thediscovery.org*.

Schoolhouse Museum

Your kids may find a new appreciation for their teachers after a few minutes in this one-room schoolhouse staffed by costumed schoolmarms and school masters, who greet visitors with the same kind of disciplined tone that teachers reserved for their charges back in the 1800s. The room itself is slightly larger than 1,000 square feet, which in and of itself will surprise your kids if they're used to attending a multigrade suburban school.

There are seasonal events listed on the museum's Web site, *www.scoe.net/oldsacschoolhouse*. Look for things such as a winter gingerbread house–decorating competition, a spring Easter bonnet promenade, and a summertime spelling bee. The museum is open Monday through Saturday from 10 A.M. till 4 P.M., and on Sunday from noon until 4 P.M. All hours are based on the availability of volunteers, so call ahead if you want to be sure of a full experience.

Shopping in Old Sacramento

There are more than 100 stores in the Old Sacramento district, and they sell everything from antiques to fine chocolates to rare books. There's also an open-air public market that operates Tuesday through Sunday with vendors selling produce, flowers, and specialty foods.

≡FAST FACT

According to Old Sacramento's Rocky Mountain Chocolate Factory, recent studies show that hot chocolate has almost twice the antioxidants as red wine. So you may want to skip Napa Valley and enjoy a glass of hot chocolate instead, maybe while you nibble on a chocolate-dipped apple or a box of freshly made fudge.

Some of the shops that are most likely to tickle your kids' imaginations (and have them tugging at your pocketbook strings) are Chez Poochie—which has dog accessory couture shows—and Fun and Games, where you can find jigsaw puzzles of up to 18,000 pieces as well as science projects, educational toys, and mind-teasing games for brains of all ages.

Also be ready to be dragged into Turtles, a unique store for turtle lovers. You'll find water globes, ceramic banks, and even cookie jars. The shop even makes homemade fudge to help you keep your energy up while browsing the offerings on its shelves.

Dining in Old Sacramento

There are nearly three dozen restaurants in Old Sacramento that serve everything from casual eats to candlelit gourmet meals. There's an Irish pub, a tea salon, a sports café, an espresso bar, and even a Subway sandwich shop for kids who are hesitant to try something new.

If you're looking for something a bit more elegant, check out California Fat's Steakhouse and Asian Grill at *www.fatsrestaurants.com*. Its appetizers include tequila lime beef skewers, there are countless steaks on the main menu (including a "drunk steak" marinated in brandy, garlic, and ginger), and entrées range from honey-walnut prawns to chicken chow mein.

Downtown

In between visits to Old Sacramento and the Capitol Park area, you may find yourself face-to-face with the Westfield Downtown Plaza mall. There are more than 100 stores here, not as kitschy as what you'll find in Old Sacramento but high-quality brands such as Gap, Gymboree, Macy's, and Wilson's Leather. You'll also find typical "mall restaurants" such as Quiznos Subs in this building, plus higher-end offerings such as Morton's Steakhouse.

RAINY DAY FUN

The Westfield Downtown Plaza mall is home to the Century Theatre Downtown Plaza 7, a digital surround-sound movie theater right next to the food court on the mall's upper piazza level. Keep your parking ticket with you when you buy your movie tickets, and the theater will validate your parking for up to four hours.

There's a children's carousel inside the mall if your little ones need a little indoor break from all your walking around. Mall hours are 10 A.M. till 9 P.M. Monday through Saturday, and 11 A.M. until 6 P.M. on Sunday. For a complete list of stores, restaurants, and other information, go to *www.westfield.com*.

Capitol Park Area

The main part of Sacramento's downtown includes the capitol building and at least four interesting museums your family might enjoy. It will be hard for you to miss the capitol's gold dome reaching up toward the sky, letting you know that you've made it to the heart of Sacramento.

A Day at the Capitol

The capitol building itself sits on the grounds of the California State Capitol Museum, which is on the National Register of Historic Places. You can tour quite a bit of the facility, including the offices of the governor, attorney general, secretary of state, and treasurer. There also are exhibits on-site, as well as opportunities to watch the state legislature in action during the months when it is in session.

Free tours are offered on the hour at the Capitol Museum, which includes murals, governors' portraits, and paintings created from 1870 through 1950. The tours also include a look at the building's architectural highlights, including the seal of California and the golden poppy mosaic floors.

Also part of the site is the outdoor Capitol Park, which comprises some forty acres and includes memorials to Civil War and Vietnam War veterans. There's also a separate California Veterans Memorial, honoring those who served in the Mexican-American War, the Spanish-American War, World Wars I and II, the Korean War, and the Persian Gulf War. There are some excellent interactive tours, as well as additional information about both the California Legislature and the museum grounds, available at *www.capitolmuseum.ca.gov.*

≡ **FAST FACT**

Arnold Schwarzenegger was elected governor of California in 2003, becoming one of the most internationally known governors in American history. The former bodybuilder and film actor was previously known for his roles in the *Terminator* movie franchise, which is how he quickly earned the nickname "the Governator" while walking the corridors of executive power in Sacramento.

The California Museum for History, Women, and the Arts

Located a block from the Capitol inside the building housing the State Archives, this museum now exists on the site that used to hold the California State History Museum. More than 20,000 square feet of exhibit space features rotating exhibitions such as "Treasures from Hearst Castle" and "Pioneers' Quilts and Textiles."

The museum is open daily, Monday through Saturday from 10 A.M. till 5 P.M. and Sunday from noon till 5 P.M. Admission is $7.50 for adults, $5 for children between the ages of six and thirteen, and free for children younger than five. Look for information about upcoming exhibits and events at *www.californiamuseum.org.*

California State Indian Museum

This museum is closer to Sutter's Fort than to the capitol building, and it tells the stories of the more than 150 tribes that originally settled the California region. It is believed that a half million Native Americans lived in the area before Europeans arrived and spoke some sixty-four languages.

At this museum, you can see baskets, beadwork, clothing, and exhibits that explain what life was like for the area's original inhabitants. There's a hands-on area where you can try out tools, perhaps grinding down some acorns the way Native Americans did centuries ago to make food. The museum is open daily except for major holidays such as Thanksgiving, Christmas, and New Year's Day. Look for information about upcoming exhibits and hours at *www.parks.ca.gov*.

Leland Stanford Museum

Yes, this institution is part of the California State Parks system, but it's a mansion more than a museum. It is the former home of tycoon, California governor, and university founder Leland Stanford. As any good tycoon might, Stanford required some 19,000 square feet of space to feel comfortable before going to bed at night. His former home includes 17-foot ceilings, crystal and bronze light fixtures, and gilded mirrors. The state of California purchased the land as a state park in 1978, and the mansion became noted as a National Historic Landmark in 1987. There was a fourteen-year, $22 million restoration that led to its opening as a museum for the public. It also serves as a welcome center for dignitaries who visit California from around the world.

FAST FACT

Leland Stanford made his fortune in a variety of businesses that took hold during modern California's early years. He owned a couple of wineries, was the president of Southern Pacific Railroad, and owned thoroughbred racehorses, which led to Stanford University's acquisition of the nickname "the farm."

Tours start on the hour daily between 10 A.M. and 4 P.M., and the mansion is open until 5 P.M. The museum is open year-round except for major holidays including Thanksgiving, Christmas, and New Year's Day. Admission rates are $8 for adults, $3 for children between six and seventeen years old, and free for children younger than five.

Towe Auto Museum

Montana banker Edward Towe at one point owned 180 Ford vehicles—which is why what is today known as the Towe Auto Museum in Sacramento used to be almost exclusively an homage to Ford models. The museum has since evolved into a facility that educates visitors about cars in general instead of just focusing on one man's personal collection.

Here you'll find everything from a 1919 Model T to a 1923 Model T Roadster to a 1966 Shelby GT350. Various car collectors loan their personal collections to the museum for short periods of time, so it's impossible to say exactly what will be on display during your visit. The museum is open daily from 10 A.M. until 6 P.M., though the last admissions accepted are at 5 P.M. The fee is $7 for adults and $3 for kids. Look for upcoming exhibits and events online at *www.toweautomuseum.org*.

Lodging and Restaurants

There is no shortage of places to stay or eat in Sacramento. Here are some suggestions you might want to consider. Each suggestion is marked by one, two, or three dollar signs.

For lodging:
$ = a room costs less than $100
$$ = a room costs from $101 to $200
$$$ = a room costs more than $200

For restaurants:
$ = entrées cost less than $15
$$ = entrées cost from $16 to $30
$$$ = entrées cost more than $30

Lodging

Best Western Sutter House
1100 H Street
(916) 441-1314
http://book.bestwestern.com
$$

Clarion Hotel Sacramento
700 16th Street
(916) 444-8000
www.clarionhotel.com
$$

Delta King Hotel
1000 Front Street
(916) 444-5464
www.deltaking.com
$$

Doubletree Hotel Sacramento
2001 Point West Way
(916) 929-8855
http://doubletree1.hilton.com
$$–$$$

Four Points Sacramento International Airport
4900 Duckhorn Drive
(916) 263-9000
www.fourpoints.com
$–$$

Hawthorn Suites
321 Bercut Drive
(916) 441-1200
www.hawthorn.com
$$

Holiday Inn Sacramento
300 J Street
(916) 446-0100
www.sacramentohi.com
$$

Homestead Sacramento—South Natomas
2810 Gateway Oaks Drive
(916) 564-7752
www.homesteadhotels.com
$

Hyatt Regency Sacramento
1209 L Street
(916) 443-1234
www.hyatt.com
$$

Radisson Sacramento
500 Leisure Lane
(800) 333-3333
www.radissonsac.com
$$

Ramada Limited Discovery Park
350 Bercut Drive
(916) 442-6971
www.ramada.com
$

Red Lion Hotel Sacramento
1401 Arden Way
(916) 922-8041
www.redlion.rdln.com
$

Sheraton Grand Sacramento
1230 J Street
(916) 447-1700
www.starwoodhotels.com
$$$

Vagabond Inn
909 Third Street
(800) 804-6835
www.vagabondinn.com/sacramentoproperties
$

Vizcaya Inn
2019 21st Street
(916) 455-5234
www.sterlinghotel.com
$$

Restaurants

Brew It Up Brewery & Grill
801 14th Street
(916) 441-3000
www.brewitup.com
$$

The Broiler Steakhouse
1201 K Street
(916) 444-3444
www.thebroilersteakhouse.com
$$–$$$

Buca di Beppo
1249 Howe Avenue
(916) 922-6673
www.bucadibeppo.com
$$

Chanterelle
1300 H Street
(916) 442-0451
www.sterlinghotel.com
$$

Cornerstone Restaurant
2330 J Street
(916) 441-0948
www.cornerstonerestaurant.net
$

Enotria Café & Wine Bar
1431 Del Paso Boulevard
(916) 922-6792
www.enotria.com
$$

Ettore's European Bakery & Restaurant
2376 Fair Oaks Boulevard
(916) 482-0708
www.ettores.com
$–$$

The Firehouse
1112 Second Street
(916) 442-4772
www.firehouseoldsac.com
$$–$$$

The Kitchen Restaurant
2225 Hurley Way, No. 101
(916) 568-7171
www.thekitchenrestaurant.com
$$–$$$

La Trattoria Bohemia
3649 J Street
(916) 455-7803
www.latrattoriabohemia.com
$–$$

Melting Pot Restaurant
814 15th Street
(916) 443-2347
www.meltingpot.com
$$

Mikuni Sushi
1530 J Street
(916) 447-2112
www.mikunisushi.com
$–$$

Morton's: The Steakhouse
521 L Street
(916) 442-5091
www.mortons.com
$$–$$$

Pyramid Alehouse
1029 K Street
(916) 498-9800
www.pyramidbrew.com
$

Rick's Dessert Diner
2322 K Street
(916) 444-0969
www.ricksdessertdiner.com
$–$$

CHAPTER 10

The Central Valley

NORTHERN CALIFORNIA'S CENTRAL VALLEY REGION, sometimes called the Great Valley, is a 400-mile stretch of flatlands that runs from north to south between the Sierra Nevada range and the western Coast Ranges. It starts up near the towns of Red Bluff and Chico and heads south beyond the region east of San Luis Obispo, making it someplace you're likely to at least cross through during any northern California vacation itinerary. It's a definite must if you want to see where much of America's food is grown.

Regional History

If you were up in space looking down on northern California, you would see what looks like a vertical, verdant field in between the Pacific Coast Range and the Sierra Nevada. It would look as if someone had scooped out the mountains from the middle of the state and replaced them with a long strip of green grass.

The reality is that this long strip used to be blue instead of green, when snowmelt from the surrounding mountains filled it with water and turned it into an inland lake. The soil beneath that water became rich with life and nutrients, and as the lake drained to create the Central Valley, farmers soon discovered that the fertile land could grow many crops.

The region was first populated with farmers who set up shop after losing out on the gold rush and others who came specifically to lay the groundwork for what would become today's agribusiness empires.

FAST FACT

Immigrants have long been, and continue to be, a huge part of the population in the Central Valley. They typically come from Asia, Mexico, Central America, and the former Soviet Union nations to work in the fields picking everything from cotton to tomatoes. There are hundreds of thousands of immigrants in the area during the harvest seasons alone.

Fruit Basket of the World

So many things grow in the Central Valley that it is often referred to as the fruit basket of the world, a play on the Midwest's moniker, the breadbasket of the world. In the Central Valley you'll find everything from cotton, rice, tomatoes, and almonds to raisins, grapes, apricots, and asparagus. By some estimates, Central Valley farms produce a quarter of all the food consumed in the United States.

The desire of large corporate farms to make the most of this fertile land has led to the creation of a huge agribusiness industry that depends on massive irrigation efforts as well as redirection and damming of existing rivers, tributaries, and streams. One of the earliest examples of this trend was the Central Valley Project, created in 1935 by the federal Bureau of Land Reclamation to send more water into the drier, southern end of the valley, where it could, among other things, create hydroelectric power for larger farming operations.

Environmental Challenges

Such redistribution of the water supply has been successful in aiding the farming community, but it has left environmentalists concerned about the potential harm to plants, animals, and humans alike.

TRAVEL TIP

The majority of groundwater contamination in the Central Valley is in the southern San Joaquin Valley, where water was redirected over the years to try to help the agribusiness industry. Tulare County, in particular, has closed the most drinking water wells due to contamination, which is why you should do as its residents do: Drink only bottled water during your visit.

Also of concern is the fact that the Central Valley is the fastest-growing region in California in terms of population. Some 6.5 million people call the area home, and that number may not include the annual influx of more than a half million immigrants during the harvest season. The additional land development required for housing, plus the increased strain on the water supply, are the subject of much governmental concern.

Local Overview

In terms of places to visit, the Central Valley has three distinct regions:

- The Sacramento Valley to the north
- The San Joaquin Valley to the south
- The Delta region that connects the two valleys

The largest city in the Central Valley is Sacramento, which you read about in Chapter 9. This chapter focuses on smaller cities such as Yuba City, Stockton, and Modesto, as well as the outlying regions of the Sacramento Valley, the San Joaquin Valley, and the Delta. Of course, any of these destinations can be easily included as part of an itinerary that also includes Sacramento.

It's about 170 miles (or a three-hour drive) from Chico in the north to Modesto in the south. It is possible to traverse the entire length of the Central Valley in a day, but you certainly won't have time to stop and see everything along the way.

Getting Here, Getting Around

Interstate 5 is the main north-south thoroughfare through the Central Valley. It connects to Interstate 80 from San Francisco, so driving to this part of northern California is quite simple. The journey from San Francisco to Yuba City, for instance, is about a two-hour drive, the majority of it along the interstate.

Train travel is also an option. Amtrak serves Sacramento, Chico, Davis, Grass Valley, and other Central Valley stations. For full schedules and routes, visit the Amtrak Web site at *www.amtrak.com*.

Practical Considerations

If you plan to drive to the Central Valley, the two things you have to consider are fog and dust storms. The thick fog that frequently descends on the Central Valley is so well known that it has its own name: tule fog. It is named for the tule grass wetlands from which it rises. Tule fog is most common during the rainy season from November to March. Sometimes, a blanket of tule fog stretches the entire length of the Central Valley, creating what looks like a giant inland cloud in satellite pictures.

 TRAVEL TIP

Visibility in tule fog is typically less than an eighth of a mile—and it can drop to nearly zero in a matter of seconds when you're driving. Try to slow down, but do not stop short if you encounter thick fog; that reaction has been blamed for several massive traffic accidents. One of the largest involved an eighty-car pileup that killed two people in 2002.

The rainy season does end, typically in April, which ushers in the dry season that lasts until about Thanksgiving. As the wetness brings fog with it, the dryness brings dust storms—particularly in the San Joaquin Valley, which would be naturally bone dry without all the manmade irrigation channels and water redistribution efforts.

As with fog, dust storms can sneak up on you quickly when you're driving down the highway. Do your best to slow down without stopping short, keep your low beams on, and get out of harm's way if there's a lot of traffic on the road around you.

Smaller Cities

You will likely want to incorporate a day or two in Sacramento into any itinerary you plan for the greater Central Valley, which will help determine how much time you have left to visit its other, smaller cities, such as Yuba City, Stockton, and Modesto.

Yuba City

Yuba City, which is about forty miles north of Sacramento, officially turned 100 years old in January 2008. Its history continues to live in its downtown, which includes Plumas Street, lined with 1920s buildings that are now home to more than 100 shops and stores. On Second Street, you can see the courthouse built in 1899 as well as the county hall of records built in 1891. The city continues to be the seat of Sutter County.

As with most cities and towns in the Central Valley, Yuba City is the home of at least one major agricultural company: Sunsweet Growers Incorporated. It's the largest prune-packing plant in the world, though it's also known for dried fruits and juices made from apricots, pineapples, mangoes, and other fruits.

What sets Yuba City apart from its Central Valley neighbors is that it is also home to one of the largest Sikh populations outside of Punjab, India. If you plan your visit to Yuba City during early November, you can attend the annual Sikh parade, which draws tens of thousands of Sikhs from the United States, Canada, Britain, and India. There are also a couple of interesting attractions worth noting just outside Yuba City, including Sutter Buttes, the Sleep Train Amphitheatre, and the Bok Kai Temple.

FAST FACT

Yuba City–based Sunsweet produces more than 50,000 tons of prunes each year. Its plant in northern California produces an average of 40,000 cases of Sunsweet products each year for distribution around the world. The company controls more than two-thirds of the entire worldwide prune market and buys prunes from more than half the growers in the Central Valley.

Sutter Buttes

Sutter Buttes, located northwest of Yuba City, is the one place where the Central Valley isn't flat. It's a series of eroded volcanic lava domes that stretches for about ten miles from north to south. The highest peak is just over 2,000 feet tall—certainly not majestic when compared with northern California's major mountain ranges, but definitely impressive in the middle of the agricultural plains.

It's believed that Sutter Buttes was formed a million and a half years ago by a now-extinct volcano. Today, cattle and sheep ranchers control much of the land around the mountains, but you can take walking tours with groups such as the Middle Mountain Foundation, which incorporates local Native American lore about the mountains into its presentations. Learn more online at *www.middlemountain.org*.

Sleep Train Amphitheatre

If you head south of Yuba City for about ten miles along Forty Mile Road, you'll come to the Sleep Train Amphitheatre. It's an open-air music center with about 8,000 seats plus an area where concertgoers can bring lawn chairs at a reduced price. The lawn area also includes a "Kid Zone" where smoking and drinking alcohol are prohibited.

For a look at the acts that will be there during your visit, go online to *www.livenation.com*. You can also scroll through the Ticketmaster Web site, *www.ticketmaster.com*, for a look at the upcoming schedule.

Bok Kai Temple

It's not often that you find a significant Chinese monument that describes its location as "two buildings behind the Silver Dollar restaurant." Such is the case with the Bok Kai Temple in Marysville, which is less than two miles outside the Yuba City limits, just across the Feather River.

The original temple was built in 1854, about five years after the first group of Chinese laborers arrived in California to work in the newly created gold mines. The temple that stands today was constructed in 1880 and remains the only one of its kind in the entire United States, since no other temples pay tribute to Bok Eye, the "water god" or "god of the dark north" who has the power to banish evil.

 RAINY DAY FUN

You can tour the Bok Kai Temple, but only with an appointment because of continuing work to prevent the structure's collapse in the face of intense rainy seasons. The temple's Web site, *www .bokkaitemple.org*, includes excellent information to help familiarize you with the Chinese system of gods before you arrive at the temple itself.

Even if you don't want to tour the temple, you can take part in the springtime Bok Kai Festival, whose date changes every year with the lunar calendar. The festival includes a parade filled with dancers and dragons, plus children's activities, food, and games. Learn more at *www.bokkaifestival.com*.

Stockton

If you're a sports fan, then you know that Stockton is the home of the San Francisco 49ers training camp. It's about an hour and a half east of the bigger city, well within a day's driving range if you want to make Stockton your only stop in the Central Valley. A lot of people do just that every April, when the city hosts its annual Asparagus Festival.

Close to 300,000 people live in Stockton, which is home not just to agricultural companies but also to other industrial headquarters, helping to keep its economic base diversified. There are a few interesting highlights within the city limits, some geared toward adults and others designed to keep the whole family happy.

Bob Hope Theatre

Previously known as the Fox California Theatre, this venue has hosted musicians, dancers, and other acts since first opening its doors in 1930. It's received hundreds of thousands of dollars in funding for recent renovations and now has one of the most innovative sound systems of its kind.

═══FAST FACT

When the Bob Hope Theatre first opened in 1930, it boasted a massive Wurlitzer pipe organ that cost $40,000, which is the equivalent of about $400,000 when adjusted for inflation today. The total renovations of the theater cost nearly twice that, including the addition of a first-of-its-kind Meyer Sound Laboratories electronic speaker system.

All kinds of acts still come here to perform, from big-name comedian George Lopez to dancer Michael Flatley and his Lord of the Dance troupe. You can also see musicals, musicians, and individual singers depending on what dates you're in town. For directions, a schedule of upcoming performances, and information about how to buy tickets online, go to *www.bobhopetheatre.com.*

Haggin Museum

The Haggin Museum is a "grown-up" institution, focused on preserving great works of art instead of building interactive exhibits. Its art collection includes pieces by noted painters including Albert Bierstadt, while its history displays showcase the work done by local residents such as Benjamin Holt, who invented the Caterpillar-type tractor. There are also rotating exhibits with titles such as "Pre-Colombian Art" and "The Age of Armor."

The museum is open from 1:30 P.M. till 5 P.M. Wednesday through Sunday, and from 1:30 P.M. till 9 P.M. on the first and third Thursday of every month. Admission is $5 for adults and $2.50 for children between ten and seventeen years old. Children younger than ten get in for free.

Children's Museum of Stockton

If your kids are more interested in playing with their art than looking at it, then you should skip the Haggin Museum and head straight for the Children's Museum of Stockton. It features a tiny "town" where kids can play at being everything from the local postmaster to the town's banker.

This isn't an all-day museum, but you'll find enough fun here to keep your kids entertained for at least an hour or two, depending on their ages. Admission is $4.50, with children younger than two getting in for free. Learn more at *www.stocktongov.com*.

Minor League Sports

If you can't get in to see the San Francisco 49ers train during their summer camp, then you might want to check out the local minor league soccer, baseball, ice hockey, and arena football teams.

The Stockton Ports are perhaps the best known. They are a minor-league affiliate of Major League Baseball's Oakland A's. The Ports play their home games at Banner Island Ballpark, which opened in 2005 and seats about 5,000 people. For tickets, go online to *www.bannerislandballpark.com*.

The Stockton Arena is the home for minor league soccer's California Cougars, minor league hockey's Stockton Thunder and arena football's Stockton Lightning. For tickets to any of their games, check out the Web site *www.stocktontickets.com*.

 RAINY DAY FUN

Even if it's raining, you can still find your fill of sports in Stockton during most months of the year. The schedules for teams that play indoor games at Stockton Arena are: California Cougars soccer, October through April; Stockton Thunder hockey, October through April; and Stockton Lightning arena football, March through July.

Pixie Woods

Pixie Woods is sometimes called a small amusement park, and sometimes it's known as a children's playground. Regardless of its description, it's always fun, having entertained kids for more than half a century now. Located inside the city's Louis Park, Pixie Woods has rides like a Merry-Go-Round and a Pixie Express Train that are meant to put smiles on the faces of your youngest children.

Days of operation during the summer are Wednesday through Sunday, from 11 A.M. till 5 P.M. on weekdays and 11 A.M. till 6 P.M. on weekends. Admission is $3 for children ages twelve and younger and $3.50 for everybody else. In addition, you have to buy tickets for the rides. They're $1.75 apiece, or $4.25 for three. Learn more at *www.stocktongov.com/pixiewoods*.

Modesto

Modesto is one of the southernmost towns in northern California's Central Valley region, with a population just shy of 200,000. Getting here is easy by car or by train; the city grew up as one of the original stops on the earliest railroad lines. It actually developed quite a reputation for being wild with brothels and opium houses, which have been replaced during the past century with establishments of a more proper business nature—assuming that you consider wine to be in that category. The Gallo Winery is one of the biggest in the region, with its headquarters based in Modesto.

≡ **FAST FACT**

Before he went on to make the *Star Wars* movies, filmmaker George Lucas grew up in Modesto, which he used as inspiration for one of his earlier groundbreaking films, *American Graffiti*. His hometown pays tribute to him by calling its downtown area George Lucas Plaza, where you can have your picture taken with the bronze sculpture that was dedicated in his honor.

Gallo Center for the Arts

Giving back to the community where its headquarters is located, the winemaking Gallo family endowed $10 million to help create the Gallo Center for the Arts in Modesto. It opened in September 2007 following a decade's worth of research and planning.

The facility has two venues, the 1,250-seat Mary Stuart Rogers Theater and the 444-seat Foster Family Theater, both named for patrons of the center. Events include live theater, music, dance, corporate gatherings, and wedding receptions. For a list of upcoming shows and ticket availability, go online to *www.galloarts.org*.

McHenry Mansion

The Gallo family also has quite a lot to do with the existence of the McHenry Mansion, which the Julio R. Gallo Foundation bought and donated to the city of Modesto in 1976. Now on the National Register of Historic Places, the mansion dates back to 1883, which is the period from which its current antiques are taken. It's open for tours as well as special events such as weddings. Learn more at *www.mchenrymuseum.org*.

Great Valley Museum of Natural History

The Great Valley Museum of Natural History is part of Modesto Junior College. It has permanent as well as rotating exhibits that focus on plants and animals. A "discovery room" lets you look at a snake skin under a microscope, work on a five-foot puzzle, and more.

 RAINY DAY FUN

The Great Valley Museum of Natural History offers many classes and tours, including some that are geared toward children between three and twelve years old. "Science for Tots" is one such program, teaching nature and science through arts and crafts. To see a full events calendar as you organize your personal travel dates, go to *www.gomjc.org*.

Note that the museum is closed during the month of August (remember, it's part of a college campus). Its regular hours are 9 A.M. till 4:30 P.M. Tuesday through Friday, and 10 A.M. till 4 P.M. on Saturday. Children six and younger get free admission. General admission prices are $1 per person or $3 per family.

Sacramento Valley

The Sacramento Valley is the northern section of the Central Valley. Chico and the Wilbur Hot Springs resort are two of the main attractions.

Chico

Chico is home to Bidwell Park—one of the twenty-five largest municipal parks in the United States. It's named for John Bidwell, who was part of the first wagon trains that reached California in 1843, when he headed west to work for gold pioneer John Sutter.

The city has grown quite a bit since then. It now has a branch of the California State University system and all the restaurants and businesses that you'd expect to go along with it. Two must-see spots for tourists are the Chico Air Museum and the National Yo-Yo Museum.

Chico Air Museum

The Chico Air Museum opened in 2004, boasting indoor artifacts as well as an outdoor aircraft display. Its particular focus is on local aviation history, which includes aerial firefighting—a great resource given the prominence of California wildfires.

Special events at the museum include presentations by legendary pilots, as well as demonstrations of aircraft maneuvers. Learn more at *www.chicoairmuseum.org*.

National Yo-Yo Museum

Admission is free at the National Yo-Yo Museum, where you can see Big-Yo, the world's largest working yo-yo, which weighs a staggering 256 pounds. It's more than four feet wide and reads "No Jive" along its side—no doubt making it the most popular photo op in town.

═══ **FAST FACT**

The yo-yo is not at all a modern invention. Its earliest reference is believed to be from 5000 B.C. in Greece, where it was called a disc. Many years later, in the 1700s, it gained popularity as a stress-reliever among France's elite. It seems to have come to the United States in the 1860s, when two men from Ohio received a patent for their version of the toy.

If you happen to be visiting Chico during the first Saturday in October, you can attend the National Yo-Yo Contest that's held at the museum. Learn more at *www.nationalyoyo.org*.

Wilbur Hot Springs

The Wilbur Hot Springs is an 1,800-acre private nature preserve in the town of Wilbur Springs, which is about an hour and a half southwest of Chico. It takes advantage of the natural hot springs from which the town got its name, adding to Mother Nature's offerings with its own hotel, massage spa, and yoga classes. This is a resort for anyone interested in connecting with nature on a spiritual level. Details, rates, and room descriptions can be found online at *www.wilburhotsprings.com.*

The Delta

The Delta is the midsection between the Sacramento and San Joaquin valleys. Most of its towns are tiny, with many serving as bedroom communities for commuters who work in Sacramento and San Francisco. Still, you can find a handful of things to do in places like Rio Vista and the Grizzly Island Wildlife Area.

Rio Vista

Rio Vista is a small town of about 4,500 souls on the Sacramento River. It's not exactly a travel and tourism hot spot, but it is the closest town to the Western Railway Museum, which offers electric train trips over the historic main line of the Sacramento Northern Railway.

There are more than fifty restored railcars on display, plus additional exhibits and a picnic area where your family can enjoy a prepacked lunch. Admission is $7 for children between two and fourteen years old, and $10 for adults. Hours are 10:30 A.M. until 5 P.M. Saturday and Sunday, with expanded hours in the summer. For details, go to *www.wrm.org.*

Grizzly Island Wildlife Area

About ten miles southeast of Fairfield, you'll find the Grizzly Island Wildlife Area, a 10,000-plus-acre region encompassing two islands where you can fish, take photographs, and sightsee among the birds, reptiles, and amphibians.

San Joaquin Valley

The San Joaquin Valley is the southernmost portion of the Central Valley. Like its northern neighbors, it is filled mostly with agricultural pastures and bedroom communities. Even so, the towns of Atwater and Fresno are worth a look; each offers activities for the whole family to enjoy.

Atwater

The Castle Air Museum is the place to visit in Atwater, a city of about 30,000 people that's best known as a driving stopover point in between Monterey Bay and Yosemite National Park.

≡FAST FACT

The Castle Air Museum, like Castle Air Force Base before it, is named for General Frederick W. Castle. He led a 2,000-strong aircraft bomber formation over Europe in December 1944, when he was just thirty-six years old. He died as the assault squadron passed over Belgium, where his plane lost an engine and was attacked by German fighters.

A group of enthusiasts opened the museum following the closing of the Castle Air Force Base in 1994. There's an indoor section full of exhibits as well as an outdoor area where you can look at several dozen World War II, Korean War, and Vietnam War–era aircraft. There's a hangar where additional aircraft are on display because some of the older planes have fabrics that don't hold up well in the open elements.

The museum is open year-round, though hours vary by the season. Admission is $10 for adults, $8 for children between six and seventeen years old, and free for children five and younger. More information is available at *www.elite.net/castle-air*.

Fresno

Art is the name of the game in Fresno, which is California's sixth-largest city. As with most metropolitan hubs, you'll find museums here that are much higher in quality than those of the surrounding towns. Two fine examples are the Fresno Metropolitan Museum of Art and Science and the Fresno Art Museum.

Fresno Metropolitan Museum of Art and Science

This museum's fantastic mission statement is to "serve the community of the curious." It opened in 1984 and has since welcomed more than 2 million visitors in person, plus countless others online at *www.fresnomet.org*, where there are special Web-only exhibits.

Look to this museum for exhibits featuring everything from dinosaurs to the paintings of Georgia O'Keeffe. Hours are 11 A.M. till 5 P.M., Wednesday through Sunday. Admission is $8 for adults, $5 for students, $3 for children between three and twelve years old, and free for infants and toddlers.

Fresno Art Museum

Not to be confused with the Fresno Metropolitan Museum of Art and Science, the Fresno Art Museum places a special emphasis on Mexican artwork and artifacts. It's a modern art museum that offers exhibits, films, concerts, lectures, tours, and more. A couple of times each year, the museum hosts "family days" with free admission. For seasonal hours, admission rates, and upcoming exhibitions, check out *www.fresnoartmuseum.org*.

Lodging and Restaurants

There is no shortage of places to stay or eat in the Central Valley. Here are some suggestions you might want to consider. Each suggestion is marked by one, two, or three dollar signs.

For lodging:
$ = a room costs less than $100

$$ = a room costs from $101 to $200

$$$ = a room costs more than $200

For restaurants:

$ = entrées cost less than $15

$$ = entrées cost from $16 to $30

$$$ = entrées cost more than $30

Lodging

YUBA CITY
Hampton Inn & Suites
1375 Sunset Boulevard
(530) 751-1714
www.hamptoninn.com
$$

Holiday Inn Express
894 West Onstott Road
(530) 674-1650
www.ichotelsgroup.com
$$

Knights Inn Yuba City
545 Colusa Avenue
(530) 671-1151
www.knightsinn.com
$

STOCKTON
La Quinta Inn Stockton
2710 West March Lane
(209) 952-7800
www.lq.com
$

Red Roof Inn
1707 West Fremont Street
(209) 466-7777
www.redroof.com
$

Stockton Grand Hotel
2323 Grand Canal Boulevard
(209) 957-9090
www.stockton-grand-hotel.pacificahost.com
$$$

MODESTO
Days Inn Modesto
1312 McHenry Avenue
(209) 527-1010
www.daysinn.com
$

DoubleTree Hotel Modesto
1150 Ninth Street
(209) 526-6000
http://doubletree1.hilton.com
$$–$$$

Ramada Modesto
2001 West Orangeburg Avenue
(209) 521-9000
www.ramada.com
$

Travelodge Modesto
722 Kansas Avenue
(209) 524-3251
www.travelodge.com
$

CHICO
Chico Days Inn
740 Broadway Street
(530) 343-3286
www.daysinn.com
$

Courtyard by Marriott Chico
2481 Carmichael Drive
(800) 321-2211
www.marriott.com
$$–$$$

Oxford Suites Chico
2035 Business Lane
(530) 899-9090
www.oxfordsuiteschico.com
$$

Vagabond Inn Chico
630 Main Street
(800) 522-1555
www.vagabondinn-chico-hotel.com
$

Restaurants

YUBA CITY
Lucio's Restaurant & Bar
890 Onstott Road
(530) 671-2050
www.luciosrestaurant.com
$$

Red Robin Gourmet Burgers
1200 Colusa Avenue
(530) 751-1012
www.redrobin.com
$–$$

STOCKTON
Marie Callender's
2628 March Lane
(209) 952-0054
www.mcpies.com
$$

Outback Steakhouse
1243 West March Lane
(209) 954-9615
www.outbacksteakhouse.com
$$

Valley Brewing Company
157 West Adams Street
(209) 464-2739
www.valleybrew.com
$$

MODESTO
Galletto Ristorante
1101 J Street
(209) 523-4500
www.galletto.biz
$$

Hazel's Elegant Dining
431 12th Street
(209) 578-3463
www.hazelsmodesto.com
$$–$$$

CHICO
California Pasta Productions
East Avenue and Esplanade
(530) 343-6999
www.calpastachico.com
$

Casa Ramos Mexican Restaurant
2490 Fair Street
(530) 893-5050
www.casaramos.net
$–$$

Hemingway's
250 Cohasset Road
(530) 345-7330
http://hemingways-chico.tripod.com
$$

Red Tavern Restaurant
1250 The Esplanade
(530) 894-3463
www.redtavern.com
$$

Riley's Bar
702 West Fifth Street
(530) 343-7459
www.rileysbar.com
$

Monterey Bay Coastline

CHAPTER 11

The South Coast

NORTHERN CALIFORNIA'S SOUTH COAST runs from just below San Francisco to just north of the Big Sur region. It includes the world-famous, sixty-mile-long, 10,000-foot-deep Monterey Bay and its exceptional hands-on aquarium, as well as the enchanting cities of Monterey, Santa Cruz, and Carmel. Whether you want to explore unique shops or spend time on the water getting close to nature, this part of northern California has a lot to offer.

Regional History

For the purposes of defining the South Coast as a region, this chapter focuses on the area from the northern edge of Monterey Bay at the city of Santa Cruz to the south end of the bay and Monterey Peninsula, where you'll find the cities of Monterey and Carmel. You might argue that the region extends a bit more to the north or to the south, but when it comes to planning your family vacation, these are the spots you're most likely going to want to visit. One special note: Many people consider the Big Sur region to be part of the South Coast, but you'll learn more about that scenic wonderland in Chapter 16, which focuses on key national and state park areas.

This part of northern California is known for nature more than anything else. The Monterey Bay has exceptionally deep underwater valleys and canyons full of rare fish, octopus, and jellyfish, the kind you see in barely lighted zoo exhibits because the creatures have never been touched by daylight. The geography of the area is just as fascinating as its animals, which is why more than 5,000 square miles along about 400 miles of coast have been protected as the Monterey Bay National Marine Sanctuary.

 TRAVEL TIP

If you want to watch the California gray whales migrating along the South Shore, then plan your vacation between October and January. That's when the whales—which can grow to 40 tons—move south from the Alaskan to the Mexican coastlines to mate. You can catch them heading north along the coast between February and June, which is the best time to look for mothers traveling with calves.

The cities in this area sprang up differently. Monterey was originally a large port city, Santa Cruz a smaller port city, and Carmel a place where wealthy people and artists alike converged to make the most of the stunning seaside views.

FAST FACT

Pebble Beach is a public golf course—but don't let that designation fool you in terms of pricing. Often ranked as the top public course in the entire United States, Pebble Beach commands rates starting at $475 per person for a single round of golf (and that doesn't include the cart fee). If that's not too steep for your wallet, you can reserve a tee time at *www.pebblebeach.com*.

Though the Pacific is certainly spectacular along this stretch of coast, it is also dangerous—and on occasion filled with great white sharks. Surfers come here from around the world to catch big waves, which should be a warning if you're traveling with small children who might easily get sucked into one of the Pacific's vortex-like undertows. Pay close attention to lifeguards and posted signs if you plan to get interactive with the sea. Safety should be as much on your mind as sunny weather and beach barbecues. There's no reason to stay out of the water altogether, but remain mindful of what Mother Nature is cooking up offshore.

On the other hand, there's plenty to do that's perfectly safe along the beach itself, from the boardwalk in Santa Cruz to the Monterey Bay Aquarium to playing a few rounds at the world-renowned Pebble Beach Golf Course in Carmel.

Local Overview

A good way to plan a vacation in this part of northern California is by car, since scenic Highway 1 runs right through Santa Cruz, down around Monterey Bay, and into the cities of Monterey and Carmel. Though the distance from Santa Cruz to Carmel is only about fifty miles, you'll want to leave at least an hour or two for the drive. With the scenic views and overlooks along the way, the odds are that you'll be stopping to take photographs just as often as you're hitting the gas pedal.

You can catch Highway 1 in San Francisco and follow it south to this region (Santa Cruz is about seventy-five miles south of San Francisco), then perhaps take an eastern route back, following Highway 101 through San Jose (which is about thirty miles from Santa Cruz). If you throw in a side trip down Highway 1 to the Big Sur area, you'll have seen a pretty good selection of natural landscapes and cityscapes alike.

RAINY DAY FUN

If it starts to drizzle while you're making your way toward Santa Cruz and the Monterey Bay beyond, consider a short detour to the town of Felton, where you'll find the Bigfoot Discovery Project. This museum is dedicated to offering proof of the creature's existence, such as plaster hand- and footprints. Explore the myth before you visit at *www.bigfootdiscoveryproject.com*.

There are two universities along this route if you're traveling with an older teenager who is interested in touring campuses. First, to the north, you'll find the University of California at Santa Cruz. A bit farther down the bay is California State University at Monterey Bay.

Santa Cruz

Santa Cruz County, created in 1850, was one of the original twenty-seven counties in existence when California became part of the United States. Santa Cruz has always been a tourist area because of its beautiful beaches and natural scenery, but the area was also known in its earlier days for logging, agriculture, and fishing. The city was born in 1876, and things progressed rather smoothly in terms of development until more than a century later, in 1989, when the 6.9-magnitude Loma Prieta earthquake destroyed many of the original historic buildings. Restoration efforts continue, but they remain incomplete.

More than 50,000 people live in the city of Santa Cruz, most of them water-sports enthusiasts who are drawn to the easily accessible swimming, fishing, and sailing. Surfing is of particular interest in Santa Cruz, which local legend says was the first location for taking out redwood boards in California. Enthusiasts worldwide know Santa Cruz's eleven surf breaks the way kids in northern climates know their neighborhoods' best sledding hills.

The downtown has its good and bad areas, but for the most part is a fine city to explore with the kids holding your hand. You'll find interesting shops as well as café-style eateries, many of them serving "California-style" health food such as sprouts and sushi.

Santa Cruz Beach Boardwalk

It's been a full century since the Santa Cruz Beach Boardwalk was created in 1907, and today the pier, full of rides and games, is California's oldest amusement park. It's also one of just two remaining seaside amusement parks on the entire West Coast; the other is Santa Monica Pier, near Los Angeles. This boardwalk is much less like Disneyland than it is like New York's Coney Island—still with hot dog vendors instead of full-service restaurants, and still with cute rides instead of death-defying ones.

FAST FACT

The boardwalk certainly draws an interesting cast of characters. The wildly popular 1987 movie *The Lost Boys*—about teenagers who become vampires—takes place with the Santa Cruz boardwalk as a backdrop. The boardwalk is also seen in the 1983 Clint Eastwood film *Sudden Impact* as well as in the 1971 cult classic *Harold and Maude*.

Two of the rides at the boardwalk are designated as National Historic Landmarks. The Charles D. Looff Carousel was built in 1911 and still contains its original 342-pipe organ as well as a brass ring machine that lets riders reach for the brass loops to hurl into a clown's mouth (although today the rings are made of steel). The Giant Dipper wooden roller coaster, built in 1924, has made more than 50 million people smile and scream on its dips and loops over the years. The original designer, Arthur Looff, said he wanted it to be a "combination earthquake, balloon ascension, and aeroplane drop." He'd surely be proud of how long it has thrilled the masses.

Newer rides at the boardwalk include the 125-foot-high Double Shot, which launches riders skyward above the Monterey Bay coastline at upward of three-G force. As the ride falls back toward the beach, riders feel weightless (and their stomachs seem to fly a little higher than the rest of their bodies).

There are water rides, too, in case your vacation coincides with the warmest days of July and August. There's laser tag and miniature golf, and about a dozen of the boardwalk's rides are designed for younger children, including the Kiddie Speed Boats.

 TRAVEL TIP

The Santa Cruz boardwalk is open daily from Memorial Day through Labor Day, but its outdoor attractions are open only on weekends and holidays during the fall and spring. (The arcade, mini-golf, and bowling centers are open year-round.) If you want to beat the crowds—and the heat—think about a weekend visit during September or October. That's when the locals tend to visit to make the best of the scene.

For a full list of rides, attractions, and online passes for daily or seasonal visits, go to the boardwalk's Web site at *www.beachboard walk.com.*

Santa Cruz Surfing Museum

If ever there were a city suitable for a surfing museum, Santa Cruz is it. You can spend an afternoon watching modern-day pipe-seekers out on the water, then head inside to learn about the century's worth of Moondoggies who came before them.

The Santa Cruz Surfing Museum is located inside the Mark Abbott Memorial Lighthouse, which was built in 1967 and named for an eighteen-year-old who drowned while bodysurfing nearby in 1965. The museum houses examples of surfboards dating back to the days of redwood planks—including a surfboard that survived a shark attack—as well as photographs and videos that show the changing nature of the sport and its surrounding culture throughout the years. There is of course also a museum store where you can buy hats, T-shirts, and surfing gear that will help you feel like a member of the local club yourself.

 JUST FOR PARENTS

Okay, okay, T-shirts are for children of all ages. But the reproduction of the 1938 Santa Cruz Surf Club's T-shirt will cost you a boffo $110 at the Santa Cruz Surfing Museum. Get the kids the $20 modern-logo version and save the really cool design for yourself, perhaps wearing it beneath a tuxedo jacket at your next black-tie event.

From July 4 through mid-September, the museum is open from 10 A.M. until 5 P.M. except for Tuesday, when it is closed. The rest of the year, the museum's hours are noon till 4 P.M., closed on Tuesday and Wednesday. Learn more at *www.santacruzsurfingmuseum.org*.

University of California at Santa Cruz

Locals know the University of California at Santa Cruz simply as UC Santa Cruz, home to about 15,000 students pursuing degrees in some sixty-two majors. There are campus tours available if you're traveling with a teenager, but you must make reservations in advance through the university's Web site, *www.admissions.ucsc.edu*.

The campus also has a healthy arts and lectures schedule each year, offering everything from musical performances to lectures by well-known correspondents from National Public Radio. For an updated events listing and links to purchase tickets, go to *http://artslectures.ucsc.edu*.

Skate Parks

Skateboarding didn't become a sport—or even a pastime—in the United States until the 1950s, when it started to make a name for itself alongside surfing in California. The city of Santa Cruz embraced anyone who wanted to practice their ollies, slides, grinds, and other popular moves by building the first public skate park in America. Today, there is also a new park in Santa Cruz where boarders can show off their decks and hone their moves alongside amateurs and pros alike.

FAST FACT

An ollie is a skateboarding trick invented in 1976 by Alan "Ollie" Gelfand. It involves launching the skateboard airborne without touching it and then landing right back where you started. The highest ollie on record, starting from flat ground, is forty-four and a half inches high (nearly four feet in the air!), a jump made by British skateboarder Danny Wainwright.

Derby Skate Park

Derby Skate Park was the first public skate park in the United States, built in the early 1970s. It's considered a classic among skateboarding aficionados, a free place to "get your carve on," as the trusted reviewer Caliskatz puts it, but lacking in large pipes and other modern marvels that let tricksters leap and twist higher than ever before. The park is open from dawn till dusk. It's by the beach, too, so you can send your teenager over to skate while you catch some rays with the rest of the family.

Derby Skate Park was designed by Ken Wormhoudt, who went on to become an active Santa Cruz citizen and world-renowned skate park designer until his death in 1997. The city recently named a new skate park in his honor: the Ken Wormhoudt Skate Park at Mike Fox Park.

Ken Wormhoudt Skate Park at Mike Fox Park

Local Santa Cruz skateboarders loved Ken Wormhoudt because he would give them a stack of modeling clay, ask them what they wanted in their next skate park, and then help them create realistic (and safe) versions of their dreams. This new skate park named in Wormhoudt's honor, opened in February 2007, is a generation beyond the Derby facility, with 15,000 square feet of launching ramps such as a full pipe, two bowls, hubba ledges, wall rides, metal rails, and a street course with steps.

The park is open from 9 A.M. until sunset daily. Helmets are mandatory, as are elbow and knee pads. Only composite wheels are allowed on skateboards here. Learn more from the Santa Cruz Parks and Recreation Department at *www.ci.santa-cruz.ca.us.*

Downtown Monterey

Even if you've never heard of the city of Monterey, you've probably at least heard of Monterey Jack cheese, which originated here and was made popular when it was mass-marketed by a man named David Jack during the 1800s. There are a lot of variations on Monterey Jack cheese today, and they range from mild to spicy—just like the offerings in the city itself.

 TRAVEL TIP

If driving down California's famous coastal Highway 1 is on your must-do list, then Monterey is as good a final destination as any when heading south from San Francisco. Monterey is about 115 miles from its sister city, making it close enough to incorporate into a round-trip itinerary if your flights are into and out of San Francisco during a weeklong vacation.

Monterey was actually the region's capital city from 1777 to 1849, when what is now northern California was controlled by Spain and

Mexico. The city boasts a lot of America's "firsts," including its first theater, public library, and printing press. Today, it is best known for the Monterey Bay Aquarium in the northern part of the city, but the downtown area has plenty to offer tourists as well, including a fine art museum and the bustling Fisherman's Wharf.

Annual events draw thousands of tourists to the city of Monterey. One of the longest-running and most popular is the Monterey Bay Blues Festival, held each June at the Monterey Fairgrounds. Details are online at *www.montereyinfo.org*. Every July, you can enjoy the Scottish Games and Celtic Festival (*www.montereyscotsgames.com*) and the Obon Festival, which features Japanese food and exhibits. Also don't miss the Monterey Jazz Festival, held for a half-century each September (*www.montereyjazzfestival.org*).

Fisherman's Wharf

Working trawlers still call Wharf 2 home at Monterey's Fisherman's Wharf, so it's a great place to explore if you want to combine touristy restaurants and shops with a bit of real-life fisheries scenery.

Lots of on-the-water Monterey Bay activities launch from Fisherman's Wharf, including glass-bottom boat tours, whale-watching tours, and deep-sea fishing boats. Even so, eating is the primary activity here; it's hard to get seafood any fresher. You'll find all kinds of variety, from places called Crabby Jim's with standard favorites to spots known as Cabo's Wild Mexican Seafood, where sweet mole is a favorite ingredient.

 JUST FOR PARENTS

Want to learn to sail? Monterey Bay Sailing offers Intro to Sailing and Seamanship courses starting at $120. You'll steer the boat, work the sails, tend the lines, and get a good feel for what sailing is all about. If you enjoy this course, you can work your way up to others that will take you well beyond Fisherman's Wharf and the greater Monterey Bay. Learn more at *www.montereysailing.com*.

Fisherman's Wharf has so much to offer that it has its own Web site, *www.montereywharf.com*, for directions, a calendar of upcoming events, and links to shops, restaurants, and services.

Presidio of Monterey Museum

If you're a student of military history or a history buff in general, then you won't want to miss a trip to the Presidio of Monterey. Under U.S. control since the early 1900s, the Presidio has been around since the 1700s, when Spain dominated the area. The Presidio was declared inactive in 1944, but it did serve as a staging and holding area for troops preparing to occupy Japan during World War II. Today, the Presidio's role is to provide base support services that help U.S. forces become mission-ready.

The on-site museum takes you through the area's history from a military viewpoint, including the Presidio's important role as a training base today. Hours are Monday from 10 A.M. till 1 P.M., Tuesday through Saturday from 10 A.M. till 4 P.M., and Sunday from 1 P.M. till 4 P.M. Learn more at *www.monterey.org*.

Maritime Museum of Monterey

As you might imagine, the Maritime Museum of Monterey focuses on local maritime history. It opened in 1992 and houses more than 50,000 photographs, including an impressive collection of ship photography. Seven exhibit areas house permanent and rotating exhibits, and some are interactive to keep younger travelers engaged. The Monterey History and Art Association oversees this museum, which you can learn more about at *www.montereyhistory.org*.

Monterey State Beach

The city of Monterey actually shares this beach with the town of Seaside to the south. It's a favorite for fishermen and scuba divers, thanks to the abundance of aquatic life below Monterey Bay's surface. The beach is flat, which attracts volleyball players and kite-flyers—an excellent way to spend an afternoon outdoors following a morning of museum tours downtown. For directions and details, go to *www.parks.ca.gov*.

Monterey Museum of Art

The Monterey Museum of Art is a repository of American art, particularly works by Monterey Bay and West Coast artists, including the world-famous photographer Ansel Adams. Paintings, photography, and contemporary art fill the permanent collection, which is enhanced by lectures, seminars, and rotating exhibitions year-round.

 RAINY DAY FUN

The Monterey Museum of Art offers a rotating schedule of hands-on workshops and other activities that are designed to help the whole family better relate to the works in the permanent collection and rotating exhibits. To see what's coming up during your vacation, go to the "education" section of the museum's Web site, *www.montereyart.org*.

Hours are 11 A.M. until 5 P.M. Wednesday through Saturday, and Sunday from 1 P.M. till 4 P.M. The museum is closed Monday and Tuesday. Adult admission is $5, and kids younger than twelve can enter for free. Military personnel pay a discounted admission fee of $2.50.

A Short Drive Away

Though the National Steinbeck Center is a short, seventeen-mile drive away in the town of Salinas, most tourists incorporate it into their itinerary when planning to visit Monterey. You know Steinbeck's books even if you haven't read them, from *East of Eden* to *The Grapes of Wrath* and *Of Mice and Men*. At the museum, these titles and more come alive through interactive exhibits and themed theaters.

Steinbeck was born in Salinas and lived there until his college years, when he attended Stanford University to the city's north. He left California for New York in his twenties but returned after failing to get any of his writings published. Thus, you can imagine the love this "hometown crowd" has for its native son, who went on to prove the critics wrong with bestsellers and even a Nobel Prize for Literature. Each August, the center sponsors a Steinbeck Festival that includes films, speakers, panels, theater, and tours that celebrate the noted author. Learn more at *www.steinbeck.org*.

Monterey Bay Aquarium Area

The world-famous Monterey Bay Aquarium is north of Monterey's main downtown area on Cannery Row, which is more of a food and wine adventure than a look back at the fishing industry that first developed there. If you have two days to spend in Monterey, you might do best to enjoy downtown on your first day before heading toward the aquarium on your second day. That way, you can spend the morning exploring the aquarium and working up an appetite before heading over to Cannery Row's restaurants and the Monterey County Wine Country Museum.

Monterey Bay Aquarium has a full-service restaurant and bar if your children are too young to enjoy strolling along Cannery Row and sampling its more exotic gastronomic offerings. There's also a self-service café at the aquarium where you can buy ready-made sandwiches and pizza.

Monterey Bay Aquarium

The Monterey Bay Aquarium has a simple mission: to inspire conservation of the oceans. Serious discussions about building the aquarium began in the late 1970s, and the facility opened in October 1984 with more than 10,000 visitors on day one. Within five months, 1 million patrons had visited the aquarium, and nearly 2.5 million people checked out the exhibits by the end of the aquarium's first year—an attendance record for all United States aquariums.

By 2006, more than 7 million people a year visited the aquarium's Web site (*www.mbayaq.org*), in addition to the continued flow of traffic that makes purchasing advance tickets almost mandatory for a visit to the aquarium.

The aquarium's exhibits focus on animals, plants, and ocean education. The daily sea otter program is a longtime favorite, letting you watch trainers in action with the rescued pups. There's also a twenty-eight-foot kelp forest that's full of fish and sharks, a giant octopus exhibit where you can watch a live feeding, and a million-gallon Outer Bay exhibit that's home to sea turtles, hammerhead sharks, giant blue-fin tuna, and the largest permanent collection of jellyfish in the United States.

You can take guided and behind-the-scenes tours of the aquarium, or you can sign up for Aquarium Adventures, which are daily programs for all ages that range from working alongside naturalists onboard a sailboat in Monterey Bay to surface scuba diving that gives kids a fish-eye view of the aquarium's tide pool from just beneath its surface.

 RAINY DAY FUN

The Monterey Bay Aquarium has several online-only exhibits that you can check out with your kids on days when you can't get to the aquarium itself. They have names such as "Saving Seahorses" and "Sharks: Myth and Mystery" and are sometimes based on previous aquarium exhibits that have since closed. Learn more at *www.mbayaq.org*.

The museum is open from 10 A.M. until 6 P.M. daily, and from 9:30 A.M. until 6 P.M. on holidays except Christmas Day, when the facility is closed. Tickets are $15.95 for children between three and twelve years old, $22.95 for students between twelve and eighteen years old, and $24.95 for adults ages nineteen and older. You can purchase tickets online—which the aquarium recommends, especially during the peak summer season. The best times to avoid crowds are during the fall and winter or after 2 P.M. from Tuesday through Thursday during the summer months.

Cannery Row

Cannery Row runs from the Monterey Bay Aquarium southeast to the lower section of the Presidio of Monterey, right along the bay. It is, in many ways, what you make of it, since you'll find everything from romantic hotels to kid-friendly face-painting along the stretch. The eight blocks that encompass the row are easily walkable, so you need not worry about transportation in the area. If you want to, you can even book a hotel right along the row to give yourself a central location from which to explore the nearby Monterey Bay Aquarium and downtown Monterey sights.

 JUST FOR PARENTS

Want to be Gary Cooper for a day? Consider stopping by Cannery Row's Monterey Rent-a-Roadster, which offers convertibles such as the Model A Ford Roadster, Mercedes 55K, and Ford Phaeton. The Fords seat four to five people, but the Mercedes seats just two and makes for a spectacularly romantic couple's drive along the California coast. Maps are included. Learn more at *www.rent-a-roadster.com*.

Some of the more family-friendly enterprises along the strip include an eighteen-hole miniature golf course and a stuffed bear-building store. Adults might enjoy a trip to Aqua Massage, where you get into a tanning-bed-style contraption that gives you a water-jet rubdown. There's also the Culinary Center of Monterey, where you can sign up for a hands-on cooking class, and the Monterey County Wine Country Museum, which is near a few stores that offer wine tastings. For a complete list of shops, restaurants, and hotels along Cannery Row, go to the street's official Web site, *www.canneryrow.com*.

Monterey County Youth Museum

The Monterey County Youth Museum is about a block and a half inland from Cannery Row, making it an easily accessible stop during a day of touring the shops, restaurants, and even the nearby Monterey Bay Aquarium. Founded in 1997, the museum has a plethora of kid-friendly, hands-on exhibits such as Creation Station for budding young artists, a Magnet Table, Water Blocks for toddlers, Body Works and Pet Vet for would-be doctors and veterinarians, and a Giant Loom for weaving.

MCY Museum is open from 10 A.M. until 5 P.M. Monday, Tuesday, and Thursday through Saturday, and from noon until 5 P.M. on Sunday. The museum is closed on Wednesday. Tickets are $5.50.

Carmel

The town of Carmel, south of Monterey, is the last outpost of pure civilization before you get into the Big Sur wildlife area. Carmel is probably best known for its world-famous public golf course at Pebble Beach, where professionals play side by side with duffers who can afford to spend upward of $400 for a single round of golf.

As you might expect with such a tony clientele, shopping is the main draw downtown, where there are plenty of upscale restaurants as well. Parking is a real bear, so if you plan to visit, expect to leave the car and do a lot of walking—either to the greens or to drop a good number of greenbacks.

Pebble Beach

Pebble Beach is actually more than just a stretch of four golf courses; it's also a full-scale resort with three separate hotels, restaurants, shops, and a spa. But it's the links that have brought worldwide fame to this Carmel establishment, which regularly hosts the U.S. Open and a celebrity-filled pro-am in addition to other well-known golf tournaments. The main par-72 course runs right along the rugged California coast, offering exquisite views as well as mind-bending shots.

You'll pay for the privilege of making memories here, with rooms starting at $565 per night and going up to $2,000 per night for suites. Those prices do not include golfing; that's an extra $475 per round, plus a separate cart fee if you're not a hotel guest. Private lessons are available, and the Golf Academy offers one- and two-day programs in addition to a Golf 101 introduction to the sport. Reservations, rates, and additional information are available at *www.pebblebeach.com*.

 TRAVEL TIP

Several of the hotels at the Pebble Beach resort complex offer winter stay-and-play package deals that will knock at least a few dollars off the cost of a visit. It's still not an inexpensive adventure—two-night, three-day deals run around $1,800 per golfer— but it's at least a little bit better than the high-season summer rates, which are as high as your worst day's golf score.

Carmel Mission

The official name of this establishment is the San Carlos Borroméo de Carmelo Mission. It was founded in 1771 and still operates as a parish that hosts regular services, weddings, and other events. The mission is open to the public Monday through Saturday from 9:30 A.M. until 5 P.M., and on Sunday from 10:30 A.M. until 5 P.M. Adult admission is $5, and children ages seventeen and younger pay $1.

There are self-guided as well as docent-led tours, and there is a $7 fee for the guided look around. The schedule for guided tours changes on a monthly basis, in part based on advance requests. If you think you might want a guided tour, go to *www.carmelmission .org* to contact the mission before your visit.

Lodging and Restaurants

There is no shortage of places to stay or eat on the South Coast. Here are some suggestions you might want to consider. Each suggestion is marked by one, two, or three dollar signs.

For lodging:

$ = a room costs less than $100

$$ = a room costs from $101 to $200

$$$ = a room costs more than $200

For restaurants:

$ = entrées cost less than $15

$$ = entrées cost from $16 to $30

$$$ = entrées cost more than $30

Lodging

SANTA CRUZ
Inn at Pasatiempo
555 Highway 17
(800) 230-2892
www.innatpasatiempo.com
$

Paradise Inn by the Beach
311 Second Street
(831) 426-7123
www.santacruz.com/hotels
$

Ramada Limited Santa Cruz Water Street
516 Water Street
(831) 426-6111
www.ramada.com
$

Santa Cruz Beach Inn & Suites
600 Riverside Avenue
(831) 458-9660
www.scbeachinn.com
$

MONTEREY
Best Western Monterey Inn
825 Abrego Street
(877) 373-5345
www.montereyinnca.com
$$

Casa Munras
700 Munras Avenue
(800) 222-2446
www.hotelcasamunras.com
$$$

Hyatt Regency Monterey
1 Old Golf Course Road
(831) 372-1234
www.hyatt.com
$$$

Monterey Marriott
350 Calle Principal
(831) 649-4234
www.marriott.com
$$$

Spindrift Inn
652 Cannery Row
(800) 841-1879
www.spindriftinn.com
$$$

CARMEL

Carmel Mission Inn
3665 Rio Road
(800) 348-9090
www.carmelmissioninn.com
$$$

Highlands Inn
120 Highlands Drive
(831) 620-1234
www.hyatt.com
$$$

La Playa Hotel & Cottages
Carmel Real at Eighth Avenue
(831) 624-6476
www.laplayahotel.com
$$–$$$

Tickle Pink Inn
155 Highland Drive
(800) 635-4774
www.ticklepinkinn.com
$$$

Tradewinds Carmel
Mission Street at Third Avenue
(831) 624-2776
www.tradewindscarmel.com
$$$

Wayside Inn

Seventh and Mission Streets

(800) 433-4732

www.innsbythesea.com

$$$

Restaurants

SANTA CRUZ

O'Mei Chinese Cuisine

2316 Mission Street

(831) 425-8458

www.omeifood.com

$–$$

Rosie McCann's Irish Pub & Restaurant

1220 Pacific Avenue

(831) 426-9930

www.rosiemccanns.com

$$–$$$

Saturn Cafe

145 Laurel Street

(831) 429-8505

www.saturncafe.com

$

Soif Wine Bar

105 Walnut Avenue

(831) 423-7020

www.soifwine.com

$$

MONTEREY
Café Fina
47 Fisherman's Wharf
(831) 372-5200
www.cafefina.com
$$

Crown & Anchor
150 West Franklin Street
(831) 649-6496
www.crownandanchor.net
$–$$

Stokes Restaurant & Bar
500 Hartnell Street
(831) 373-1110
www.stokesrestaurant.com
$$

PACIFIC GROVE
Fishwife
Sunset Drive at Asilomar
(831) 375-7107
www.fishwife.com
$–$$

Passion Fish
701 Lighthouse Avenue
(831) 655-3311
www.passionfish.net
$$

CARMEL
Anton & Michel
Mission Street between Ocean and Seventh

(831) 624-2406
www.carmelsbest.com/antonmichel
$$–$$$

Bouchée Restaurant and Wine Bar
Mission Street between Ocean and Seventh
(831) 626-7880
www.boucheecarmel.com
$$–$$$

The Grill on Ocean Avenue
Ocean Avenue between Delores and Lincoln
(831) 624-2569
www.carmelsbest.com/thegrill
$$–$$$

Mission Ranch
26270 Dolores Street
(831) 624-6436
www.missionranchcarmel.com
$$

Portabella
Lincoln and Monte Verde
(831) 624-4395
www.carmelsbest.com/portabella
$$–$$$

Tutto Mondo Trattoria
Dolores Street
(831) 624-8977
www.mondos.com
$$–$$$

CHAPTER 12

The Northern Mountains

THE CALL OF THE WILD, as much as the rush for gold, helped bring civilization into the northern mountainous terrain that stretches up to the California-Oregon border. The peaks reach elevations of 5,000, 7,000, and even 9,000 feet, making them a massive natural obstacle to development. That's a good thing for the locals who want to enjoy hiking, camping, and fishing in peace, as well as for visitors who want a real taste of unscathed wilderness—with a few tourist-friendly towns thrown in just in case you get lost along the way.

Regional History

The Shasta Cascade, California's northernmost mountain region, is a bit hard to define. In general, it stretches from just inside the Pacific Coast all the way across California to the Nevada border, with a northern boundary at the Oregon border and a southern edge around the town of Redding and Lassen Volcanic National Park.

No matter where you draw the lines on a map, this is a land where wilderness still rules. The word *avalanche* is part of winter weather reports, and a handful of ill-prepared tourists lose their lives each year trying to hike to the top of snow-covered peaks. That's not to say the northern mountains are unwelcoming to adventure-seeking tourists. Just the opposite: If your family vacation plans include whitewater rafting, fishing, backpacking, or climbing, then this part of northern California is going to seem like your Mecca, particularly during the warmest times to visit, from June through August.

 TRAVEL TIP

Anglers, take note: The Web site *www.shastacascade.org* posts a weekly fishing report that covers the lakes and rivers in all eight northern mountains counties, along with tournament information and links to local outfitters where you can pick up tackle and bait supplies.

It's believed that fur trappers were the first European settlers to inhabit this part of northern California; they made their way south from Oregon or north from what would become the San Francisco area. The gold rush came this far north in 1851, first in what is now the town of Yreka (hence the name—they found gold there, just as in Eureka) and later in surrounding areas. Not too long afterward, timber became the main draw in terms of economic opportunity, thanks to the incredible stretches of dense forests that line the base of the mountain ranges. Those magnificent vistas are still in the area today, unlike in parts of northern California where the timber industry decimated the redwood forests.

Indeed, the Shasta Cascade rage has always kept its wilderness ways, sometimes to the detriment of the people trying to bring civilization into the region. Just before World War II, a few counties in northern California and southern Oregon banded together with the intention of forming a new state. The would-be secessionist movement was fueled by demands for better access and roadways. Thankfully, cooler heads prevailed and better roadways came, linking the two main towns of Redding and Yreka with the Mount Shasta tourism area between them, plus Sacramento and San Francisco to the south and southwest.

Local Overview

Your main north-south artery into the region is Interstate 5, which comes down from California's northern border with Oregon and then passes through Yreka, Mount Shasta, and the town of Redding. It's about a four-hour drive from Yreka to Sacramento and close to five hours from Yreka to San Francisco. If you want to make the northern-most area of the mountains part of your itinerary, allow at least two or three days to recoup your energy from the driving alone—not to mention all the outdoor fun you'll have once you leave the highway and explore the lakes, rivers, waterfalls, volcanoes, and additional surrounding wilderness. In this part of northern California, there are a whopping seven national forests and parks:

- Klamath National Forest
- Lassen National Forest
- Mendocino National Forest
- Modoc National Forest
- Plumas National Forest
- Shasta-Trinity National Forest
- Lava Beds National Monument

If you're driving down to this region from Oregon instead of up from San Francisco or Sacramento, you can travel via the Volcanic Legacy Scenic Byway. The 500-mile route has connecting sections that cross the state line, and northern California's roughly 360-mile section includes parts of Interstate 5 and Highways 97, 89, and 36. The southern section of the byway makes a loop around Lassen Volcanic National Park, so you can enjoy a bit of it even if you don't want to drive all the way up to and beyond the California-Oregon border. If you have the time, though, it's worth the trip. This is one of only two Department of Transportation–designated All-American Roads in northern California, the other running along the Pacific Ocean's Big Sur Coast Highway.

Whether you take the scenic route or make a straight shot up Interstate 5, the two towns that will serve as your points of reference are Redding, in the southern part of the Shasta Cascade, and Yreka, which is the last outpost to the north. You can reach Redding via Amtrak trains, but to get to Yreka, you'll have to drive.

Redding

With just over 100,000 residents, Redding is the largest city in California north of Sacramento. It's on the Siskiyou Trail, which Native Americans traversed for centuries—followed by fur trappers and gold-seekers—until Interstate 5 was built in its shadow. Redding incorporated as an official town in 1887 and grew to more than 3,500 people within about twenty-five years after copper and iron mining. The timber industry dominated the area through the 1950s; tourism started to take hold during the late 1960s after the completion of Interstate 5. Today, tourism remains a stronghold, as do retirement settlements that lure people who are attracted to a less-expensive and quieter way of life.

≡FAST FACT

The first settler in Redding was pioneer Pierson B. Reading, but the town was named for Southern Pacific railroad businessman Benjamin B. Redding. In 1874, the locals tried to rechristen the town with the spelling Reading in honor of its first non-native settler, but the railroad stuck to its double-D version and by 1880 the name Redding was printed on most maps of the area.

Redding, like the town of Red Bluff to its south, is mainly a gateway area to Lassen Volcanic National Forest and the greater Shasta Cascade mountain wilderness areas. However, it does have a couple of annual events that draw tourists, including a hot-rod show every April and a rodeo every May. For upcoming dates, visit *www.visitredding.org*.

One of Redding's great attractions is the Sundial Bridge at Turtle Bay, a pedestrian bridge that crosses the Sacramento River and connects a trail system with Turtle Bay Exploration Park. Walking across the bridge itself is free, but you'll have to pay to enter Turtle Bay Exploration Park, a 300-acre campus that includes an aquarium, botanical gardens, a butterfly garden, an art gallery, an interpretive forest, and more.

 RAINY DAY FUN

The rotating exhibits at the Turtle Bay Exploration Park in Redding focus on the relationship between humans and nature. The curators stretch this mission statement, offering everything from "Alien Earths: Are We Alone?" to "The Art of Warner Bros. Cartoons." (Hey, Bugs Bunny did eat a lot of carrots. That's one way of interacting with nature. . . .)

Hours change from season to season, so check the park's Web site at *www.turtlebay.org*. Admission is $12 for adults and $7 for children age twelve and younger.

Yreka

About an hour and a half north of Redding along Interstate 5 is the town of Yreka, adding further proof beyond the Redding/Reading issue that spelling was apparently a major challenge for this region's early settlers. Today, the town's name is pronounced wye-REE-ka, perhaps to distinguish this town from Eureka to the south.

The town got its start when gold was found in 1851, bringing the California Gold Rush and civilization into the region. (They no doubt shouted "eureka!" and not "wye-REE-ka!" at the time, but let's not quibble.) Today, about 7,000 people live in Yreka, which has a downtown that includes a historic district with buildings preserved from the late 1800s. You can get a brochure for a walking tour from the local chamber of commerce, online at *www .yrekachamber.com*.

TRAVEL TIP

If you want to combine land and air travel in a unique way, plan your visit to the Yreka area during September, which is when the town of Montague hosts its annual Rotary Balloon Fair. You can book a special ticket for the Dawn Express onboard the Yreka Western Railroad, arriving at Montague in time to see dozens of hot air balloons rise along with the sun.

Another fun thing to do is take a ride on the Yreka Western Railroad, which steams just shy of eight miles to the town of Montague, just as it has since 1889. The ride from the historic railroad depot is about an hour long, with an extended stop in Montague so that you can walk around to the local shops and restaurants before riding the rails back to Yreka. Round-trip ticket prices start at $10 for children younger than thirteen and $20 for adults, with regular departures from May through October. Learn more at *www.yrekawesternrr.com*.

Trinity Mountains

The Trinity Mountains are often called the Trinity Alps, both because it sounds sexier and because they remain snow-covered even during July and August, just as the Swiss Alps do. Thompson Peak is the highest in the range, with an elevation of nearly of 9,000 feet.

As you might imagine, hiking and camping are big draws here in terms of tourism. The mountains overlook Trinity Lake to the east, where you can enjoy fishing, boating, and even swimming during the warmest summer months. The nearby Trinity River is popular with kayakers and whitewater rafters. There are plenty of local outfitters who can hook you up for the more popular activities (look for a list of links at *www.shastacascade.org*).

If you dig a little deeper into the area's offerings, you'll also find things like the Coffee Creek Ranch, a 367-acre dude ranch about eight miles north of Trinity Lake. The folks there have everything from horseback riding to gold-panning expeditions, not to mention a heated pool and health spa for soothing those achy muscles at the end of the day. Square dancing is a popular after-dinner activity, too, so bring those cowboy hats. The season at Coffee Creek Ranch is from Easter through Thanksgiving. Learn more at *www.coffeecreekranch.com*.

≡ FAST FACT

When you're hiking or camping in the Trinity Mountains, keep an eye out for the Trinity Alps Giant Salamander, a cryptid—or presumably extinct species—that was last reported seen in the mountains during the 1990s. It's believed to be a relative of the Hellbender, a foot-long salamander that also goes by the names *devil dog* and *snot otter* in the eastern United States.

Another interesting option in this part of the northern mountains is renting a houseboat on Trinity Lake. Trinity Alps Marina (*www .trinityalpsmarina.com*) has 36-foot to 56-foot models available at prices ranging from $900 to $4,300 per week depending on the season and the size of the boat. Three- and four-night packages are also available, as well as additional rentals of ski boats, party barges, and fishing boats to make the most of your time on the water.

Marble Mountain Wilderness

The Marble Mountain Wilderness is part of Klamath National Forest, near the city of Yreka. The forest is about 1.7 million acres strong, crossing over the California border into the state of Oregon. The Marble Mountain Wilderness section is 240,000 acres of forest (all within California's borders) and offers some of the best fishing, hiking, and backpacking in the region.

There are eighty-nine lakes stocked with trout, not to mention countless streams teeming with steelhead trout and salmon. As you might imagine, those streams are like buffets for the bears that live in the area, so take appropriate precautions when fishing, hiking, and camping. If you plan to hike, try to do so before late September and early October, when deer hunters swarm the area—or at least steer clear of the designated hunting areas.

 JUST FOR PARENTS

There are plenty of Class 2 and 3 rapids for whitewater rafting in the Trinity Mountains, but if you choose to take on the Class 4 and 5 sections of the California Salmon or Scott Rivers, consider leaving the kids at home. Older teenagers may have the physical strength to keep themselves inside the raft, but your little ones probably won't be safe, if they're allowed in the raft at all.

If you want to visit the Marble Mountain Wilderness in a more organized way, consider a stay at the Marble Mountain Guest Ranch (*www.marblemountainranch.com*). It's a dude ranch geared to family fun, combining horseback rides with whitewater rafting trips, fly fishing excursions, trap and sporting clays shooting, and more.

Mount Shasta

If the town of Redding is the heart of civilization in this region, Mount Shasta is the heart of nature. Standing 14,000-plus feet, Mount Shasta is California's fifth-highest peak, visible from some 150 miles away on the clearest of days. That's because everything around it is 10,000 feet shorter, making the peak seem even taller than it already is. There are seven named glaciers on the snow-covered mountaintop, adding to its fantastic beauty.

Mounts Shasta hasn't erupted for at least 200 years. The U.S. Geological Survey says the volcano is dormant—which is different from being extinct—and presumes that it will erupt again. That's not the biggest danger to tourists, though. The primary concern is preparedness for hiking to the snow-covered top, which many amateurs try between June and September only to end up in distress or serious danger. If hiking to the summit is part of your plans, make sure you have the experience and the athleticism for the climb. This is no tiny hill.

 TRAVEL TIP

The Forest Service offers an avalanche advisory and mountain condition report for Mount Shasta that applies to all hikers. Learn more at *www.fs.fed.us*. You also can learn about safety information and local conditions from stores like the Fifth Season Sports in Mount Shasta City, which has a 24-hour climbing report. That store's Web site is *www.thefifthseason.com*.

The Mount Shasta Chamber of Commerce Web site, at *www.mtshastachamber.com*, offers a helpful list of popular hiking routes complete with difficulty ratings and average times for completion. The hikes range from fifteen minutes to more than two hours. Most popular among the routes to the top is Avalanche Gulch, which is also called the John Muir route, named for the late-1800s preservationist who wrote compelling books about northern California's natural beauty before founding the Sierra Club. The Avalanche Gulch route is labeled as beginner-intermediary, which means you have to know how to handle crampons and an ice axe. The steepest angle is 33 degrees—enough for beginners to slip and fall when the terrain is loose from rainfall and glacial runoff.

If you'd rather experience Mount Shasta's beauty without quite as much exertion, consider booking a ticket onboard the Shasta Sunset Dinner Train, whose vintage cars wind around the mountain during a three-hour tour. You get a choice of entrées ranging from beef Wellington to mushroom pesto salmon, which you can enjoy while sitting in a restored train car that was originally built in 1916. Tickets start at $89 per person and go a little higher for special events such as wine tasting and mystery-theme trains. If you want a private table for two, you'll have to pay an extra $60 fee. Learn more at *www.shastasunset.com*.

≡**FAST FACT**

The first man to be recorded in history as climbing to the top of Mount Shasta was Elias Pearce in 1854. The first women to reach the top of the peak followed two years later in a group that included Harriette Eddy and Mary Campbell McCloud. Today, thousands of people try to follow their paths each summer. About half make it to the top.

Shasta Lake

Shasta Lake is actually not a lake at all, but a reservoir that came into existence after the Shasta Dam was completed in 1945. It's a bit smaller than Lake Tahoe to its east, but not by much. In fact, when the reservoir is at full water capacity, it boasts more shoreline than all of San Francisco Bay.

Some 2 million people come to Shasta Lake each summer for camping, hiking, fishing, boating, and—for those with thicker or warmer skin—swimming. You'll find hotels, motels, RV parks, houseboat rentals, and pretty much everything else you'd expect in this kind of wilderness tourist area, with many links to reputable businesses at *www.shastalake.com*.

Because Shasta Lake forms the core of the Shasta-Trinity National Recreation Area, you can also find information about it through the U.S. Forest Service at *www.fs.fed.us*. There are links from that site to everything from low-water safety restrictions to permit requirements and events calendars.

TRAVEL TIP

If you're into off-roading, bring your bike to the Chappie-Shasta Off-Highway Vehicle Area, which boasts 200 miles of roads and trails. You need a permit, but they're free through the Shasta Dam Bureau of Reclamation (*www.usbr.gov*). The permits are required by the U.S. Department of Homeland Security, so don't try to get by without one.

Lake Shasta Caverns

Lake Shasta Caverns, on the east side of the lake, are an interesting option for tourists. Since they opened to the public in 1964, more than a million people have toured them. Though you can get to them by car or by boat, the most popular option is a "three-in-one" tour that combines boating, a bus ride, and an underground walk. Tours of the Lake Shasta Caverns are available year-round, but hours of operation decrease substantially during the winter months. Adult prices start at $20, while children younger than fifteen pay $12. Details are available online at *www.lakeshastacaverns.com*.

Camping

If you want to enjoy the great outdoors above as well as below ground, you'll find no shortage of campsites in the Lake Shasta area. The U.S. Forest Service maintains more than a dozen campgrounds on the surrounding shores, and there are just as many private campgrounds in the area, many of which accommodate RVs.

Camping is a popular activity around Lake Shasta, especially during the summer months, so many of the campgrounds have amenities including volleyball and basketball courts, laundry facilities, and convenience stores. If you want to "rough it" in the truest sense, you may have to go a bit farther out from the lake. Look for a list of all local campgrounds at *www.shastalake.com*.

Lassen Volcanic National Park

The National Park Service describes Lassen Volcanic National Park as a place that lets you witness "a moment in the ancient battle between the earth-shaping forces of creation and destruction in northern California." That's pretty heady stuff, especially given that the last major events were less than a century ago, from 1914 until 1921, when the peak experienced a series of eruptions, including one that blew clouds of smoke and dust seven miles into the air.

The sights you're likely to see during a visit to Lassen Volcanic National Park today are far less threatening, and often they'll be part of a tour or a ranger-led program from one of the visitor centers. This is one of the rare wilderness areas whose primary features can be seen or reached from the manmade roads, meaning you can take younger children with you and not have to worry about them walking into areas where they might get tired or hurt.

 RAINY DAY FUN

There are two Junior Ranger programs that meet inside the Manzanita Lake Amphitheater in Lassen Volcanic National Park. One teaches seven- to twelve-year-old visitors about becoming a junior ranger, while the other teaches the same age group about becoming a junior firefighter and about the role of wildfires in national parks—a timely topic given California's continuing, statewide battles with wildfires.

The rangers at Lassen Volcanic National Park put on an impressive number of programs and activities designed to help you better understand everything you'll see around you. All of the programs are free with admission to the park, and most last forty-five minutes to an hour. Some topics include:

- The American mountain lion
- Local seismic activity
- Geology basics
- Wildlife tracks and trails
- Predators and prey

There are two visitor's centers in the park where you can find information such as trail maps and program notes. The main center is at park headquarters in the town of Mineral, and it is open year-round with shorter hours during the winter months. The second visitor's center, located in the Loomis Museum on Manzanita Lake, is open from June through September. You can find information about both at the Web site *www.lassen.volcanic.national-park.com.*

Exploding Sites

One of the greatest things about Lassen Volcanic National park is that it still shows hints of life. There are hissing fumaroles (holes with vapor rising from them) as well as boiling mud pits that will fascinate even the most easily bored kids. The National Park Service calls these spaces "active hydrothermal areas." But let's face it: "Boiling mud pits" sounds a whole lot more interesting!

 TRAVEL TIP

If you want to ensure that you'll get a chance to walk the trail to Bumpass Hell, consider visiting Lassen Volcanic National Park in August or even September. During colder years, the trail can remain impassable due to thick snow well into the month of June or even early July. The best way to find out about current trail conditions is to call the information desk at (530) 595-4444.

Bumpass Hell has the most active hydrothermal areas in the park; a round-trip walk from the Bumpass Hell parking lot takes about two hours. The location is named for an early settler who burned his leg after falling into a boiling pool—which is of course not easily accessible from the well-marked trail that the National Park Service recommends.

Boiling Springs Lake is another popular active hydrothermal area, with multiple underground steam vents that keep the lake at a temperature of about 125 degrees. The mud pits that line the lake's southeast shore are considered among the best in the entire park. You can reach Boiling Springs Lake on foot after parking your car west of the Warner Valley Campground; it's about three miles round-trip. The trail is mostly wooded and home to many birds, so have your camera with zoom lens handy.

Snowshoeing

Every year is a good year for snowshoeing at Lassen National Volcanic Park, even if you're a beginner. Rangers offer guided snowshoe tours and hikes from January through April, and you can enjoy some easier trails or—if you're experienced at the sport—take on a path like Bumpass Hell. Sometimes, you can join a hike led by a park-designated naturalist, thus combining the exercise with information about animal and plant behavior during the colder months.

If you decide to try the more difficult trails, consider attending one of the park's wilderness survival presentations. Should that sound too scary, stick to the well-marked snowshoe and ski-touring routes, including the main road through the park, which remains unplowed and unavailable to cars during the winter months. Details, maps, and more information are available online at the National Park Service's Web site, *www.nps.gov.*

Lodging and Restaurants

There is no shortage of places to stay or eat in this region. Here are some suggestions you might want to consider. Each suggestion is marked by one, two, or three dollar signs.

For lodging:

$ = a room costs less than $100

$$ = a room costs from $101 to $200

$$$ = a room costs more than $200

For restaurants:

$ = entrées cost less than $15

$$ = entrées cost from $16 to $30

$$$ = entrées cost more than $30

Lodging

REDDING
Ameri Host
2600 Larkspur Lane
(530) 722-9100
www.amerihostinn.com
$$

Best Western Hilltop Inn
2300 Hilltop Drive
(530) 221-6100
http://book.bestwestern.com
$$

Best Western Twin View Inn & Suites
1080 Twin View Boulevard
(530) 241-5500
http://book.bestwestern.com
$–$$

Bridge Bay Resort
10300 Bridge Bay Road
(530) 275-3021
www.sevencrown.com
$$

Fawndale Lodge & RV Resort
15215 Fawndale Road
(800) 338-0941
www.fawndale.com
$

Holiday Inn Express Hotel & Suites
1900 Hilltop Drive
(530) 221-7500
www.ichotelsgroup.com
$$

Redding's Bed & Breakfast
1094 Palisades Avenue
(530) 222-2494
www.reddingbedandbreakfast.com
$$

Tiffany House Bed & Breakfast Inn
1510 Barbara Road
(530) 244-3225
www.tiffanyhousebb.com
$$

Value Inn & Suites
533 North Market Street
(530) 241-2252
www.valueinnredding.com
$

YREKA
Best Western Miner's Inn Yreka
122 East Miner Street
(530) 842-4355
www.bestwestern.com
$–$$

Comfort Inn Yreka

1804 B. Fort Jones Road

(530) 842-1612

www.comfortinn.com

$

Econo Lodge Inn & Suites Yreka

526 South Main Street

(530) 842-4404

www.econolodge.com

$

Rodeway Inn Yreka

1235 South Main Street

(530) 842-4412

www.rodewayinn.com

$

Yreka Super 8 Hotel

136 Montague Road

(916) 842-5781

www.super8.com

$

SHASTA LAKE

Shasta Dam Motel

1529 Cascade Boulevard

(530) 275-1065

$

Restaurants

REDDING
Applebee's
1801 Hilltop Drive
(530) 221-1888
www.applebees.com
$–$$

Black Bear Diner
2605 Hilltop Drive
(530) 221-7600
www.blackbeardiner.com
$–$$

Buz's Crab
2159 East Street
(530) 243-2120
www.buzscrab.com
$$

Cattlemen's
2184 Hilltop Drive
(530) 221-6295
www.cattlemensrestaurants.com
$$–$$$

Cheesecakes Unlimited
1344 Market Street
(530) 244-6670
www.visitredding.com
$–$$

C.R. Gibbs American Grille
2300 Hilltop Drive
(530) 221-2335
www.crgibbs.com
$$

Gironda's Restaurant
1100 Center Street
(530) 244-7663
www.girondas.com
$$

Home Town Buffet
1380 Churn Creek Road
(530) 224-1711
www.oldcountrybuffet.com
$–$$

IHOP Restaurant
2495 Hilltop Drive, Redding, CA
(530) 221-5130
www.ihop.com
$

Jack's Grill
1743 California Street
(530) 241-9705
www.jacksgrillredding.com
$$

Mari Time Seafood & Grill
1600 California Street
(530) 229-0700
www.maritimeredding.com
$$

Papa Murphy's Take 'n' Bake
1355 Churn Creek Road
(530) 223-4223
www.papamurphys.com
$–$$

Pico Loco
1135 Pine Street 96001
(530) 246-2111
www.picoloco.com
$$

Red Robin Gourmet Burgers
1035 Dana Drive
(530) 222-5999
www.redrobin.com
$–$$

CHAPTER 13

The Sierra Nevada

THE SIERRA NEVADA MOUNTAIN RANGE, sometimes called the high Sierras, dominates the landscape of eastern California from just north of Lake Tahoe to well south of Yosemite National Park, delineating much of the border with the state of Nevada in a way that no manmade barrier ever could. The name *Sierra Nevada* is Spanish for "snowy range," and it lives up to the moniker with majestic beauty all twelve months of the year. If you're looking to be awed by nature's grace and power, this is the place to visit.

Regional History

The Sierra Nevada range owes its spectacular beauty to shifting tectonic plates and massive, melting glaciers. The mountains are believed to have existed in a less-impressive form, during their early stages of creation, some 65 million years ago. It's estimated they continued to rise, shift, and tilt with the movement of tectonic plates along the Pacific Coast until about 2.5 million years ago, when they were covered during the most recent Ice Age. The melting glaciers then carved out the range as it is today, leaving Lake Tahoe, Mono Lake, the Mammoth Lakes, and Yosemite Valley in their wake.

Unlike the rest of nothern California, the Sierra Nevada region didn't experience an influx of settlers during the late 1840s and early 1850s. Gold Country, to the west of the mountains, was a much easier place for most of the newcomers to settle their wagon trains, what with flatter land and easier access to the good stuff buried in the ground. It wasn't until the 1860s that the state sent researchers into the Sierra Nevada for sheer exploration purposes, and such mountaineer expeditions continued well into the early 1900s as the early map of California continued to take shape.

≡FAST FACT

The Sierra Club takes its name from the Sierra region. It was founded by early preservationist John Muir, who wrote about his adventures as one of the region's first mountaineers during the late 1800s. His books captivated the nation with titles such as *The Mountains of California* and *The Yosemite*. In honor of his efforts, many schools, trails, and museums in California bear his name.

Scars of Industry

That's not to say that there wasn't mining here; on the contrary, hydraulic methods were employed to blast through the rock of the Sierra Nevada in the search for gold. Copper, aluminum, and other valuable minerals have also been found in the range, and the businessmen who couldn't compete in those categories soon turned to logging, just like their contemporaries in the northwest corner of the state.

The scars of early industrialism are less prominent in the Sierra Nevada region than they are in other parts of northern California, but they do exist, and they still affect natural habitats and ecosystems. Soil erosion and water pollution are two of the more common effects.

Today's Business

Today, development is beginning to encroach on the Sierra Nevada region just as it is throughout the rest of the state, much to the dismay of preservationists and conservationists who want to protect the natural habitat. Agriculture continues to maintain a strong foothold in this region; in the southern foothills, you can find apples, cherries, almonds, walnuts, grapes, olives, and cereal crops. The logging and timber operations are also active, although they face stricter scrutiny than ever before thanks to the public's desire to see parklike areas preserved for recreational use.

Indeed, in recent years tourism has become the main draw for this part of the state, but tourism brings traffic, congestion, smog, and new parking lots where natural beauty used to be. These issues are raising new questions in the minds of preservationists and conservationists, especially in popular areas such as Lake Tahoe and Yosemite National Park.

FAST FACT

Some 15 million people visit the Lake Tahoe and Yosemite National Park areas of the Sierra Nevada each year. That's the same number of people who live in the cities of New York and Los Angeles combined. These kinds of numbers terrify preservationists, as the impact of so many people—even conservation-minded ones—is difficult to balance against the natural landscape.

Another often-debated topic is wildfires, which seem to be increasing in frequency and size across all of California. The giant sequoias that tower some 250 feet high in the Sierra Nevada region are a different species from the giant redwoods in the northwestern part of the state and can live more than 3,000 years. That is, unless they are felled by loggers or burned by wildfires, which some experts believe are more common and more intense because of timber industry practices. The debate continues as fewer than 100 groves of the giant sequoias continue to create a towering canopy across the region, drawing tourists from across the United States and beyond.

Local Overview

As you might imagine, sheer physics makes it nearly impossible to create a north-south route along such an impressive mountain range. Mount Whitney, at 14,505 feet tall, is the highest peak in the contiguous United States, and it is just one of many peaks along the Sierra Nevada that tower more than 10,000 feet into the sky. Even if somebody did build a road here, you'd need a heck of a transmission to get up and down its peaks and valleys.

For planning your itinerary, think of Interstate 5 in the Central Valley as your main north-south route. Yes, it's quite a bit over to the west of the Sierra Nevada, but from it you can access local highways to get to different parts of the range, as well as Interstate 80, which will get you to the northern shore of Lake Tahoe.

 TRAVEL TIP

Mono Lake and the Mammoth Lakes are located east of Yosemite National Park, inside national forest parkland. If you plan to visit either of the lake areas, consider doing so as part of a trip that includes a ride through Yosemite. That's the easiest direct route, especially if you're coming from San Francisco, San Jose, or Sacramento.

The two main southern tourist areas in the Sierra Nevada that this chapter covers are Mono Lake and the Mammoth Lakes, which are to the south and southeast of Yosemite and are both accessible from the north-south Highway 395 route. You can continue south from there to Kings Canyon National Park as well as Sequoia National Park, both of which are detailed in Chapter 16.

Another option, to go to Mono Lake or the Mammoth Lakes from San Francisco to the west instead of from Lake Tahoe to the north, is to follow Highway 120 through Yosemite National Park, connecting to Highway 395 on its eastern side. From the city to Mono Lake is about 250 miles, which can be driven in about five hours' time unless you hit big summer traffic jams.

Mono Lake

Mono Lake is beautiful to visit, but it is primarily known for its role in California's Water Wars, which began in 1898. That's when the city of Los Angeles, in southern California, got a new mayor and water department superintendent. The two shared a vision for helping the city grow despite its location in a semi-arid part of the state, and they set about tapping into runoff from the Sierra Nevada by creating an aqueduct to Los Angeles from the Owens Valley, which is where Mono Lake is located. The aqueduct was completed in 1913, diverting so much water from the valley that its beautiful lakes began to fall. At least one dried up completely by 1924.

☰FAST FACT

Local farmers in the Sierra Nevada foothills tried to stop the aqueduct system from redirecting water toward Los Angeles, in one case using dynamite to blow holes through the pipes and tunnels carrying the water. Their efforts slowed the local damage caused by the system in the early 1920s, but they could not stop the aqueduct from operating at full capacity just a few years later.

The rebellions, lawsuits, calls for change, and pumping of water continue to this day. Since the mid-1970s, volunteers have focused a lot of their studies on Mono Lake, where they have shown that pumping water away from feeder streams has had a negative impact on the lake's ecology. The lawsuits stemming from those findings continued well into the 1990s, and arguments continue today about when the lake will return to its natural level.

Salty, for the Birds

That's not to say that Mono Lake is in any way lacking in buoyancy. In fact, because it is fed by streams that collect salt as they run off the Sierra Nevada, the lake is referred to as having "hypersalinity." There is such a concentration of salt in the water that no fish are native to Mono Lake, though it is well known for its population of small brine shrimp. They're not the kind of shrimp you might order at a restaurant, but they're a key food source for birds, which is why Mono Lake is a favorite destination for bird watchers from across America.

Nearly 2 million birds—dozens of species—spend at least part of the year at Mono Lake. You can see the second-largest population of California gulls (after Great Salt Lake in Utah), plus American avocets, sandpipers, snowy plovers, and phalaropes.

 RAINY DAY FUN

If your kids are old enough to read Mark Twain's *Roughing It*, consider giving them a copy to peruse on a rainy day before visiting Mono Lake. Two of the chapters from the 1872 work describe the lake as Twain saw it in his time, before civilization had encroached and water had begun to be redirected out of the region toward Los Angeles.

Fun Things to Do

There is good hiking, as well as some nice beaches, along Mono Lake—and given its saltiness, it's the right place to take a dip to clear out your nasal passages if you're suffering from a summer cold. Just be prepared to be surrounded by tens of thousands of birds, especially during midsummer when the brine shrimp population matures.

Mono Lake is famous for its tufa formations. They're tall, odd-shaped limestone pillars that jut out of the lake almost like fingers reaching toward the sky. They are created by precipitation from the lake's salt-rich waters. It takes years for a tufa formation to grow, in a similar time scale to a coral reef. Mono Lake's tufa formations are some of the best known in the world; there are others in Armenia and Southern Italy. Historically, the Romans used tufa to build many structures because it was relatively soft and thus easier to cut than other types of rock or granite. Today, the formations are primarily the stuff of great pictures.

 TRAVEL TIP

Tufa is pronounced TOO-fah, but the locals get a big kick out of the many tourists who arrive at Mono Lake each year and ask for directions to the "tofu." If you want to see the greatest concentration of the formations at the lake, skip the misdirected food query and head for South Tufa Grove just off Highway 120, near the southern end of the lake.

As with most photography, the best pictures are to be had during sunrise and sunset, when the tufa formations cast gorgeous shadows across the water in beautiful orange-red colors. They can be interesting when shot as close-ups, thanks to their craggy and porous nature, or when shot with the Sierra Nevada mountains behind them in the distance for scale. If you have a panoramic camera, this is the place to bring it for impressive shots that can be framed both vertically and horizontally as souvenirs when you get back home.

Mammoth Lakes

Mammoth Lakes is a town as well as a region, located just southeast of Yosemite National Park off of Highway 395. It includes more than 100 lakes that offer terrific hiking, fishing, camping, canoeing, kayaking, and more. Mountain biking is also popular during the warmer months, as are hot air balloon rides that offer a mesmerizing view of the Sierra Nevada range.

The Mammoth Lakes region is renowned for its wintertime fun more than its summertime offerings, with several ski centers and a recently renovated Mammoth Mountain Ski Area (*www.mammoth mountain.com*) that offers dining, shopping, and entertainment in addition to guided snowboard tours, snowmobile adventures, and the like. In general, the greater Mammoth Lakes area offers wintertime activities including:

- Downhill skiing
- Cross country skiing
- Dog sledding
- Snowboarding
- Snowmobiling
- Snowshoeing

What's interesting to note, though, is that the geological forces that created this downhill wonderland of snow and ice are still very much at play beneath the earth's surface—a fact you can learn about up close and personal at places like the Long Valley Caldera and Hot Creek.

Long Valley Caldera

The Long Valley Caldera is just north of Mammoth Lakes, next to Mammoth Mountain. If you didn't know it was the remnants of a long-ago volcanic eruption, then you might think it was a valley carved out by glaciers within the Sierra Nevada range. That's because it's so big—some nineteen miles long by ten miles wide. That's more square footage than some towns in this part of northern California.

There has been no volcanic activity from the Long Valley Caldera for tens of thousands of years, but there has been seismic activity in the area, including what scientists called an "earthquake swarm" in May 1980. It included four magnitude-6 earthquakes. There have been additional swarms since that time, leading scientists to begin a careful study of what's happening geologically in the area. Clearly, Mother Nature isn't done with this region yet—and if you need confirmation of that, you can head on down to Hot Creek.

Hot Creek

Hot Creek is a geothermal area within the Long Valley Caldera, whose active hydrothermal system also includes steam vents. That's right: Steam boiling right out of the earth, in this case heating water that discharges into a creek where tourists tend to go swimming, or at least wading. The idea is to find a part of the cold creek where the hot spring water mixes in to create warmth.

 JUST FOR PARENTS

The springs that feed into Hot Creek can scald human skin if you fail to find a spot where the incoming water isn't cooled by the colder creek. Officials do not recommend swimming in the creek, but their warnings are regularly ignored. If you must take a dip, leave the kids behind. Their skin is softer than yours, and it won't be able to withstand a step in the wrong direction.

The possibility of turning your rump into rump roast doesn't deter many tourists from donning bathing suits and splashing into the water, though. A good rule, if you're new to the experience, is to look for the area where people have congregated with smiles and cameras, and head straight for it. Odds are that if they were boiling beneath the surface, you'd be able to tell by the looks on their faces.

Devils Postpile National Monument

Ah, the sane way to see Mother Nature at work: a trip to check out the Devils Postpile National Monument. The rock formation gets its name from its appearance; it looks as if a pile of posts (some of them sixty feet tall) has been inlaid along the side of a mountain. The posts, or columns, are made of columnar basalt. Because of their rarity they were protected from destruction by presidential proclamation in 1911. In the United States, the only place where you can see a similar formation is Wyoming. There are others scattered about the world's volcanic regions, including in Armenia, Italy, New Zealand, and Russia.

≡ **FAST FACT**

It's easy to think that the columns at Devils Postpile National Monument were carved by humans, since many of them have an almost perfect six-sided shape. But if you look closely, you'll see that some have three, four, or seven sides. It just goes to show you that out in the wilderness, you really don't need all that geometry they tried to teach you in high school.

You can walk about two and a half miles from the Devils Postpile National Monument down to Rainbow Falls, which drop just over 100 feet and often display rainbows in their mist. It's the highest waterfall on the middle fork of the San Joaquin River, according to the National Park Service. And if you get tired while looking at it, you'll be happy to know that there's a shuttle bus stop nearby. For specific directions and information about other trails that you can access along the way, go to the National Park Service Web site at *www.nps.gov*.

Lodging and Restaurants

There is no shortage of places to stay or eat in Mammoth Lakes. Here are some suggestions you might want to consider. Each suggestion is marked by one, two, or three dollar signs.

For lodging:

$ = a room costs less than $100

$$ = a room costs from $101 to $200

$$$ = a room costs more than $200

For restaurants:

$ = entrées cost less than $15

$$ = entrées cost from $16 to $30

$$$ = entrées cost more than $30

Lodging in Mammoth Lakes

1849 Condos at Canyon Lodge

826 Lakeview Boulevard

(760) 934-7525

www.1849condos.com

$$$

Alpenhof Lodge

6080 Minaret Road

(760) 934-6330

www.alpenhof-lodge.com

$

Austria Hof Lodge

924 Canyon Boulevard

(760) 934-2764

www.austriahof.com

$–$$$

Cinnamon Bear Inn

113 Center Street

(760) 934-2873

www.cinnamonbearinn.com

$$

Juniper Springs Resort
4000 Meridian Boulevard
(760) 924-1102
www.mammothmountain.com
$-$$

The M Inn Mammoth
75 Joaquin Road
(760) 934-2710
www.mammothcountryinn.com
$$

Mammoth Lakes Travelodge
54 Sierra Boulevard
(760) 934-8892
www.travelodge.com
$$

Mammoth Mountain Inn
1 Minaret Road
(760) 934-2581
www.mammothmountain.com
$$$

Quality Inn Mammoth Lakes
3537 Main Street
(760) 934-5114
www.qualityinn.com
$$

Rodeway Inn Sierra Nevada
164 Old Mammoth Road
(760) 934-2515
www.rodewayinn.com
$$

Shilo Inn Mammoth Lakes
2963 Main Street
(760) 934-4500
www.shiloinns.com
$$

Sierra Lodge
3540 Main Street
(760) 934-8881
www.sierralodge.com
$$

Silver Bear Condos
527 Lakeview Boulevard
(800) 336-6543
www.hotels.com
$$$

The Westin Monache Resort
50 Hillside Drive
(760) 964-2526
www.westin.com/mammoth
$$$

Restaurants in Mammoth Lakes

Alpenrose Restaurant
343 Old Mammoth Road
(760) 934-3077
www.mammothweb.com
$$

Anything Goes
645 Old Mammoth Road
(760) 934-2424
www.anythinggoescatering.com
$–$$$

Base Camp Cafe
3325 Main Street
(760) 934-3900
$$

Chart House Restaurant
106 Old Mammoth Road
(760) 934-4526
www.chart-house.com
$$–$$$

Grumpy's Sports Restaurant
361 Old Mammoth Road
(760) 934-8587
www.grumpysmammoth.com
$–$$

Lakefront Restaurant
Twin Lakes Road
(760) 934-3534
www.tamaracklodge.com
$$–$$$

Mogul Restaurant
1528 Tavern Road
(760) 934-3039
www.themogul.com
$$–$$$

Old New York Deli & Bagel
6201 Minaret Road, No. 105
(760) 934-3354
www.oldnewyork.com
$–$$

Paul Schat's Bakery
3305 Main Street
(760) 934-6055
$–$$

Pita Pit
6201 Minaret Road, No. 149
(760) 924-7482
www.pitapitusa.com
$–$$

Restaurant Lulu
1111 Forest Trail
(760) 924-8781
www.restaurantlulu.com
$$$

Restaurant Skadi
587 Old Mammoth Road
(760) 934-3902
www.restaurantskadi.com
$$–$$$

Sherwin's
1 Sherwin Creek Road
(760) 924-7222
www.sherwinsfolly.com
$$

Thai'd Up
587 Old Mammoth Road
(760) 934-7355
www.thaidup.net
$

Lake Tahoe Area

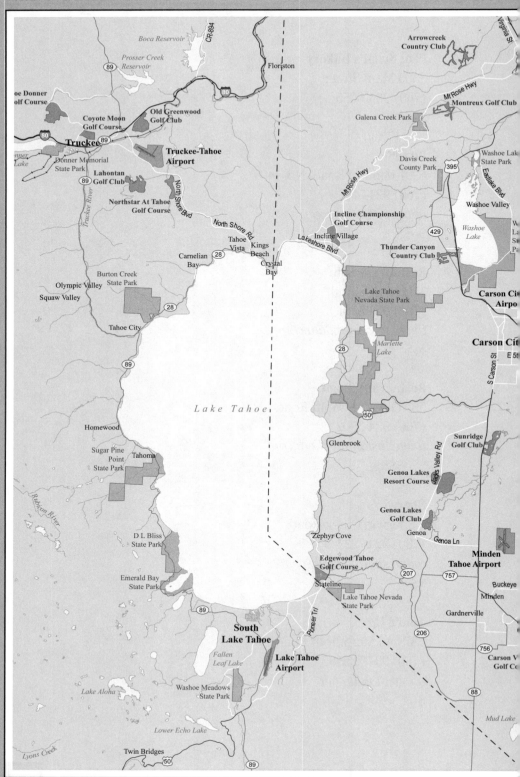

CHAPTER 14

Lake Tahoe Area

MOST OF NORTHERN CALIFORNIA is best known for its summertime tourism, but it's the winter season that tends to draw the crowds at Lake Tahoe, which straddles the California-Nevada border near Reno and Carson City. Even though snow lovers have made the area so popular, Lake Tahoe is a year-round destination, a stunning oasis amid the Sierra Nevada boasting spectacular panoramic views from virtually every inch of shore. Whether you want to ski down mountainsides or across a boat's wake, Lake Tahoe is a great option. There's a reason it's known as the geologic crown jewel of the Sierra Nevada region.

Regional History

Glaciers created much of modern-day Lake Tahoe during the ice age, long after the geologic upheavals that created the Sierra Nevada and its surrounding valleys. Mother Nature wasn't fooling around with Lake Tahoe, either. Its deepest point is 1,645 feet below sea level, making it the third-deepest lake in North America and the second-deepest in the United States, after Crater Lake in Oregon. Some scientists believe the lake is deep enough to create a tsunami should an underground earthquake strike. So far, thankfully, there is no modern-day evidence to prove that theory.

Though inhabited by Native Americans for years, the first records of Lake Tahoe stem from the mid-1800s, when people of European descent started flocking westward across what would become the United States of America. For many years, the body of water went by the name Lake Bigler, in honor of John Bigler, who served as California's governor from 1852 until 1856. Nearly a century later, in 1945, the name officially changed to Lake Tahoe. It stuck, just like the state border that runs right through the lake's middle.

 TRAVEL TIP

If you want to gamble during your visit to Lake Tahoe, then you'll have to book a hotel room on the Nevada side of the lake—gaming is illegal in California. The folks from Nevada are happy to oblige anyone needing a blackjack or slot machine fix with some half-dozen casinos in the South Shore town of Stateline alone.

The mountains surrounding the lake are just as dramatic as the crystal-clear water itself, with peaks seeming to climb one higher than the next in an effort to make the skyline as dramatic as possible. There's Mount Pluto at more than 8,600 feet tall, which seems high until you learn that Mount Rose is close to 11,000 feet tall. That's the height of a dozen full-length cruise ships stacked up bow-to-stern.

As with most seasonal spots, there are major temperature shifts from summer to winter. During the warmest months, you can expect anything from 70 to 90 degrees Fahrenheit—which is not enough to warm the water all that much, given the lake's great depth. It's considered something of a miracle if Lake Tahoe reaches even 70 degrees at its surface, which for most people is a swimming environment about as hospitable as a giant tub of ice water.

The average winter temperatures around Lake Tahoe are in the mid-30s during the day and of course much colder at night. And it's not just the temperature that'll get you come winter, but the precipitation—Tahoe is known for its blizzards. The average annual snowfall is about 12 feet, enough to reach the roofs of most single-story buildings (and to please all the snowboarding fans who fly in from around the world to pound the fresh snow).

≡FAST FACT

One of the reasons Lake Tahoe is considered so beautiful is that its water is incredibly clear, rated in many spots at the same purity levels as distilled water. There has been a League to Save Lake Tahoe since the 1950s, when automobile pollution began to wreak havoc on the water's clarity. "Keep Tahoe Blue" is the local battle cry.

Lest you think the Lake Tahoe area is all about ski resorts and summertime hot spots, it is still very much a wilderness—complete with wild animals for which you should keep watch. Black bears, mountain lions, coyotes, and bobcats are among the local residents, not to mention woodpeckers that can drive you crazy if they take up residence outside your hotel room or cabin. On the other hand, you can also see soaring American bald eagles, which frequent popular locations such as Emerald Bay and Kiva Point.

Local Overview

Lake Tahoe is about two hours from Sacramento by car, or about three and a half hours from San Francisco. If you'd prefer to start your northern California vacation in the Lake Tahoe area and then drive west into California, your best bet is to fly into the Reno-Tahoe International Airport, which is a half-hour to an hour from Lake Tahoe, depending on which shore you choose for your stay. Though it's not a huge airport, it does have flights from a good number of major and minor carriers, including:

- Alaska Airlines
- Allegiant Air
- American Airlines
- Continental
- Delta and Delta Connection
- Frontier
- Horizon Air
- Southwest
- United
- Ted
- U.S. Airways

If you choose to drive to Lake Tahoe during the winter months, be sure to have snow chains for your tires, just in case of a blizzard. Trains are also an option. Amtrak's California Zephyr operates between the San Francisco Bay area and Chicago, Illinois, with a stop in Truckee, a small town just north of Lake Tahoe on Interstate 80. You'll need a rental car or a car service to get you from Truckee to Tahoe, but if you want to avoid flying with the crowds, the train is a good option.

Once you get to the lake, you'll see that it has multiple personalities depending on which shore you choose to explore. You can also head a bit farther east to the Nevada hotspots of Reno and Carson City, which are best known as "Little Las Vegas" and the Nevada state capital, respectively.

Tahoe City and the North Shore

Tahoe City resides on the northwest shore, along the stretch of Lake Tahoe that connects directly to Highway 89—thus delivering tourists by the carload before they head farther up the North Shore to Tahoe Vista and Kings Beach, or farther down the West Shore to Sunnyside, Homewood, Tahoma, and Meeks Bay.

Tahoe City

Tahoe City's proximity to the highway from western California made it the first real town along the northwest shore to draw tourists in mass numbers. Now that it's more than a century old, it has grown up, but it still retains its old-school charms through such details as cobblestone streets and outdoor movie nights at the beach during the summer. There are dog-friendly beaches, family picnic areas, and a marina where you can indulge in a boat ride out on the lake.

 TRAVEL TIP

Want to save a few bucks on entertainment in Tahoe City? There are free concerts at Commons Beach during summer Sunday nights from 4 P.M. to 7 P.M. Performers include local acts as well as touring groups, and the whole family is welcome—except Fido. Picnics are encouraged, as are low-back lawn chairs. Look for a lineup of upcoming acts at *www.visittahoecity.com.*

There's plenty of shopping as well. Tahoe City has everything from wine stores to sports shops that can outfit you with the latest outerwear for whatever season you visit. There are also at least a dozen restaurants—everything from McDonald's to elegant water-front options. For a complete list of annual events, accommodations options, and more, go to the city's Web site, *www.visittahoecity.com.*

The North Shore

The rest of the North Shore towns offer similar scenery but with different attractions, such as gambling in Nevada spots like Incline Village and golf courses at Squaw Valley—home of the 1960 Winter Olympics (which tells you the skiing is pretty darn good, too).

Alpine Meadows is also known for great skiing, while boating is the main draw in Carnelian Bay. Crystal Bay has a couple of casinos, Kings Beach is the hip hangout for the cool kids, and Tahoe Vista is a favorite among bicycle fans.

If you plan to travel with the kids, consider a visit to the West Shore town of Homewood, which is home to the Tahoe Maritime Museum. Founded in 1988, the museum actually looks like an old boathouse and blends into the picturesque surroundings.

 RAINY DAY FUN

The Tahoe Maritime Museum has interactive exhibits that help kids understand what boating is all about. They can learn to tie a line, do art projects such as painting and drawing, and even get their hands a little dirty while learning the craft of boatbuilding. There is a dedicated children's activity room on the premises, as well. Details are at *www.tahoemaritimemuseum.org*.

Inside, exhibits focus on the maritime history of Lake Tahoe dating back to the 1800s. The museum's memorabilia includes information about the first steam and passenger ferries. There are also exhibits about the gentlemen's races of years gone by, including classic boats by builders such as Chris-Craft, Gar Wood, and Stephens.

East Shore

The East Shore of Lake Tahoe runs from about Incline Village in the north down toward South Lake Tahoe, which is a California town just past the Nevada town of Stateline. The southern stretch is far more scenic than the area to the north, which is developed with resorts and casinos. Traveling down the Lake Tahoe shoreline, you'll come to Lake Tahoe Nevada State Park, which offers backcountry rental cabins built in Scandinavian log style. South of the park is the Humboldt-Toiyabe National Forest, just to the east of Route 50, which hugs the lake's coast.

Canoeing and kayaking are the big draws here during the warmer months, since the shoreline is largely unblemished and the wildlife is plentiful. During the winters, cross-country skiers tend to populate this shore, since there's an entire area devoted to the sport in the town of Glenbrook. Downhill skiing is also an option, as it is all around Lake Tahoe thanks to the mountainous terrain.

 TRAVEL TIP

You can save a rental car fee by flying into the Reno-Tahoe International Airport and catching a ride with South Tahoe Express down to any of the South Lake Tahoe casino/resorts. The fee is $24 for adults and $12.50 for children traveling one way, and there are eleven daily departures each way beginning well before sunset and ending after midnight. Details are at *www.southtahoeexpress.com.*

Along the East Shore, two of the spots you'll want to consider visiting are Lake Tahoe Nevada State Park and the town of Stateline.

Lake Tahoe Nevada State Park

Sand Harbor is the most popular tourist magnet inside Lake Tahoe Nevada State Park, since it has a little bit of something to suit different ideas of outdoor fun. If you are bringing a boat on a trailer, you can launch it here. You can also find some great fishing, snorkeling, scuba diving, and a self-guided hike (with trail maps available from the nature center, which also has a concession stand).

As you might imagine, Sand Harbor takes its name from the fact that it's one of the finest sand beaches on the East Shore; other beaches can be rocky and tough on bare toes. If you want to lay out a beach blanket or even take a dip in the 65-degree Lake Tahoe water, this is as good a place as any.

Also inside Lake Tahoe Nevada State Park is Spooner Lake, which is a favorite stop for picnicking during the summer months and a must-visit location for cross-country skiers come wintertime. At the Spooner Lake Cross Country Ski Area, there are a couple of cabins that you can rent plus a day lodge with a fireplace and snacks if you just need to make a pit stop. The ski area alone encompasses some 9,000 acres of land, and there are beginner trails for downhill skiing if you're new to the sport. Learn more about Spooner Lake at *www.spoonerlake.com.*

═══ FAST FACT

The self-guided Sand Point Nature Trail is about a third of a mile long and is wheelchair accessible. It's an easy enough trail to do with even small children, and there are interpretive signs along the way to help you understand all the flora and fauna you see interspersed with the views of Lake Tahoe.

Another popular spot within Lake Tahoe Nevada State Park is Cave Rock, near Zephyr Cove. Fishermen and photographers are the most regular visitors; since the cave is actually part of an extinct volcano, it makes for both a good fishing hole and a memorable take-home picture.

RAINY DAY FUN

If you happen to be in Lake Tahoe on a day when you can't enjoy Cave Rock for its natural beauty, you can at least drive by and tell your kids about Tahoe Tessie, the creature that calls Cave Rock its home if local lore is to be believed. She's not as famous as the Loch Ness Monster, but she'll be a memorable yarn for your kids to tell their friends when you get home.

Each section of Lake Tahoe Nevada State Park requires you to pay an entrance fee, and those fees are all less than $10 per car (and sometimes only $2 or $4 per car). There are some other basic tidbits of information—such as bear warnings and seasonal fire restrictions—that will help you plan your visit depending on which time of year you arrive. You can learn more at the park's official Web site, *www.parks.nv.gov.*

Stateline

The town of Stateline, Nevada, is at the bottom of Lake Tahoe's East Shore, just south of the intersection between Highway 50 and Highway 207. As towns along Lake Tahoe go, Stateline has quite a lot of hotels, resorts, and casinos. This is the place to find a bit of social interaction after a day or two of enjoying the sights in the state park to the north.

Four of the six casinos in Stateline are resorts, some with big names such as Harrah's and MontBleu. Other casinos are smaller, catering to penny-slot bettors and low-betting blackjack players. If you want to gamble but aren't sure of your budget, this is a good place to come. No matter how much you choose to risk, there will be a dealer or a glitzy machine ready to accommodate your dreams of a big payday—and they're all located pretty close to one another, so you can move from casino to casino as your luck ebbs and flows.

Some of the larger casino-resorts offer package deals for your visit, including everything from free buffets to show tickets and gaming credits. The MontBleu and Harrah's, for instance, each have an on-site spa, and they sometimes incorporate daily treatments into their reservation rates. To find out what's being offered during the dates of your visit, you'll have to check out each casino-resort's website:

- Harrah's Lake Tahoe, Bill's Casino Lake Tahoe, and Harvey's Lake Tahoe are all at *www.harrahs.com*
- Horizon Casino Resort, *www.horizoncasino.com*
- Lakeside Inn and Casino, *www.lakesideinn.com*
- MontBleu, *www.montbleuresort.com*

There is of course outdoor fun to be found in and around Stateline as well, including some great hiking and sightseeing along the shore of Lake Tahoe. If you're a golfer, you'll want to check out the Edgewood-Tahoe Golf Course, which is the home of the annual Celebrity Golf Championship. A round of golf will run you anywhere from $100 to $225 here, depending on the time of year. There are "Stay and Play" packages available in conjunction with some of the casino-resorts in Stateline, as well as some of the standalone hotels in town. Go to *www.edgewood-tahoe.com* to learn more.

South Shore

South Lake Tahoe is the main town along the South Shore, on the California side of the lake near the intersection of Highway 89 and Highway 50. The town is one of the biggest on Lake Tahoe, with some 25,000 residents as of the last census. (That's compared with other Lake Tahoe towns that have fewer than 5,000 permanent residents after the summer influx dies down.)

Since the town is in California, you won't find any casinos here, but you will find pretty much every activity imaginable, from camping to sportfishing in the summer to snow skiing in the winter.

Camping

There are more than a half-dozen campgrounds in South Lake Tahoe, each offering a little something different.

Camp Richardson Resort, for instance, is quite big—with a full-service marina, bicycles for rent, a bar and grill, more than 300 campsites, a hotel, lakefront cabins for rent, and dozens of RV spaces. The Campground by the Lake, on the other hand, offers a swimming pool, gymnasium, basketball courts, volleyball courts, and a crafts room. You can choose a roughing-it-in-the-wild camping experience, a camping-in-luxury option with a private cabin, or pretty much anything in between within the South Lake Tahoe town borders. To learn about all the local camping options, go to *www.tahoeinfo.com.*

 **TRAVEL TIP**

When comparing amenities, be sure to ask whether all the advertised services are available year-round. The South Lake Tahoe KOA Campground, for instance, does offer a heated pool and cable television—but only from Memorial Day weekend through Labor Day weekend.

Fishing

Tahoe Sport Fishing Company is the place to go for fishing in South Lake Tahoe. It offers year-round sportfishing excursions that will get you out on the lake instead of casting a line from a local beach. There are morning departures, afternoon departures, all-day excursions, and private or group boats available. Prices start at $85 per person, and you can bring a friend who doesn't fish for half price. The rate includes gear, tackle, bait, coffee, rolls, soda, and beer.

Salmon and trout are the fish you'll be trying to attract. The law allows unlimited catch-and-release or as many as five fish per trip to take home. You will need a day-fishing license, which is available through the company for an extra charge. For details about seasonal options, look online at *www.tahoesportfishing.com*.

Snow Sports

Just as with every other town on the lake, South Lake Tahoe turns into a snow sports paradise every winter. There are at least a dozen companies that offer everything from snowshoes to cross-country and downhill skiing equipment, plus snowboards, boots, and everything else you need to brave the blizzards in style. Some of the companies will even drop off the equipment at your hotel upon arrival and then collect it for you at the end of your vacation so you can concentrate on making the most of your time in Lake Tahoe.

There's an excellent listing of all South Lake Tahoe snow-sports equipment providers at *www.tahoeinfo.com*.

Reno

Reno, Nevada, is about 20 miles northeast of Lake Tahoe. It's one of the biggest cities in Nevada, ranked second or third behind Las Vegas depending on whose figures you trust. And it takes that ranking seriously, since the city's motto is "The Biggest Little City in the World." It's almost as well known for its casinos as Sin City to the south, but Reno's proximity to Lake Tahoe gives it a definite edge in the summer and winter outdoor fun department. That's a good thing for the city, since its older casinos are closing down at a faster rate than Las Vegas's new ones are being built. Increasingly, Reno is becoming known for more than just gaming.

≡FAST FACT

Before gambling became one of the main economic forces in Reno, the city drew a lot of tourists who wanted to end their marriages. The city was one of the first in the United States to pass liberal divorce laws, so people came from near and far to call it quits before going out to try rolling the dice again.

Even though Reno is close to Lake Tahoe on the map, its topography is entirely different. The city is located in the high desert, which means that while there is some snow during the winters, there's nothing like the deluge that blankets Lake Tahoe and its surrounding mountains. In the summers, Reno offers plenty to do that is different from Lake Tahoe—so you can make the city part of an itinerary that includes both places without getting, well, bored.

Whitewater Park

Reno citizens voted to spend $1.5 million on a downtown whitewater park that opened in 2004, boasting Class 2 and 3 rapids as well as drop pools for rafters and kayakers who want to practice advanced skills. Since the park is downtown, you can walk to it from many hotels—a bit of an odd feeling, but a convenience nonetheless.

It's not exactly a huge run, taking just two to three minutes to paddle if you go straight through, but experienced kayakers often stay for hours, hanging out at a single drop pool to hone their moves.

Spectator Sports

If watching people take on athletic challenges is more your speed than actually performing them, consider buying tickets to watch the Golden Baseball League's Reno Silver Sox play at William Peccole Park. The team came to Reno in 2006 and set the bar pretty high for themselves by winning the championship during their inaugural year in town. For the upcoming season's schedule and ticket prices, go to *www.goldenbaseball.com.*

There's also the University of Nevada-Reno Wolf Pack, which has had good teams in recent years in men's basketball and football and women's volleyball. As you might imagine, volleyball tickets are your least expensive option at just $7 for adults and $4 for children ages twelve and younger. Men's football tickets start at more than twice that amount, $18, and go up from there depending on where you choose to sit within Mackay Stadium.

 JUST FOR PARENTS

If you want to tailgate before a men's football game at Mackay Stadium, stick to the parking lots instead of the parking structures, where tailgating is prohibited. Also expect to go inside to root on the Wolf Pack at some point, since come the post-halftime kickoff, university staff patrol the parking lots and politely ask tailgaters to call it a day.

For information about tickets to all University of Nevada-Reno games, go to *www.nevadawolfpack.com.*

Nightlife

Reno has no shortage of nightclubs, both inside and outside its casinos. From comedians like Joe Piscopo to crooners like Frank Sinatra Jr., you can find big-name touring acts and city fixtures alike on the stages around town.

The Web site *www.reno.com* not only provides a listing of scheduled performances around town, but also offers links to all the individual casinos' entertainment schedules—plus upcoming acts at the Reno Events Center, the Reno-Sparks Convention Center, and more. If you want to see who'll be in town or even nearby during the dates of your vacation, this is the place to do your research with the fewest possible keystrokes.

Carson City

Carson City is Nevada's capital, much to the chagrin of schoolchildren everywhere who shout out "Las Vegas!" when asked to name the state's seat of control. Carson City is about thirty miles south of Reno on Lake Tahoe's eastern side.

The city started as a small town in the late 1850s as settlers pushed westward into California during the gold rush. The history of those founding years is on display at the city's museums, which offer everything from railroad history to hands-on exhibits. But if you'd rather learn by walking the streets where that history was made, you can follow the Kit Carson Trail, a two-and-a-half-mile path that winds through some of the city's most impressive historic homes.

Museums

There are three main museums in Carson City—some better than others for families with small children—and all offer something that's likely to entertain at least a few members of your group. You can find information about each of the following museums at *www.carson-city.org*.

Nevada State Museum

The Nevada State Museum was the home of the U.S. Mint for more than two decades, turning the ore from Comstock Lode into gold and silver coins for American citizens. You can see some of the original equipment, including Coin Press No. 1, which was built and sent from Philadelphia and minted coins from 1870 until 1893.

There's also an Earth Science Gallery at this museum, along with a replica of a ghost town that just may give you chills. Remember, Carson City was at one time part of the Wild West Frontier. She may be a respectable city today, but she's a lady with a past, for sure. Hours are 8:30 A.M. until 4:30 P.M. daily. Admission is $5 for adults and free for children ages seventeen and younger.

Nevada State Railroad Museum

The Nevada State Railroad Museum offers just what you'd expect based on its name: A look at the history of the railroads that helped to build not just Carson City and Nevada, but the entire western portion of the United States.

 RAINY DAY FUN

From spring through fall, the Nevada State Railroad Museum offers rides on a restored steam train as well as a classic steam car. Departures are every thirty to forty minutes daily between 10 A.M. and 4 P.M., and tickets are free for children ages six and younger. Adults pay $4 or $5, depending on which railway you choose to ride.

There are some sixty-five railcars in the museum's collection, and forty of those were built before 1900. Some actually had to be purchased from Hollywood studios, which had snapped them up after some of the early rail lines in the region went bust. The museum also offers occasional lectures and special events. Check the online calendar at *http://dmla.clan.lib.nv.us/docs/museums/cc/carson.htm* to see what's coming up during your vacation dates.

Northern Nevada Children's Museum

Hands-on is the mantra at the Northern Nevada Children's Museum, which has everything from dress-up costumes to a walk-in kaleidoscope. There's a section called Wee World for toddlers, so you don't have to worry that your older kids will have all the fun. Programs are geared for kids of all ages, including the Baby Signs class that helps you communicate with infants before they learn how to talk.

 RAINY DAY FUN

Every Tuesday from 10 A.M. until 11:30 A.M., the Northern Nevada Children's Museum hosts "Books & Brags," a program that's included free with your museum admission fee. Your child will join others as they read a book and then make a craft to brag about what they've just read. All ages are welcome, as are walk-in participants.

Admission is $5 for anyone age fourteen or older; $3 for children between two and fourteen; and free for toddlers and infants. Hours are from 10 A.M. until 4:30 P.M. daily. More details are available online at *www.cmnn.org*.

Kit Carson Trail

Kentucky-born frontiersman Kit Carson—for whom Carson City is named—has been the subject of comic books, television shows, and movies. The museum that honors him is in the state of New Mexico, but Carson City offers the Kit Carson Trail. It's a walking path through the city's residential area that features more than sixty landmarks.

There's a downloadable trail map available online at *www .carson-city.org*, which also has interesting links to podcasts by the

"Talking Houses of Carson City." Some are the same houses you'll see along the walking trail, offering 90-second anecdotes about the lives and times that the houses have "experienced" throughout the city's history. Some are really quite unexpected, such as the story narrated by John Wayne about the Krebs-Petersen house, where the beloved Western actor filmed his last movie, *The Shootist*.

Lodging and Restaurants

There is no shortage of places to stay or eat in the Lake Tahoe area. Here are some suggestions you might want to consider. Each suggestion is marked by one, two, or three dollar signs.

For lodging:

$ = a room costs less than $100

$$ = a room costs from $101 to $200

$$$ = a room costs more than $200

For restaurants:

$ = entrées cost less than $15

$$ = entrées cost from $16 to $30

$$$ = entrées cost more than $30

Lodging

NORTHERN QUEEN INN

400 Railroad Avenue, Nevada City, CA 95959

(800) 226-3091

www.northernqueeninn.com

$$

Emma Nevada House

528 East Broad Street, Nevada City, CA 95959

(800) 916-3662

www.emmanevadahouse.com

$$$

National Hotel
211 Broad Street, Nevada City, CA 95959
(530) 265-4551
www.thenationalhotel.com
$$–$$$

Outside Inn
575 East Broad Street, Nevada City, CA 95959
(530) 265-2233
www.outsideinn.com
$–$$

Nevada City Inn
760 Zion Street, Nevada City, CA 95959
(800) 977-8884
www.nevadacityinn.net
$$

Piety Hill Cottages
523 Sacramento Street, Nevada City, CA 95959
(800) 443-2245
www.pietyhillcottages.com
$–$$

Parsonage Bed & Breakfast
427 Broad Street, Nevada City, CA 95959
(530) 265-9478
www.theparsonage.net
$–$$

Golden Chain Resort Motel
13413 State Highway 49, Grass Valley, CA 95945
(530) 273-7279
www.hotels.com
$

Best Western Gold Country Inn
11972 Sutton Way, Grass Valley, CA 95945
(800) 780-7234
www.bestwestern.com
$-SS

Stagecoach Motel
405 South Auburn Avenue, Grass Valley, CA 95945
(530) 272-3701
www.historichwy49.com
$

Sonora Days Inn
160 South Washington Street, Sonora, CA 95370
(866) 732-4010
www.sonoradaysinn.com
$

Holiday Lodge
1221 East Main Street, Grass Valley, CA 95945
(800) 742-7125
www.holidaylodge.biz
$

Courtyard Suites
210 North Auburn Street, Grass Valley, CA 95945
(530) 272-7696
www.gvcourtyardsuites.com
$–$$

The Pine's Resort
54432 Road 432, Bass Lake, CA 93604
(559) 642-3121
www.basslake.com
$$–$$$

Best Western Sonora Oaks
19551 Hess Avenue, Sonora, CA 95370
(800) 780-7234
www.bestwestern.com
$$

Restaurants

Friar Tuck's Restaurant & Bar
111 North Pine Street, Nevada City, CA 95959
(530) 265-9093
www.friartucks.com
$$

New Moon Cafe
203 York Street, Nevada City, CA 95959
(530) 265-6399
www.thenewmooncafe.com
$$

Posh Nosh
318 Broad Street, Nevada City, CA 95959
(530) 265-6064
www.myposhnosh.com
$$

Citronee Bistro and Wine Bar
320 Broad Street, Nevada City, CA 95959
(530) 265-5697
www.citroneebistro.com
$$–$$$

Lefty's Grill
221 Broad Street, Nevada City, CA 95959
(530) 265-5837
www.leftysgrill.com
$$

Port of Subs Express Market
407 Hollow Way, Nevada City, CA 95959
(530) 478-1788
www.portofsubs.com
$

Dos Banditos
101 Broad Street, Nevada City, CA 95959
(530) 265-4840
www.dosbanditos.com
$–$$

California Organics
135 Argall Way, No. A, Nevada City, CA 95959
(530) 265-8025
www.californiaorganics.com
$

Five Mile House
18851 State Highway 20, Nevada City, CA 95959
(530) 470-8849
www.5milehouse.com
$$

Top Floor Tea Room
210 Main Street, Nevada City, CA 95959
(530) 265-2668
www.topfloortearoom.com
$–$$

Chief Crazy Horse Inn
230 Commercial Street, Nevada City, CA 95959
(530) 470-8443
www.chiefcrazyhorseinn.com
$–$$

Sopa Thai Cuisine
312 Commercial Street, Nevada City, CA 95959
(530) 470-0101
www.sopathai.com
$–$$

Arietta's at the Holbrooke
212 West Main Street, Grass Valley, CA 95945
(800) 933-7077
www.holbrooke.com
$$

Cousin Jack Pasties
100 South Auburn Street, Grass Valley, CA 95945
(530) 272-9230
www.historichwy49.com
$–$$

Larry & Lena's Pizza $ Grill
15690 Johnson Place, Grass Valley, CA 95945
(530) 272-1095
www.historichwy49.com
$–$$

CHAPTER 15

Gold Country

THERE IS PERHAPS NO REGION more important in the history of northern California than the area we know today as Gold Country, which runs along the California-Nevada border from places as far north as Hallelujah Junction to towns in the south such as Yosemite Village, and as far west as Sacramento. Sometimes called "Mother Lode Country," this is the place where so many of the area's first settlers flocked in search of earth-buried treasure. It's also the place that boasts so much of the region's early history—with a lot of it nicely preserved for tourists.

Regional History

You've read quite a lot about the gold rush and how the influx of would-be millionaires eventually spread out into what would become the cities of San Francisco and Sacramento, as well as agricultural meccas such as Napa and Sonoma counties. But in the beginning, they all came here, to the eastern part of the state where the gold-fields were found. Today's Gold Country is also yesteryear's gold country, in more ways than one.

Some people believe there's still gold in them thar hills of the Sierra Nevada, and local tour operators continue to lure thrill-seekers who come to pan for a nugget of gold to take back home. There are dreamers who believe that as the price of gold rises in modern markets, some of the hard-to-reach deposits might be worth mining even yet. Heck, even the state of California itself is still getting in on the action; the state motto "Eureka" comes from the gold rush days. (It means "I have found it.")

That's an impressive impact on modern history, given that the gold rush lasted just seven years, from 1848 until 1855. Then again, any time 300,000 people relocate to one place on earth in such a short span, it's bound to leave an impact for generations to come.

═══ **FAST FACT**

> When gold was first discovered in northern California, the region was still under control of the Mexican government. The Mexican-American War ended in February 1848, but California itself did not become a state until September 1850—a year after the gold rush began. The land where the goldfields lay was technically there for anybody's taking, which is why so many people clamored to get their share.

More than anywhere else in northern California, this region is dominated by the gold rush, past and present. That's true not just in the minds of people who come for covered wagon rides or the locals who keep the Old West alive in spirit, but also in the landscape that continues to heal after more than a century of mining.

Mining, Past and Present

The most accessible gold, such as large quantities of nuggets that could be recovered through river panning, was all but found as the early 1850s rolled around. Northern California's early fortune seekers did well, recovering what by some estimates would be gold worth more than $7 billion today.

You can imagine how such early successes whetted fortune seekers' appetites for more of the same. Yet the easy-to-come-by gold that practically floated atop riverbeds seemed to be a literal flash in the pan, meaning folks had to get more creative quickly if they wanted to get rich.

Hydraulic Mining

Miners and entrepreneurs believed there was more gold deep in the earth. By 1853, they began to use a technique known as hydraulic mining. It's a method of forcing high-pressure water, like a massive hose, into a gravel bed to push out the valuable metal. And it worked, accounting for another $6 billion or so of gold adjusted for modern-day prices, but also pushing river silt and gravel into mounds that could no longer serve as suitable growing environments for plants, fish, or other life.

Dredging

Dredging came along in the 1890s to try to get whatever gold might be left in even deeper parts of the rivers, and it, too, produced fantastic financial results: about $12 billion at today's prices by some estimates. But again, the recovery took its toll on the natural landscape; waterways were sometimes damaged and diverted past the point of recovery.

Hard-Rock Mining

As the gold got harder to pry from the earth, techniques for finding it got more aggressive, including simply blasting with dynamite. The explosions left small chunks of gold-laced rock, which could be crushed to extract whatever gold they contained. The approach is called hard-rock mining, and it was even more financially successful—and environmentally destructive—than either hydraulic mining or dredging.

By 1855, six years after the frenzy began, it was over for everyone except larger companies that could afford to employ such powerful methods in search of fortune. A lot of people moved on to the cities and countryside to start new lives, laying the groundwork for industries and communities that continue to flourish today.

Environmental Impact

The folks who stayed in this part of the state were left to deal with the effects of the mining techniques, which were sometimes severe. Environmental problems began to come to a head in 1884, when a lawsuit led to the prohibition of hydraulic mining after several mountain slopes destabilized, caused floods, and destroyed farmers' lands. As modern-day environmentalists continue to investigate what the mining companies left behind and washed into the watershed, they found large amounts of mercury, arsenic, cyanide, and acid.

Time, as the saying goes, heals all wounds, and the natural landscape is beginning to recover. Today, there is lovely scenery alongside historic towns that try to focus on the excitement of the old days, providing tourists with an enjoyable peek at the Wild West veneer of an age whose true impact will be felt for generations.

Local Overview

The 321-mile Highway 29 is the north-south artery that runs through Gold Country. It passes through the town of Coloma, where the foreman at Sutter's Mill first found gold in 1848, and it connects many of the Mother Lode towns in the counties of Amador, Butte, Calaveras, El Dorado, Mariposa, Nevada, Placer, Sacramento, Sierra, Tuolumne, and Yuba. Highway 29 will also get you close to Columbia State Historic Park in the town of Sonora, where the business district has preserved many buildings from the mid-1840s and turned them into a good-size tourist attraction.

 TRAVEL TIP

One section of Gold Country is not any "better" than the next, so try to organize your itinerary around other sites that interest you. If Sacramento is on your must-visit list, then visit the midsection of Gold Country to the city's east. If you're dying to visit Yosemite, then head for the southern section of Gold Country, which is nearest the national park.

The sheer length of Highway 29 should be a bit of a reality check for you; seeing every inch of Gold Country during a northern California vacation is probably an impractical itinerary. Think of Gold Country as having a top, middle, and bottom, and then focus your projected path in just one of those areas.

The main town in the northern part of Gold Country is Nevada City. It's just west of Tahoe National Forest and makes a good base for exploring historic Gold Country sights as well as some of the region's natural beauty. North of Nevada City is Malakoff Diggins State Historic Park, the site of California's largest hydraulic mine.

In Gold Country's midsection, you'll find the town of Sonora as well as Columbia State Historic Park, which is well worth a visit. Its businesses have embraced the past, using the preserved buildings to create a slice of gold rush–era history for visitors to enjoy.

In Gold Country's southern section, west of Yosemite National Park, you'll find Yosemite Sierra, where you can ride the Sugar Pine Railroad just as prospectors and loggers did. There are also a few boutique winemakers popping up in this region to help you combine modern culture with the experiences of days gone by.

Nevada City

Nevada City embraces Gold Country's history with its nickname, "Queen of the Northern Mines." With an award-winning historic district that is on the National Register of Historic Places, the city offers a true look at what life was like back in the days when mining towns—like early Nevada City—were still coming into their own. This particular mining town quickly became one of the most impressive in the region, which it dominated until the early 1950s with a population of several thousand people.

The number of year-round residents hasn't changed much since then, which of course means that Nevada City is now small potatoes compared with other cities in northern California. But its size is a great part of its charm, since walking down Main Street feels like walking down a true Main Street, instead of down an old country road that's preserved in the center of a modern metropolis. This is a gold mining town. Always has been, probably always will be.

Miners Foundry Cultural Center

The Miners Foundry Cultural Center is a vaulted- and beamed-ceiling building whose antique fixtures and heavy metal doors were once the accouterments of miners. The foundry opened in 1855 and helped the area surrounding Nevada City become one of the world's greatest gold-producing regions.

 JUST FOR PARENTS

Want to tie the knot in a romantic part of Gold Country? The Miners Foundry Cultural Center is available for event rentals, with halls that seat from 50 to 250 people. Its beauty makes it such a popular spot for weddings that there is a nine-page downloadable PDF on the center's Web site, *www.minersfoundry.org*. If you want to reserve a weekend date, get in touch at least a year in advance.

The public is welcome to tour the center Monday through Friday from 10 A.M. until 4 P.M. Self-guided tours are the most popular, but you can arrange for a docent to show you around if you call at least a week in advance: (530) 265-5040.

Nevada County Narrow Gauge Railroad and Transportation Museum

Here you'll also find the Nevada County Narrow Gauge Railroad and Transportation Museum, which offers free admission (though donations are appreciated). The museum's mission is to preserve the local railroad history, specifically anything that concerns artifacts from the narrow gauge railroad that operated from 1876 until 1942 and hauled some $200 million worth of gold.

The museum's hours during the summer months are 10 A.M. till 4 P.M. Friday through Tuesday. It is closed Wednesday and Thursday. From November 1 through April 30, the museum's hours are Saturday and Sunday only, 10 A.M. till 4 P.M. You can read quite a bit about the railroad's history at the official Web site, *www.ncngrrmuseum.org*.

Malakoff Diggins State Historic Park

Nevada City is a good base from which to head north to Malakoff Diggins State Historic Park, the site of California's largest hydraulic mine and a place where you can see the environmental impact left behind by the rush to find gold in the hills. The farmers who lived downstream from this mine eventually sued to end use of the mining technique altogether. Don't expect a typical park here. Prepare yourself mentally to see the earth gouged and scarred on such a scale that it's difficult to appreciate unless you view it yourself.

 **RAINY DAY FUN**

During the summer months, you can take tours through parts of what remains of North Bloomfield, a town that supported Malakoff Diggins mining operations. You'll step inside the general store, drugstore, church, schoolhouse, and a home furnished with period pieces. Be sure to call ahead for tour hours: (530) 265-2740.

Fortunately, Malakoff Diggins is a state park for reasons other than just what's left of the mid-1800s mining efforts. All around the remains of the old mine and the ghost town that used to be its supporting civilization of North Bloomfield, you can enjoy some 3,000 acres of hiking trails, plus picnic areas, a campground, and cabins that are available for rent. This park is not fully wheelchair accessible, something the state of California says it's working to improve.

Grass Valley

Just south of Nevada City is Grass Valley, a city of 12,000 people that is best known as the home of the Empire Mine, which produced 5.6 million ounces of gold between the time it opened in the mid-1800s and the time it closed in 1956. It's been owned by the state of California since 1975 and is now part of a nearly 800-acre park.

What's interesting about Grass Valley is that its gold rush immigrants came largely from Cornwall, England, where workers accustomed to deep tin mining learned that their skills could be put to more profitable use in the newly discovered California goldfields. That Cornish heritage is still part of the fabric of life in Grass Valley, where there is an annual Cornish Christmas celebration and where you can buy pasties—a traditionally baked pie filled with meat, sliced potato, and onion. There are several interesting options for sightseeing in Grass Valley, including the Empire Mine State Historic Park and a couple of museums.

Empire Mine State Historic Park

Although Empire Mine produced a staggering amount of gold and is considered one of the richest mines in northern California, some experts say that more than 80 percent of the available ore is still buried in the mine, waiting to be recovered. That's not likely to happen anytime soon now that the state has turned the site into a park that's popular with hikers, horseback riders, and bikers, but there's nothing wrong with dreaming while you're wandering the grounds.

During weekends from May through October, there are living-history days at the park, complete with people in period dress portraying everything from miners to blacksmiths. There's also an annual Miners' Picnic every August, originally begun to benefit miners' widows and orphans but now held to raise money for projects and programs that benefit all Empire Mine State Historic Park visitors. For additional information, go to *www.empiremine.org*.

RAINY DAY FUN

If the history of mining technology and methods interests you, be sure to check out the film *Tears from the Sun*, which is shown regularly as part of the public offerings at Empire Mine State Historic Park. You'll see hydraulic and hard-rock mining in action to help you better appreciate how the landscape was changed after constant use of such erosive methods.

North Star Mining Museum

The North Star Mining Museum is devoted to preserving the tools that miners across the region used. You'll learn the difference between a headframe and a skipjack, and you'll get to see the largest-ever Pelton wheel, which is a type of water turbine that was used to generate electricity for mining operations. A headframe, by the way, is also known as a gallows frame and sits atop a mine shaft. A skipjack is—well, you don't want to know everything before you get to the museum, do you? The best source of additional information about the museum is the Grass Valley Chamber of Commerce, whose Web site is *www.grassvalleychamber.com*.

Columbia State Historic Park

Columbia State Historic Park, which is about three miles north of Sonora, just off Highway 49, gives you a look at another aspect of historic Gold Country life—the fun that people were having in the western towns that sprang up during the great rush.

The park is actually a business district full of shops and restaurants that have been so well preserved that they still look much as they did during the mid-1800s. The area became a park in 1945, when those in a position of power realized that Columbia was one of the few remaining gold rush–era towns that had not succumbed to fire, earthquake, or other tragedy.

Today, shop owners and restaurateurs embrace Columbia's history, often dressing in period costume. Here, you can ride on a 100-year-old stagecoach or take your chances with the other prospectors by panning for gold. It's hard to resist the fun when even the folks running the bowling alley show up in costume.

═══FAST FACT

If you want to film a movie or television show that takes place in the Old West, the place to come is Columbia. It's been the backdrop for *Hopalong Cassidy*, *The Lone Ranger*, *High Noon*, *Little House on the Prairie*, and *Pale Rider*. Hey, if the place is authentic enough for John Wayne and Clint Eastwood, how can you resist?

You'll find all kinds of shops on the streets of Columbia, many pegging their businesses to the downtown theme of yesteryear. Parrott's Blacksmith offers handmade, coal-forged gifts and puts on live demonstrations. The Fancy Dry Goods and Clothing Store sells traditional quilts and period-style clothes that you can take home to play dress-up. At Columbia Candle and Soap Works, you can watch the wares being made in an open studio. Columbia Booksellers and Stationers sells historical books, period stationery, and old-style maps.

The period fun can continue long after you're done shopping for the night if you choose to book a room at the Columbia City Hotel, an authentically restored 1800s inn. The rooms are filled with Victorian antiques, and some rooms have balconies where you can sit and watch the goings-on along Main Street, just as people did during the old days.

The official Web site of Columbia State Historic Park is at *www .parks.ca.gov*, and there's also a great deal of helpful information online at the site sponsored by the local chamber of commerce, *www.columbiacalifornia.com*.

Yosemite Sierra

Yosemite Sierra is in the southern part of Gold Country, making it an excellent choice if you also have plans to visit Yosemite National Park to the east. This region isn't quite as blunt about its historical ties to the gold rush as the areas farther to the north, but you'll find nods to the days gone by intermixed with stunning scenic retreats and even a few gourmet delights.

Yosemite Mountain Sugar Pine Railroad

The Yosemite Mountain Sugar Pine Railroad is a restored section of the Madera Sugar Pine Lumber Company Railroad, which operated it from 1899 until 1931. It was used more for the logging industry than the transport of gold, but it still offers a glimpse into what life was like when the forty-niners were scattering all about the region.

You can take a regular old ride here, or you can step things up a notch and sign up for the Moonlight Special, which runs on Saturday and Wednesday nights during the summer and on Saturday nights only during spring and fall. The evening begins with a barbecue dinner and live music followed by a ride into the dark woods—where masked horsemen sometimes appear out of nowhere in search of gold shipments and passengers carrying loot that's ripe for "stealing."

 TRAVEL TIP

If you plan to visit the Yosemite Mountain Sugar Pine Railroad between November and March, make sure you call ahead to see whether the facility will even be open. Unlike other months of the year, the winter season is especially slow—and hours can vary from day to day depending on weather predictions. The number for information is (559) 683-7273.

Hours and schedules change from month to month for the various attractions at Yosemite Mountain Sugar Pine Railroad, so check out your options in advance at *www.ymsprr.com*. Adult train ride fares start at $13, and kids' fares start at $8.50. For the Moonlight Special, adults pay $45 and children twelve and younger are charged $22.50.

Bass Lake

Less than 1,000 people lived in Bass Lake as of the last census, and you can bet that darn near every last one of them had something to do with the tourism industry. Unlike larger inland bodies of water such as Lake Tahoe to the north, Bass Lake is considered warm by northern California standards—getting up to 80 degrees during July and August. People flock here for swimming, water skiing, and wakeboarding during the summer the way they flock to northern scenic lakes for snow-skiing during the winter.

The freshwater lake is actually a hydroelectric reservoir for the Pacific Gas and Electric Company, and most of the undeveloped land around it is part of the Sierra National Forest, which extends for more than a million acres full of oak trees and alpine hills.

⎯⎯FAST FACT

Bass Lake doesn't have quite the resume that the town of Columbia does when it comes to appearing in television shows and major motion pictures, but it does boast its role as the backdrop for the 1988 film *The Great Outdoors* starring John Candy and Dan Aykroyd—in which many critics said the scenery was the best thing to watch onscreen.

Camping is a big draw in the Bass Lake area, thanks to the unspoiled scenery and smaller crowds that you'll find as you get closer to Yosemite National Park. The Bass Lake Chamber of Commerce promotes eight different campsites within short driving distance of the lake, each with different owners, fees, and regulations.

You can review each site's facilities and requirements online at *www .basslakechamber.com.*

Madera Wine Trail

The Madera Wine Trail, so named for its location in Madera County, consists of ten boutique wineries that are known for producing award-winning wines as well as Ports. See if you recognize any of the names from labels at your local store:

- Birdstone Winery
- Ficklin Vineyards
- Lamanuzzi & Pantaleo
- Chateau Lasgoity
- Mariposa Wine Company
- Oak Hollow Winery
- Pacific Crest
- Quady Winery
- Westbrook Wine Farm
- Vineyard 208 (a Whelchel Ruffalo family winery)

 JUST FOR PARENTS

Every February, the vintners that make up the Madera Wine Trail hold a "Wine and Chocolate Weekend." You can buy a tasting glass for $15 at any participating location, and then take it with you from winery to winery as you sample not only the local bottlings, but also specially paired chocolates such as truffles and chocolate cheesecake squares.

Even if the names are new to you, they may soon become well-known favorites thanks to the tasting rooms and tours that many of the wineries offer. Given the vastly different terrain, you're going to find a good deal of different tastes. You'll also find varietals that may be new to you. Mixed in among the Chardonnay and Cabernet are Barbera, Muscat, Petite Sirah, Madera Port, and dessert wines such as Muscat, Essensia, and Elysium.

There are downloadable maps of the wine trail, as well as more in-depth descriptions of each of the wineries, available online at *www.maderavintners.com.*

Lodging and Restaurants

There is no shortage of places to stay or eat in Gold Country. Here are some suggestions you might want to consider. Each suggestion is marked by one, two, or three dollar signs.

For lodging:
$ = a room costs less than $100
$$ = a room costs from $101 to $200
$$$ = a room costs more than $200

For restaurants:
$ = entrées cost less than $15
$$ = entrées cost from $16 to $30
$$$ = entrées cost more than $30

Lodging

SOUTH LAKE TAHOE
3 Peaks Resort and Beach Club
931 Park Avenue
(866) 500-4886
www.lake-tahoe-california-hotels.com
$

Big Pines Mountain House
4083 Cedar Avenue
(800) 288-4083
www.thebigpines.com
$

Fantasy Inn and Wedding Chapel
3696 Lake Tahoe Boulevard
(800) 367-7736
www.fantasy-inn.com
$$

Forest Suites Resort
1 Lake Parkway
(800) 822-5950
www.forestsuites.com
$$

Green Lantern Inn & Suites
4097 Manzanita Avenue
(866) 456-6835
www.glmoteltahoe.com
$

Inn by the Lake
3300 Lake Tahoe Boulevard
(800) 877-1466
www.innbythelake.com
$$

Lakeland Village Beach & Mountain Resort
3535 Lake Tahoe Boulevard
(800) 544-1685
www.lakeland-village.com
$$

Royal Valhalla on the Lake
4104 Lakeshore Boulevard
(866) 493-4603
www.tahoeroyalvalhalla.com
$$

STATELINE, NEVADA
Harvey's Resort & Casino
Highway 50 and Stateline Avenue
800-HARRAHS
www.harveystahoe.com
$

OLYMPIC VALLEY
Plumpjack Squaw Valley Inn
1920 Squaw Valley Road
(530) 583-1576
www.plumpjack.com
$$$

KINGS BEACH
Ferrari's Crown Resort
8200 North Lake Boulevard
(800) 645-2260
www.tahoecrown.com
$

Sun N Sand Lodge
8308 North Lake Boulevard
(800) 804-6835
www.hotels.com
$

Tahoe Inn
9937 North Lake Tahoe Road
(800) 804-6835
www.hotels.com
$

INCLINE VILLAGE, NEVADA
Hyatt Regency Lake Tahoe Resort,
Spa and Casino
Country Club Drive at Lakeshore
(775) 832-1234
www.laketahoe.hyatt.com
$$$

Restaurants

TAHOE CITY
Bacchi's Inn
2905 Lake Forest Road
(530) 583-3324
www.bacchisinn.com
$$

Christy Hill Restaurant
115 Grove Street
(530) 583-8551
www.christyhill.com
$$

Jake's on the Lake
780 North Lake Boulevard
(530) 583-0188
www.jakestahoe.com
$$

Pfeifer House
760 River Road
(530) 583-3102
www.pfeiferhouse.com
$$

River Ranch Lodge
Highway 89 and Alpine Meadows Road
(866) 991-9912
www.riverranchlodge.com
$$

Rosie's Cafe
571 North Lake Boulevard
(530) 583-8504
www.rosiescafe.com
$–$$

Wolfdale's
640 North Lake Boulevard
(530) 583-5700
www.wolfdales.com
$$–$$$

SOUTH LAKE TAHOE
The Cantina Bar & Grill
765 Emerald Bay Road
(530) 544-1233
www.cantinatahoe.com
$

Evan's American Gourmet Cafe
536 Emerald Bay Road
(530) 542-1990
www.evanstahoe.com
$$–$$$

Fremont Bistro & Wine Bar
1041 Fremont Avenue
(866) 541-6603
www.dorysoar.com
$$

The Fresh Ketch Seafood Restaurant
2435 Venice Drive
(530) 541-5683
www.thefreshketch.com
$$

Nepheles Creative California Cuisine
1169 Ski Run Boulevard
(530) 544-8130
www.nepheles.com
$$–$$$

KINGS BEACH
Char-Pit
8732 North Lake Boulevard
(530) 546-3171
www.charpit.com
$

Lanza's Restaurant
7739 North Lake Boulevard
(530) 546-2434
www.lanzastahoe.com
$–$$

Crystal Bay, Nevada
Calneva Lodge
2 Stateline Road
(800) 233-5551
www.calnevaresort.com
$$–$$$

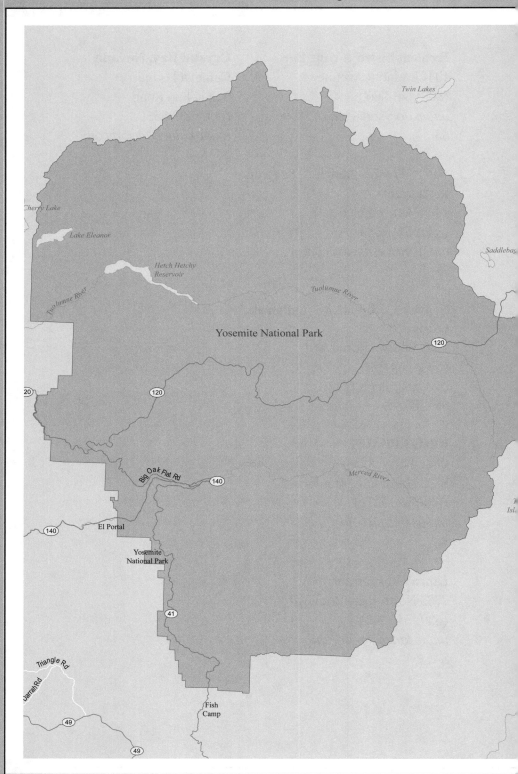

CHAPTER 16

National and State Parks

IF YOUR IDEA OF A PERFECT VACATION includes hiking, camping, or looking out across majestic vistas, then northern California has more than a few world-famous sites that should be on your must-visit list. There are towering redwood trees, spectacularly deep cliffs, and ocean-side panoramas. You can make an entire vacation out of visiting any one of the region's national or state parks, or you can spend a few weeks driving from one to the next to enjoy every last natural highlight that the area has to offer.

Regional Overview

The natural history of northern California is something to behold, even if you're not a particularly enthusiastic student of geology. Mother Nature's ability to create places like Yosemite, Big Sur, and Redwood National Forest is a study in sheer force, of land and water and air colliding furiously for centuries before settling into today's stunning vacation destinations.

There is a sense of amazement that comes with learning about the creation of redwood trees that stand more than 300 feet tall—the height of a thirty-story skyscraper. You don't have to be a scientist to be impressed by the massive tectonic plates shifting beneath Earth's surface with such violence that they birth entire mountain ranges. Even the smallest child can imagine sprawling glaciers carving out grand valleys before melting into the rivers and waterfalls that you can visit on tours of places like Yosemite. You can watch the powerful waves of the Pacific Ocean bash into places like Big Sur, eroding more and more of the land into natural rock sculptures with every crash.

=== FAST FACT

Spots like Redwood National Forest are so geologically different from any other places on Earth that they appeal to moviemakers trying to create futuristic and prehistoric backdrops. *Star Wars Episode VI: Return of the Jedi* filmed some scenes among the towering trees, as did *The Lost World: Jurassic Park*.

Each of northern California's national and state parks has a mesmerizing geologic backstory, and you can incorporate them into your vacation if you want to add an educational component to your family's sightseeing. Yosemite National Park, for instance, has easy-to-follow, online curriculum outlines designed for teachers that you can use to create pretrip lessons. These lessons will help children better understand the geology and natural history that went into creating the vistas you explore as a family.

Yosemite

Yosemite National Park is in the southeastern section of northern California, just west of the Nevada border. The geological history of Yosemite includes the creation of the Sierra Nevada, the rise of the earth led to the formation of deep canyons that were eventually filled by glaciers. The glaciers—which may have been some 4,000 feet thick at one time—eventually melted, leaving the cliffs, waterfalls, and groves of giant sequoia trees that now draw at least 3 million people to visit Yosemite each year. The park is about a three-and-a-half-hour drive from San Francisco, almost due east of the city along

Route 120. The name *Yosemite* comes from the Native American word *uzumati*, which means "grizzly bear" (and yes, hundreds of American black bears still call the park home).

 TRAVEL TIP

Traffic congestion has become a major concern at Yosemite during the peak summer season. You can pay $20 to enter the park in your car, or you can leave it in a nearby parking area and instead use the park's free shuttle bus system, which is less expensive, better for the environment, and designed specifically to help tourists see the sights without damaging them.

Planning Your Visit

The numbers alone speak volumes about Yosemite National Park's size and scope:

- More than 760,000 square acres—nearly 1,200 square miles—of parkland
- More than 3,000 lakes, ponds, and reservoirs
- Some 1,600 miles of rivers and streams
- About 800 miles of hiking trails
- Nearly 350 miles of roads

In fact, the seven-square mile area known as Yosemite Valley, which is where most people visit during one-day trips to Yosemite, makes up just one percent of the entire park's area. Just think of everything you might miss if you follow that crowd. Some of the river canyons in the outlying areas are 3,000 to 4,000 feet deep, carved by great glaciers centuries ago. Some of the waterfalls are more than a thousand feet high, including the 2,425-foot Yosemite Falls, which is the highest in all of North America.

You can get to Yosemite Falls and other sites deeper within the park, beyond the popular Yosemite Valley area, but you may need the help of a guide, or at least some assistance from the National Park Service. Its Web site is full of information about safety and restrictions at *www.nps.gov*, where you'll also find a season-by-season listing of popular activities and climate information—some of which may surprise you.

 TRAVEL TIP

If you want to see Yosemite National Park's waterfalls rushing at their fullest, plan your visit for late spring, particularly the months of May and June. That's when water flow in the park is at its peak, thanks to the warming summer sun and the increased snowmelt at the top of the mountains, whose runoff feeds the waterfalls.

For instance, many of the park's roads remain impassable and closed due to snow well into the month of May, a time you wouldn't think winter's grip would still be so tight. If you're interested in skiing, be sure to check the section about plowing schedules, which tell you which roads the park service opens up for recreation during the coldest months—when many of the waterfalls dry up completely until the spring snowmelt begins.

Key Yosemite Attractions

Yosemite boasts quite a few landmarks that you probably know by sight even if you can't identify them by name. It's easy to see these magnificent sites when you visit the park; many views require only a few minutes' walk on short, well-maintained trails. The popular trails tend to be crowded during the summer months, but they are a great way to experience the park. If your mobility is impaired, you might also consider a guided horseback tour or an open-air tram tour, each of which can be as short as two hours. Here are a few examples of

Yosemite's offerings:

- **Glacier Point.** Enjoy a stunning view of Yosemite Valley and Half Dome from this vista. The road literally ends here, and there's a short walk to the point. Note that the road closes in the winter and does not open until May or June.
- **Yosemite Falls.** Get up close and personal with the lower fall on an easy one-mile loop.
- **Bridalveil Fall.** A paved trail drops you off at the base of this waterfall. The roundtrip journey from the parking lot to the waterfall and back is half a mile.
- **Mirror Lake.** The lake gets its name from its still, clear water that produces crystalline reflections of the surrounding wilderness and rock formations. The trail is a two-mile loop, but it is paved and easy to walk.

 TRAVEL TIP

Two of Yosemite's most recognizable landmarks, Half Dome and El Capitan, can be seen from various viewpoints around the park. Bring a pair of binoculars and let your kids try to find climbers scaling these remarkable formations; it's one way to appreciate their sheer size.

Yosemite Accommodations

For longer visits, camping is the most popular option. You can park your RV right in Yosemite Valley, though as with the trails during summertime, you should expect to have wall-to-wall company there. There are thirteen popular designated campsites throughout the park, and seven of them take reservations through the Web site *www.recreation.gov*. Be prepared for the fact that the campgrounds have no showers, and note that the farther you get from Yosemite Valley, the more peace and quiet you're likely to find.

TRAVEL TIP

The bears that call Yosemite home have an incredible sense of smell. You have to keep all food—anything with a scent—locked in an airtight container at all times. An open bag of chips in your car, left somewhere with the windows rolled down, would violate the park's policy on food. Failure to follow food-storage laws can result in fines as high as $5,000 as well as revocation of camping permits.

A more upscale sleeping option is the Ahwahnee Hotel, a National Historic Landmark that was conceived in the 1920s as a place that would draw affluent visitors to the park. Its rates aren't cheap, with basic rooms starting around $425 a night, but it's about as grand as accommodations get in a wilderness setting.

If you want to sleep indoors without breaking the bank, consider Curry Village, which the locals call Camp Curry. It offers everything from regular and heated cabins to standard motel-style rooms, with prices starting at less than $100 a night. You can learn more online at *www.yosemitepark.com*.

No matter where or how long you decide to stay, you may want to explore a bit more of this part of northern California without leaving the parks system altogether. If you are willing to drive three hours south of Yosemite, you can easily check out Kings Canyon National Park and Sequoia National Park, which are twin, contiguous operations that offer some pretty fabulous scenery of their own.

Kings Canyon National Park

Kings Canyon National Park is about 460,000 acres, much of it formed by the same glaciers that created Yosemite National Park. Its main draw is giant sequoias; the park boasts the largest natural giant sequoia grove in the world. The General Grant tree—266 feet tall—is believed to be the second-largest tree in the world. If you plan to stay at Kings Canyon for more than a day, or if you plan to visit both Kings

Canyon and Sequoia National Park, consider investing in a seven-day pass. It's $20 per vehicle or $10 per person on foot, bicycle, motorcycle, or bus.

Sequoia National Park

Sequoia National Park is about 404,000 acres immediately to the south of Kings Canyon National Park. Its premier natural feature is Mount Whitney, which, at 14,491 feet tall, is the highest mountain summit in the contiguous forty-eight states. Like the adjacent Kings Canyon Park, Sequoia National Park is also known for its groves of giant sequoia trees.

 JUST FOR PARENTS

Inside Sequoia National Park you'll find Crystal Cave, which offers a special activity called the Wild Cave Tour for people sixteen and older. The cost is $129 per person, which allows you four to six hours' worth of climbing time off the regular, subterranean trails that most tourists wander. There is a guide, and tours typically start around 4 or 5 P.M. Anyone more than thirty pounds overweight is not eligible to participate.

For additional information about either Kings Canyon National Park or Sequoia National Park, go to the official government Web site, *www.nps.gov.*

Redwood National Park

Redwood National Park is in the northwestern corner of northern California, about as far as you can get without falling into the Pacific or crossing into Oregon. The park is a little more than five hours north of San Francisco by car. Route 101 goes right through, often hugging the Pacific Ocean coastline for a fantastically scenic drive.

The park comprises about 112,000 acres that include some 45 percent of the world's coastal redwood groves. Most people don't realize that the park also is home to nearly forty miles of unspoiled Pacific Ocean shoreline. Interestingly, the national park wasn't formed until 1968, by which time nearly 90 percent of its original redwoods had been destroyed in logging operations. To help preserve the remaining trees, the national park combined on an administrative level with three state parks in 1994. Though it's all effectively one region now, the three state parks are known as Prairie Creek Redwoods, Del Norte Coast Redwoods, and Jedediah Smith Redwoods. Much of the area is still recovering from the clear-cutting that went on during the timber industry's heyday.

The main draw at Redwood National Park, as its name suggests, is the groves of redwood trees—which are closely related to the giant sequoias found in Yosemite, Kings Canyon, and Sequoia National Parks to the southeast. Coastal redwoods typically live at least 600 years and sometimes longer than 2,000 years, meaning they are some of the planet's oldest living organisms. Three of the world's ten tallest trees are located inside this park, and you'll see limbs that are sometimes the diameter of other trees' trunks. Redwood trees are also good perches for the northern spotted owl, one of several endangered species that call Redwood National Forest home. You also might catch a glimpse of a Roosevelt elk.

 TRAVEL TIP

Because of the tectonic plates that run beneath Redwood National Forest, the area is one of the most seismically active locations in the United States. There are frequent minor earthquakes, and during the 1990s the area averaged magnitude 6.0 earthquakes at a rate of almost one per year. Pay attention to the literature the park service provides; it tells you what to do should an earthquake—or a tsunami—occur while you are exploring the grounds.

There are about 200 trails running throughout the combined federal and state parks, and some of them are open to horseback riding as well as mountain biking. You can also enjoy guided nature walks if you check in at one of the park's two main visitor centers. The longest trail in the park is about thirty miles long and is called the Coastal Trail. It runs almost the length of the park itself, but you can only access it for hiking in certain sections.

If you're visiting Redwood National Park during the summer months, you also can witness an Indian dance demonstration performed by members of the Tolowa and Yurok tribes. The demonstrations are free, and they include a short lecture about tribal history in the region. Watching is a great way to help children understand the native people who lived as one with the area before the timber industry's arrival. Learn more at *www.nps.gov*.

The state of California's Department of Parks and Recreation maintains four developed campgrounds inside the park, three of them in the redwood forest and one along the ocean. They are open from May 1 until September 30, and they include restrooms but no RV hookups. You can check on availability and get more campsite information by calling (800) 444-7275.

≡**FAST FACT**

If you enjoy touring Redwood National Forest, then you might consider joining the Save-the-Redwoods League. It has helped preserve more than 177,000 acres of parks and reserves since its inception in 1918, and it now has more than 50,000 members across the United States and the world. You can join for as little as $19 through the group's Web site, *www.savetheredwoods.org*.

If you would rather stay at a hotel or motel, nearby are the towns of Eureka and Arcata to the south of the park, or Crescent City to the north. Each area has everything from bed-and-breakfast inns to inexpensive motels and proper hotels. For the southern towns, check out the jam-packed Web site *www.redwoods.info*. For Crescent City lodging options, go to *www.northerncalifornia.net*.

RAINY DAY FUN

> If the clouds come with you during your visit to Redwood National Park, you can stay in the car and enjoy the scenery in comfort. The Newton B. Drury Scenic Parkway is one of several fully paved scenic drives. It's ten miles long and goes right through old-growth forest, giving you about a half-hour to look through the trees for Roosevelt elk if you drive at a leisurely pace.

Redwood National Park has many scenic drives running through the forests and along the coastline. If you happen to choose one of the routes with an ocean view during the months of November and December or March and April, you might also get to do a bit of whale watching as the gray whales make their seasonal migrations to the north and south.

Big Sur

Big Sur is a region just south of Monterey Bay that includes a dozen state-protected reserves and parks. It also includes Cone Peak, a nearly mile-tall mountain that is the highest coastal peak in the lower forty-eight United States. The region is all but pristine, with about 1,000 residents at last count. Highway 1 runs right down the coastal side of Big Sur, meaning that you can enjoy the views without ever having to leave your automobile or RV. Just don't stop midlane. Use the frequently placed vista overlooks to ensure you stay out of traffic's way.

There are twelve state parks and reserves in the Big Sur region. The ten that have visitor's services are as follows:

- Carmel River State Beach
- Point Lobos State Reserve
- Garrapata State Park
- Point Sur Lightstation State Historic Park
- Andrew Molera State Park
- Pfeiffer Big Sur State Park
- Julia Pfeiffer Burns State Park
- Limekiln State Park
- Hearst Castle
- William Randolph Hearst Memorial State Beach

Pfeiffer Big Sur State Park

The actual park that most people think of when they consider Big Sur is the Pfeiffer Big Sur State Park. It's known for its waterfalls, which are accessible by hiking trails. It also has campsites along the Big Sur River, plus a lodge with sixty-one guest rooms, a conference center, and a grocery store on the grounds.

If you don't want to stay overnight, you can find everything from campgrounds to five-star resorts along Highway 1 on the way to or from the park—but, because of the area's protected land status, there are probably no more than 300 or so indoor rooms along the main stretch of roadway. As with the rest of California's parks in the summertime, you'll need reservations.

Hearst Castle

You'll have a far different kind of sightseeing experience at Hearst Castle, which opened for public tours in 1952 and was officially donated to the state of California in 1957. Before that, it was a private 250,000-acre wilderness that the wealthy Hearst family used for camping trips. The castle was built by 1947 with some 165 rooms and 127 acres of gardens, pools, and walkways. There are almost as many fireplaces (forty-one) in the guest areas as there are bathrooms (sixty-one). Today, Hearst Castle is one of the largest historic house museums in the United States—and it offers four separate tours, each about two hours long, to help you get a good look around:

- Hearst Tour 1 covers the first floor of the main house as well as one of the three guesthouses.
- Hearst Tour 2 includes viewing and interpretation of the main house's upper rooms.
- Hearst Tour 3 is more about construction and development, comparing the earliest-built guesthouse with the newest wing on the grounds.
- Hearst Tour 4 is designed to be accessible for people who are mobility impaired, with a look at the main house's ground floor as well as gardens, pools, and the main level of one guesthouse.

You can get more information about the tours, the castle, and the Hearst family at the castle's official Web site, *www.hearstcastle.org*.

Point Sur State Historic Park and Lighthouse

Lighthouse keepers began living in and staffing the Point Sur Lightstation in 1889. The last keeper didn't leave until 1974, when the U.S. Coast Guard finished renovations that automated the lighthouse. For lighthouse aficionados, this meant replacing the original Fresnel lens with a beacon—as has been done in lighthouses all across the United States. A restoration of the lantern room at the top of the lighthouse was completed in 2001.

Point Sur has never been one of the most treacherous places for shipping, but it was the site of numerous significant wrecks from 1894 until the mid-1950s. One of the most spectacular ship demises was in February 1935, when the 785-foot-long, helium-filled dirigible USS *Macon* crashed offshore and sank, taking eighty-one of the eighty-three people onboard to a watery grave. It was a spectacular sight from onshore, as the *Macon* was three times the size of a modern-day Boeing 747. The wreckage was later discovered, and you can view some of it during a tour of the visitor's center.

Tours last about three hours and are available year-round between 10 A.M. and 2 P.M. Rates are $8 for adults and $4 for kids between the ages of six and seventeen. Children five and younger can take the tours for free. For more information, check out the Web site at *www .pointsur.org.*

 JUST FOR PARENTS

The Point Sur State Historic Park offers "moonlight tours" on selected dates from April through October, but children younger than six are not permitted to attend. You will also have to leave the family dog behind. Not only are pets prohibited on the grounds, but there's also a restriction that says you can't leave them in a car on the premises during your visit.

Whiskeytown National Recreation Area

The Whiskeytown National Recreation Area isn't as big or well-known as Yosemite and Big Sur, but it offers a unique kind of family park fun in northern California: Whiskeytown Lake. There are nearly thirty-six miles of shoreline on the lake, where you can swim, scuba dive, kayak, fish, and rent boats for sailing or water skiing. The park also offers hiking, camping, and waterfall vistas, as well as a historic district where you can learn about the gold rush. Guided activities include ranger-led kayak tours and gold-panning expeditions.

Whiskeytown is eight miles west of Redding, located on Interstate 5 as you travel north from the Sacramento Valley up toward Shasta and Trinity lakes. In fact, the three lakes are sometimes referred to as one large recreation area for freshwater boaters and fishing enthusiasts, not to mention terrestrial tourists as well. You won't want to go swimming during the winter months, but the temperatures remain nice enough that you can enjoy horseback riding, hiking, and mountain biking all year long.

TRAVEL TIP

Unlike many other state and national parks in northern California, Whiskeytown not only encourages you to bring a car but pretty much requires it. There is no public transportation running to or within the park itself. And unless you plan on camping overnight, you'll need a car to get you to the towns of Redding, French Gulch, or Weaverville for a hotel room.

There are campsites for overnight stays at Whiskeytown, but if you want a motel or hotel, the closest big town is Redding. It has four RV parks, four bed-and-breakfast inns, and more than thirty hotels and motels ranging from bargain brands to a Hilton. The town's user-friendly Web site lists contact information for them all at *www.visitredding.org*.

Smaller Parks

While Yosemite and Redwood National Park tend to be the big draws for nature lovers in northern California, there are a good number of state parks across the region that offer interesting diversions for a day, a few days, or even a week's worth of camping and exploration. You can make many of these parks destinations or incorporate them into your broader itinerary as places to stop and stretch your legs. For a complete list of parks that you can search by region, go to *www .parks.ca.gov*.

Ahjumawi Lava Springs State Park

Located in the Shasta Cascade region, this park is mostly rugged lava rock that is accessible only by boat. There are no public roads in or out, and private vehicles are prohibited anyway. To get to the park, you can tow your boat to a public launch ramp about three miles north of the town of McArthur. The ramp is known as the "rat farm"—not exactly enticing, but certainly easy to remember if you get lost and need to ask for directions.

There are views of Mount Shasta and Mount Lassen from the park, but the unique sights are the lava tubes, craters, and freshwater springs flowing through them. The place looks almost Jurassic. If your kids are learning about geology around the time of your trip, it's a destination they'll not soon forget.

Bothe-Napa Valley State Park

What makes this state park worth mentioning is its proximity to the popular Napa Valley wineries. You'll need someplace to enjoy all those bottles of Chardonnay and Merlot that you buy during your tours, and the Bothe-Napa Valley State Park is ready to oblige with picnic tables, campsites, and hiking trails to work off the extra calories you take in.

This park also has a swimming pool that's open on weekends from Memorial Day until mid-June and then daily through Labor Day. There's also horseback riding every season except winter, with reservations available online through Triple Creek Horse Outfit at *www .triplecreekhorseoutfit.com*.

Folsom Powerhouse State Historic Park

If walking through history appeals more to your family than walking through forests, consider making a stop at the Folsom Powerhouse State Historic Park in Sacramento County.

≡FAST FACT

The Folsom Powerhouse was the first place in the United States to transmit long-distance hydroelectric power, using water from the American River to power generators that served citizens in Sacramento some twenty-two miles away. In fact, it was the second facility to harness hydroelectric power from the river altogether. The first to achieve that was Folsom Prison in 1893.

The powerhouse was built in 1885 to force American River waters to turn generators and create electricity for the growing town of Sacramento. You can still see the vintage generators during a tour of the grounds, plus the transformers that are capable of conducting as much as 11,000 volts of electricity—a charge that has been known to launch human beings at least ten feet in electrical cable accidents.

Manchester State Park

Manchester State Park is right on the Pacific coast in Mendocino County, near Point Arena, north of San Francisco. It's an ideal place to camp if you also like to fish and hike, since some of the trailheads lead to the beach as well as to Brush Creek and Alder Creek, where steelhead and salmon fishing are excellent. What's also nice about this park is that it's right next door to a KOA campground, where you can find help if you're new to sleeping in the great outdoors. Learn more at *www.parks.ca.gov.*

Best Hikes for the Whole Family

Among northern California's countless national and state parks, you'll find literally thousands of trails. Some are long, some are short, some are easy, and some are steep. If your kids are a bit older, they'll probably be able to handle some of the tougher, more spectacular trails. On the other hand, if you're traveling with wee ones, you'll likely have to limit your hiking to shorter, flatter landscapes where they'll be able to keep up.

Yosemite Four-Mile Trail

This deceptively named trail is actually closer to nine miles round-trip, but there is a shuttle bus from Yosemite Lodge that will take you up to Glacier Point so that you only have to hike the downhill section for a distance of about four and a half miles. The slope is more gradual than on some other trails, too, so you won't have the kids trying to leap from rocks that are taller than their legs.

Lady Bird Johnson Nature Loop at Redwood National Park

This one-mile loop trail runs pretty much right from the parking lot at Redwood National Park through an old-growth redwood grove. The trail is so flat and well maintained that it is wheelchair accessible—and even the littlest of legs should have a fairly easy time making their way along the route.

Pfeiffer Falls Trail at Pfeiffer Big Sur State Park

This trail is just shy of a mile and a half long and is rated easy by the Big Sur Chamber of Commerce. It takes you along a creek and through a redwood grove, leading you to a view of a 60-foot waterfall. That may not be quite as impressive to you as the falls at Yosemite, but it's still going to seem pretty darn tall to your five- or six-year-old kids.

Lodging and Restaurants

There is no shortage of places to stay or eat in northern California. Here are some suggestions you might want to consider. Each suggestion is marked by one, two, or three dollar signs.

For lodging:

$ = a room costs less than $100

$$ = a room costs from $101 to $200

$$$ = a room costs more than $200

For restaurants:

$ = entrées cost less than $15

$$ = entrées cost from $16 to $30

$$$ = entrées cost more than $30

Lodging

YOSEMITE NATIONAL PARK
Curry Village
9010 Curry Village Drive
(801) 559-4884
www.yosemitepark.com
$

Yosemite Lodge
9006 Yosemite Lodge Drive
(801) 559-4884
www.yosemitepark.com
$$

EL PORTAL
Cedar Lodge
9966 Highway 140
(209) 379-2612
www.yosemite-motels.com
$

Yosemite View Lodge
11136 Highway 140
(888) 742-4371
www.yosemite-motels.com
$$

OAKHURST
Oakhurst Lodge
40302 Highway 41
(800) 655-6343
www.oklodge.com
$

Shilo Inn Oakhurst
40644 Highway 41
(559) 683-3555
www.shiloinns.com
$

Angels Camp RV & Camping Resort
123 Selkirk Ranch Road
(209) 736-0404
www.angelscamprv.com
$$

REDDING
Americana Lodge
1250 Pine Street
(530) 241-7020
www.hotels.com
$

Oxford Suites Redding
1967 Hilltop Drive
(530) 221-0100
www.oxfordsuitesredding.com
$$

Redding TraveLodge
540 North Market Street
(800) 243-1106
www.reddingtravelodge.com
$

MONTEREY
Portola Hotel & Spa at Monterey Bay
2 Portola Plaza
(866) 711-1534
www.portolahotel.com
$$

BIG SUR
Big Sur Lodge
47225 Highway 1
(800) 424-4787
www.bigsurlodge.com
$$–$$$

Big Sur River Inn
Highway 1 at Pheneger Creek
(831) 667-2700
www.bigsurriverinn.com
$$–$$$

Fernwood Resort Big Sur
Highway 1
(831) 667-2422
www.fernwoodbigsur.com
$$

Ventana Inn and Spa
Highway 1
(831) 667-2331
www.ventanainn.com
$$$

Restaurants

YOSEMITE NATIONAL PARK
Ahwahnee Dining Room
1 Ahwahnee Road
(209) 372-1489
www.yosemitepark.com
$$–$$$

Mountain Room Restaurant
9006 Yosemite Lodge Drive
(209) 372-1274
www.yosemitepark.com
$$

Wawona Dining Room
41 Wawona Road
(209) 375-1425
www.yosemitepark.com
$$

MIDPINES
Café at the Bug
6979 Highway 140
(866) 826-7108
www.yosemitebug.com
$

GROVELAND
Groveland Hotel Victorian Room
18767 Main Street
(209) 962-4000
www.groveland.com
$$–$$$

MARIPOSA
Charles Street Dinner House
Highway 140 at Seventh
(209) 966-2366
www.yosemitelinks.com
$$–$$$

BIG SUR
Big Sur Bakery & Restaurant
Highway 1
(831) 667-0520
www.bigsurbakery.com
$$–$$$

Big Sur Roadhouse
Highway 1
(831) 667-2264
www.bigsurroadhouse.com
$$

Deetjen's Big Sur Inn
48865 Highway 1
(831) 667-2377
www.deetjens.com
$$–$$$

The Grill at Treebones Resort
71895 Highway 1
(877) 424-4787
www.treebonesresort.com
$$

Lucia Lodge
62400 Highway 1
(831) 667-2391
www.lucialodge.com
$$–$$$

The Maiden Publick House
Highway 1
(831) 667-2355
www.themaidenpub.com
$

Redwood Grill
Highway 1
(831) 667-2129
www.bigsurcoastfoods. com/redwoodgrill
$$

KINGS CANYON NATIONAL PARK
Montecito Sequoia Lodge Restaurant
63410 General's Highway
(800) 227-9900
www.mslodge.com
$$

RAGGED POINT
Ragged Point Inn
19019 Highway 1
(805) 927-4502
www.raggedpointinn.com
$$

CHAPTER 17

Seeing the Sea

THE PACIFIC OCEAN, which delineates northern California's western border, is one of the most spectacular oceans in the world. The Golden State isn't shy about promoting this natural tourist attraction, giving you opportunities to drive, hike, bicycle, sail, swim, and cruise along virtually every inch of it. Whether you want to sit behind the wheel of a shiny red convertible on top of the coastline itself or relax in a deck chair while watching the coast pass by from a distance, there are tons of opportunities for you to see the sea.

Main Junctions for Heading Inland

The easiest way to combine a drive along Highway 1 with other itineraries farther inland is to consider the main junction points along the route and plan accordingly. Here's a list of the easiest connections to make and where they'll take you, running from north to south along Highway 1:

- The Bodega Highway joins Highway 1 at Bodega Bay and turns into Route 12 near Santa Rosa.
- That same junction offers an offshoot onto Valley Ford Road, which will get you to Petaluma.
- In San Francisco, Highway 1 connects to Interstate 280, which meets Interstate 80, which is the route to Oakland.

- South of San Francisco, Highway 1 again connects to Interstate 280, which you can follow south to Interstate 880 and San Jose.
- At Santa Cruz, Highway 1 connects to Highway 17, which you can follow north to San Jose.
- In Monterey, Highway 1 connects to Monterey Road, which will take you to Salinas.

From Carmel south to the intersection with Highway 46 south of Cambria, there are no major connecting roads off Highway 1. This is a 100-mile stretch that, at peak conditions, will take about two hours to drive. There are some local roads connecting to Highway 1, but they'll take you toward Los Padres National Forest and the Hunter-Liggett Military Reserve—neither of which is known for its easy access to other major destinations.

 RAINY DAY FUN

Stuck in traffic? See which person in your car can name the most songs about California. These will get you started: "California Dreamin'" by the Mamas and the Papas, "California Girls" by the Beach Boys, "Do You Know the Way to San Jose" by Dionne Warwick, "Goin' Back to Cali" by LL Cool J, and "Californication" by the Red Hot Chili Peppers.

Great Drives Along Highway 1

For the sake of making your planning as easy as possible, this section will divide the northern California coastline into three sections, running from south to north: San Luis Obispo to Carmel, Monterey to the Point Reyes National Seashore, and Bodega Bay to Leggett, which is the northern terminus of the highway, connecting to Route 101. The most crowded parts of northern California's Highway 1 are exactly where you might expect them to be: in the San Francisco, Monterey Bay, and Big Sur areas, the most popular tourist destinations. That's especially true during the peak summer months, when drivers jam rental cars onto the highway by the hundreds of thousands.

San Luis Obispo to Carmel

If you choose to begin your Highway 1 driving in San Luis Obispo, be sure to take a few hours—or even a day—to explore what the town has to offer. There are walking and bicycling trails, golf courses, fine dining, museums, and more. Call the city "SLO," as the locals do, and take things slow before you climb into the car for the first leg of your drive up the coast.

An excellent first stop is Hearst Castle, which is forty-five miles north of San Luis Obispo, in the town of San Simeon. A lot of people driving from Los Angeles to San Francisco along Highway 1 consider Hearst Castle the midway point, so it's a popular destination for more reasons than just its tours and history. For information about tours, go to *www.hearstcastle.org.*

 TRAVEL TIP

The stretch of Highway 1 near Hearst Castle can be closed due to heavy rains during the wet season, which technically runs from November through April. Your best bet in the face of inclement weather is to click on the "highway conditions" link found on the California Department of Transportation's Web site, *www.dot. ca.gov.*

From Hearst Castle, it's about ninety-three miles to Monterey, covering what is perhaps the most spectacular section along High-way 1. This is the Big Sur region, the part of the highway where there are forty-mile stretches without so much as a single gas station. You almost have to do this long of a stretch by sheer definition of the place, especially if you want to spend your evenings in larger city-style hotels instead of roadside campgrounds or motels.

You will pass through the small towns of Gorda, Posts, and Big Sur before coming to Carmel-by-the-Sea and neighboring Monterey, but expect this leg of your drive to be almost 100 percent filled with nature. That's the beauty of the place. Start out with a full tank of gas and enjoy it to the fullest.

Monterey to the Point Reyes National Seashore

The drive from Monterey to Santa Cruz is about forty-five miles and takes you around the whole of Monterey Bay. There are a couple of towns in between, both on Highway 1 and just to its east, but for the most part the main attraction is the bay itself. Both Monterey and Santa Cruz have more than enough attractions to keep the entire family happy. You might consider a morning at the Monterey Bay Aquarium, then a drive along the coast up to Santa Cruz, where you can spend the night before buying tickets for the rides along the seaside boardwalk.

═══ FAST FACT

One of the rides at the Santa Cruz Beach Boardwalk is called "Back to the '50s." It features colorful cars that your little kids can drive backward and forward while singing along to doo-wop and Motown-era songs, thus keeping the driving theme going during your stopover between other Highway 1 destinations.

Heading north from Santa Cruz, it's about sixty miles to the town of Half Moon Bay, which is as good a place as any to stop if you don't want to continue on to San Francisco, another thirty miles to the north. There are a couple of adults-only attractions here, including a double-decker smoking bus at Cameron's Pub and the Half Moon Bay Brewing Company, where you can sample the local ales.

A lot of surfers tend to stop at Half Moon Bay along Highway 1, since the famous fifty-foot wave area known as Mavericks is about a half-mile away. This is not a place to learn the sport of surfing, but if you want to see some of the best surfers in the world, grab your long-lens camera and hit the beach. There's an annual invitation-only surfing contest, with varying dates depending on weather conditions. If you want to avoid traffic, that would be a good time to continue north to San Francisco.

 JUST FOR PARENTS

Looking for a place to blow some big bucks on a super-memorable romantic weekend? Consider the Ritz-Carlton at Half Moon Bay, an 1800s-style estate with a thirty-six-hole championship golf course and a waterfront spa with sixteen different treatment rooms. The lowest-price room during the high season in August is $500. Suites cost up to $3,500 per night.

Assuming that you stop for the night at Half Moon Bay, your next destination along Highway 1 is San Francisco. You can of course pull off the highway and do any or all of the activities described in Chapter 2, but if you just want to get a look at the Golden Gate Bridge, you needn't even hit the brakes. Highway 1 crosses right over it, bound for Sausalito and the Point Reyes National Seashore.

Bodega Bay to Leggett

After you leave the Point Reyes National Seashore in your rearview mirror, you'll come to Bodega Bay, which marks the southernmost point in the northernmost route along Highway 1. The stretch from here to Leggett, at the highway's northern terminus, is far less crowded with towns and tourist attractions. If you want to get away from the crowds and be almost alone with nature well into the redwood forests, this stretch of Highway 1 is ideal.

To do the entire stretch from Bodega Bay to Leggett, you'll cover about 150 miles—which you can do, on good days, in about three hours. That's not bad at all for a scenic drive, and if you're hoping to become mesmerized without interruption along the highway, this is the place to do it.

 TRAVEL TIP

Looking for a place to rent a house between Bodega Bay and Leggett on Highway 1? Consider the town of Sea Ranch, a planned community of weathered-wood houses built almost entirely without fences, so as to utilize the natural landscape as barriers between neighbors. Anyone with an interest in architecture will love this place.

Should you require a stop along the way, your best bet is in Mendocino, which was covered in Chapter 8. The city is just shy of 100 miles north from Bodega Bay, about two-thirds of the way up to Leggett and the intersection with Highway 101.

Up North on Highway 101

Highway 1 ends at the northern California town of Leggett, which is actually inland from the coast. In this tiny town of about 300 residents, Highway 1 connects to Highway 101, which continues north along an inland route through Humboldt Redwoods State Park before reconnecting with the shoreline north of Eureka, near the town of McKinleyville.

In some ways, it's almost as if the highway planners saved the best for last; along this stretch of Highway 101, you'll enjoy virtually simultaneous views of the Pacific Ocean to the west and Redwood National Park to the east. Route 101 is actually called the Redwood

Highway as it crosses the Humboldt County–Del Norte County line, passing through the town of Klamath and then hugging the coast again on its way to the Oregon border.

RAINY DAY FUN

You don't have to step outside your car to see the giant redwoods along Highway 101. Several offshoot roads take you to an early tourist attraction: the drive-through tree. Yes, the act of gutting centuries-old trees has left some of the redwoods in need of steel cables to ensure that they stay upright, but nothing you do will cause any additional environmental damage.

Top Pacific Coast Walks and Hikes

Of course, if you want to do as little damage as possible to the beautiful environment along the Pacific Coast, the best way to see it is on foot. You'll have the added bonus of being able to take a quick dip in the surf to cool off—at least in the areas where the waves aren't ferociously carving out cliffs from the state's western edge.

A good place to start planning any kind of walking or hiking itinerary is at the Web site *www.californiacoastaltrail.info*. It offers separate sections about great routes from San Luis Obispo, at the southern edge of the region, to Del Norte, on the California-Oregon border. The Web site is run by the Coastwalk association, which is working along the length of the state to map out and fill in sections of trails that will connect one end of California to the other via a route as impressive for walkers as Highway 1 is for drivers. The trail system, which is nearly 80 percent "safe and hikable," is known as the California Coastal Trail, or CCT.

To hike the entire CCT would require about 1,200 miles of hoofing it up or down the coast—certainly not for the out-of-shape, and probably not exactly what you had in mind for your family's vacation. Odds are you'll explore the CCT by choosing a section or two in between visiting other destinations along the way, which is exactly the way the vast majority of people get to know northern California's coastal trails each year.

≡ FAST FACT

From June through October, the group Coastwalk organizes overnight and multiday hikes for individuals and families that highlight separate sections of California coastal trails. Some of the itineraries are suited for children as young as age six, while others are more strenuous and geared toward athletic adults. Learn more at *www.coastwalk.org.*

The Lost Coast

Highway 1 never made it here, but there are some sixty-four miles of trails crossing from Humboldt County into Mendocino County. One of the prettiest areas along this route is the wilderness beach within the King Range National Conservation Area, which has the truly coastal section of the trail. Beyond the twenty-five miles or so of beach hiking, the trail moves across roads and then inland—beautiful, but not a way to see the sea if that's your primary aim.

≡ FAST FACT

Getting up close to the Pacific shore in this part of northern California is actually easier on foot than it is by car. The topography is so rugged that planners were forced to push Highway 1 and Highway 101 inland. The federal Bureau of Land Management offers some interpretive hikes here during the summer months to explain the geological details. Learn more at *www.blm.gov.*

Golden Gate National Recreation Area

If the words *Golden Gate* are in the name, then you can bet the stretch of trail runs near the city of San Francisco. The Golden Gate National Recreation Area extends far beyond the city limits and includes spectacular views of the famous bridge. What better way to see this part of the coast than to walk right over the Golden Gate Bridge? You can start at Fort Mason and walk across the bridge to Fort Point, then continue south along the coast to Sausalito (if you have the energy for a half-day workout) before returning to San Francisco via a leisurely ferry ride.

 TRAVEL TIP

The National Park Service publishes excellent full-color maps including trailhead directions and marked routes for the Golden Gate National Recreation Area. Some are available as free PDF downloads at the Web site *www.nps.gov,* which also offers seasonal information, fees and park rules, and more.

Big Sur

One of the best trails in the Big Sur region for coastal views is the Andrew Molera Loop, an 8.8-mile route that takes you inland as well as along the Pacific shoreline. This trail is long but doable for people of reasonable athletic conditioning. You don't have to be an Olympic athlete to make it to the end, but do be prepared for your muscles to let you know that they've had a good day's workout.

The easiest way to access the trailhead is by driving to Andrew Molera State Park, just north of Pfeiffer Big Sur State Park on Highway 1, about twenty miles south of Carmel. It's the northernmost in a string of trails that runs south along the Big Sur coastline toward San Luis Obispo; thus, it's the easiest to access if you're driving down from San Francisco to tour the area.

There are shorter hikes, too, that will give you the flavor of the Big Sur coastline, and you can check them out in advance via pictures on the informative Web site *www.hikinginbigsur.com*. It has a "One Day Must See" section that includes trails shorter than a mile long, in case you want to do the majority of the coast via Highway 1 with a walk along the shore as a pit stop.

CHAPTER 18

Theme Vacations

SOMETIMES IT'S FUN to throw geography out the window and plan a regional vacation based on a theme. Northern California offers plenty of opportunities for doing just that. This chapter offers ideas for theme vacations that add to some of the recommendations in previous chapters, allowing you to plan a week of activities keyed to your family's favorite activities and interests.

Kid-Friendly Education

Family vacations can be just as educational as they are fun. A lot of kids hear the word *museum* and keel over like a wilted flower, dreading being dragged through hallways where talking and touching are most definitely not allowed. That's no way to spend a holiday—or any day, especially when it's part of a family getaway.

Luckily, there are a plethora of kid-friendly museums, aquariums, and more in northern California. You can spend a week touring the region while visiting an institution or two each day, making your trip just as educational as a week at school (but without the homework, of course!). A lot of times, kid-friendly museums offer arts and crafts classes, too, so simply taking part means creating a souvenir to take home. That's an added bonus that will keep you and your pocketbook out of the nearest gift shops.

Any child (and any adult, for that matter) would find it boring to visit the same kind of educational-oriented institutions every day, no matter how kid-friendly they are. That's why this section focuses on three different kinds of institutions: living-history parks, hands-on museums, and aquariums. If you mix and match them while planning your family's vacation itinerary, then you're far more likely to keep everyone's imagination engaged.

≡FAST FACT

According to the National Education Association, children whose parents are actively involved in their education tend to do better in school. If you can organize your vacation visits around a theme that correlates to what your child is learning in school, then you will reinforce those lessons—and you'll help your child achieve more than other children who don't have the chance to receive additional information.

Living-History Parks

Many people think that anyone who dresses up in period costumes or re-enacts an event is creating a living-history experience. That's not the case. *Living history* is actually a phrase that describes an educational medium. It must have an educational component, not just a celebratory one. The men and women who re-enact Civil War battles across the United States of America, for instance, are not engaging in living-history demonstrations. They're re-creating something historic, but typically they don't do it with the educational element that is so crucial to the living-history experience.

Historians and museum workers are most often the kinds of people you'll find involved in creating living-history experiences, but in general, anyone who tries to teach others about historical events and lives by dressing up and portraying a character can be said to be taking part in a living-history demonstration. When you decide to take advantage of a living-history experience, be ready to get fully engaged. The people playing historic roles rarely drop out of character, so you'll have to commit to your role as a player on the historical stage they're trying to set.

Empire Mine State Historic Park

Empire Mine State Historic Park was mentioned in Chapter 15, which explained that living-history days are held at this Gold Country institution during weekends from May through October. Volunteers dress in costumes dating to the early 1900s, becoming everything from estate owners to the maids who served them and of course the miners who found all the gold that made the estate possible in the first place. You can talk to everyone from the guys working in the mine shaft to the men in the front office who were responsible for the miners' safety and well-being.

 RAINY DAY FUN

One of the living-history tours at Empire Mine State Park is through Bourn Cottage, a two-story home built in the style of nineteenth-century English estates. Even if it's pouring outside, you'll be warm and cozy inside as you explore the redwood interior, leaded glass windows, and towering granite walls.

There is some information on Empire Mine State Park at *www .parks.ca.gov*, but a better online resource that includes photographs is at *www.empiremine.org*.

Wilder Ranch State Park

Just north of Santa Cruz, west of Highway 1, you'll find Wilder Ranch State Park, 7,000 acres of preserved land that used to be home to a dairy ranch famous for its butter. Before that, it served as a supply site for the Santa Cruz Mission.

Some buildings were constructed in the late 1700s, and some were built as recently as the 1940s. You'll find houses (including a historic adobe) as well as barns, shops, and gardens where, during the weekends, docents demonstrate skills such as blacksmithing and baking on wood stoves. If you want to know what it was like to be an early rancher or farmer in this part of northern California, this is the place to visit.

≡FAST FACT

Wilder Ranch was driven by water power, with a water wheel that, among other things, charged three large lamps that created a fake sunrise each day. The idea was to get the cows up and moving earlier—a business idea that led some people to accuse the ranchers of cruelty to animals back in the late 1800s.

Wilder Ranch State Park is part of California's parks system. You can learn more at the official Web site, *www.parks.ca.gov*.

Hands-On Museums

Talking to people who are dressed in period costumes is fun, but for more active kids, nothing beats hands-on entertainment and education. Plenty of the cities in northern California have embraced the trend of hands-on museums, creating exhibits that encourage getting dirty, wet, and interactive with everything from yo-yos to science experiments.

Each of the museums has the word *discovery* in its name. So perhaps they're a little short on creativity in the naming department, but they're full of great ideas when it comes to the different exhibits you'll find inside.

Bay Area Discovery Museum

The Bay Area Discovery Museum first came up in the section of Chapter 3 that described the city of Sausalito. This museum is located in the Golden Gate National Recreation Area, with exhibits centered on art, science, and the environment. What's nice about this museum is that its hands-on exhibits are designed for different age groups, with some exhibits meant for children younger than five and others designed to intrigue older kids. There are indoor art studios and outdoor bay education exhibits, plus special exhibits that include everything from boatbuilding to visits with Clifford the Big Red Dog. Learn more at *www.baykidsmuseum.org*.

 JUST FOR PARENTS

The Bay Area Discovery Museum's Web site, *www .baykidsmuseum.org*, has a special section for parents that includes seasonal play tips, parenting articles, and "Ask Nurse Rona," a series of advice columns that invites you to send in questions on virtually any topic that affects kids. The parents' section of the Web site is updated quarterly.

Children's Discovery Museum

Chapter 3 first introduced San Jose's Children's Discovery Museum. It, too, has special exhibits featuring characters such as Clifford the Big Red Dog, but there are also exhibits based on everything from circles to bubbles. A few of the hands-on exhibits at this museum are sociologically oriented, teaching kids how to run a post office, a pizza parlor, and a bank. Learn more at *www.cdm.org*.

Discovery Museum in Eureka

Chapter 8 introduced the Discovery Museum in the town of Eureka, where your kids can enjoy everything from a pint-size grocery store to a 3-D planetarium exhibit. If your wee ones can't get enough activity, they can climb onto the Kid Power bicycles and see how much power they can generate by pedaling. That'll tire 'em out enough to keep still in the car as you travel to the next destination on your vacation itinerary! This hands-on museum's official Web site is at *www.discovery-museum.org*.

Discovery Museum

Sacramento is home to the Discovery Museum, which is another name for the city's Museum of History, Science, Space, and Technology. You'll find exhibits focusing on everything from the gold rush to the space shuttle, plus "imagination play stations" where your kids can put on costumes and pretend to be part of living-history exhibits.

 TRAVEL TIP

If you want to incorporate Asian history into your hands-on museum experience, consider a stop at the Discovery Museum in Sacramento. Its exhibits include "Chinese in the Gold Rush," focusing on the work and sacrifice of the Chinese immigrants during this storied era in northern California's history. The exhibit is a collaborative project with the Chinese American Council of Sausalito.

You can learn more about upcoming exhibits and events by going online to *www.thediscovery.org*.

Aquariums

So much of northern California's history and beauty is tied to the ocean, you'd be hard-pressed to create a kid-friendly educational itinerary without including at least one aquarium. Even better, this region has a couple of the best aquariums in the world, meaning that you'll enjoy the trip just as much as your children.

Aquarium of the Bay

San Francisco's Aquarium of the Bay includes exhibits that focus on all things related to San Francisco Bay, from the animals that live within it to the conservation efforts that are required to keep it in top condition.

 RAINY DAY FUN

Okay, make that rainy "night" fun—available only to kids who are working toward national badges within the Girl Scout and Boy Scout organizations. If your child fits that bill, for $55 he or she can participate in a sleepover program at the Aquarium on the Bay. Naturalists lead activities that highlight the nocturnal behavior of the bay's many creatures.

This aquarium boasts far more than just windows you can peer through. There are glass tunnels that take you beneath the bay, plus touch pools where you can get up close and personal with rays, sharks, and other harmless bay animals. Learn more online at *www .aquariumofthebay.org*.

Monterey Bay Aquarium

The world-famous Monterey Bay Aquarium has been educating children and adults alike for more than two decades. Exhibits and tours take place inside and out, on the bay and beneath it, so you can learn virtually everything there is to know about the ecologically fascinating body of water. For information about what's happening at the aquarium during your family's travel dates, log on to the Web site at *www.mbayaq.org*.

Amusement and Water Parks

All right, all right—so not every kid wants to spend a week's worth of vacation time checking out educational exhibits. For some families, theme vacations mean theme parks—complete with all the stomach-turning rides and junk food that can be packed into the hours between sunrise and sunset.

Northern California has quite a lot to offer in the theme park department, especially if you include water parks in your plans during the warmer summer months. Here's a look at some of the bigger attraction-filled destinations for thrill-seekers of all ages.

≡FAST FACT

Disneyland is by far the most famous theme park in California, but it's in the southern part of the state. Not to worry: Mickey and Minnie may not be there to greet you in northern California, but you'll find everyone from Thomas the Tank Engine to Sylvester and Tweety Bird at Six Flags Discovery Kingdom in Vallejo, near San Francisco.

Six Flags Discovery Kingdom

Anyone who is a theme park fan knows the name Six Flags. Discovery Kingdom is like many other Six Flags parks across the United States, featuring everything from roller coasters to kid zones where the rides are geared toward the tiniest of tots.

If your kids are the teenage variety, then you'll want to get in line to ride Medusa, which is billed as "the tallest, fastest, longest, and most technologically advanced roller coaster in northern California." There's no floor beneath your feet as you twist and turn down 3,500 feet of track, including seven inversions. Make sure you do this ride before eating that chili dog for lunch.

Smaller children will enjoy no-size-requirement rides such as the Road Runner Express "roller coaster" as well as the Bertie the Bus ride that swings into the air. There are also kids' games in special sections of the park that are geared toward the younger set. For a complete list of rides and other attractions, go to *www.sixflags.com.*

Gilroy Gardens

The Gilroy Gardens Family Theme Park, near San Jose, claims to be the state's only "horticultural theme park." That's right: There are multiple gardens mixed in with the rides for thrill-seekers of all ages, all designed to foster an appreciation of the natural world as well as humanity's ability to shape it.

A lot of the rides at this park are geared toward families with young children, including boat rides around gardens, a Ferris wheel, a carousel, and paddleboats. Older children who want thrills and spills will be a little out of their element here compared with a larger park like Six Flags.

 TRAVEL TIP

To make the most of a visit to Gilroy Gardens, put it on your must-visit list and then wait to choose your day of attendance based on your vacation week's weather report. A lot of the attractions and exhibits incorporate the great outdoors, including some of the rides. Rainy days are always kind of the pits at theme parks, and that's especially true for this one.

Gilroy Gardens hosts special events such as camp-out nights and educational days, as well as "build-your-own-field-trips" complete with at-home activities that will keep your vacation going long after the traveling is done. Learn more at the park's official Web site, *www.gilroygardens.org*.

Santa Cruz Beach Boardwalk

This amusement-filled boardwalk was covered in Chapter 11, which noted that it's one of just two seaside amusement parks still standing on the entire West Coast. As with Gilroy Gardens, the rides here tend to be smaller and older—more suited to families with young children than for teenagers who want to do loop-de-loops until they get bloody noses and headaches. Still, the offerings are full of time-less fun, which is of course why the boardwalk rides have lured tour-ists continually for more than a century. Details about attractions and exhibits are online at *www.beachboardwalk.com.*

Tahoe Amusement Park

Much like the Santa Cruz Beach Boardwalk and Gilroy Gardens, the Tahoe Amusement Park in South Lake Tahoe is designed for fam-ily fun, particularly including younger children. It's open from May through October, and admission is free. However, you have to buy tickets to get on the rides, much as you would at a local or county fair. Some of the rides you can expect to find here include the Tilt-a-Whirl, a carousel, a miniature train, and go-karts. The park doesn't have a Web site, but you can learn more by calling (530) 541-1300.

Water Parks

The Island Waterpark

The folks in Fresno don't have the roller coasters you'll find else-where, but they do know how to stay cool with a smile during the summer months at the Island Waterpark. Although it has a miniature golf course and an arcade, this park's main attractions are designed to leave you soaking wet—which is a good way to be after any Memo-rial Day weekend, when the park opens for the season every year.

 TRAVEL TIP

Many of the water slides at the Island Waterpark have height requirements. If your child is shorter than forty-two inches, she will not be allowed on some of the attractions. Also, every child age three and younger—whether potty-trained or not—is required to wear a swim diaper inside the park. Leave your boo-gie boards and inner tubes at home, though. They're not allowed inside the park gates.

Rides at the Island Waterpark include five different water slides, a lazy river, and a wave pool. There are about a dozen different rides and attractions in total, making this a smaller park compared with some of the larger theme parks discussed earlier in this chapter. For a complete list of rides, a park map, and additional information, go to *www.islandwaterpark.com*.

Raging Waters

There are two Raging Waters locations in northern California: Sacramento and San Jose. The Sacramento venue has more than two dozen rides and attractions for all ages, while the park in San Jose offers about half as much to do. At both parks, you'll find slides, lazy rivers, and more, all designed to keep you cool and wet during the hot and dry summer months. You can look for special pricing when buying tickets online at *www.ragingwaters.com*. The Web site also has links to park maps, age and height restrictions, and additional information.

Miner Fun for Minors

No, you shouldn't send the little ones down into a dark shaft with a lighted helmet and a canary, but there's plenty of fun panning for gold in local rivers and riding the rails just as the locals did back when trains were the only way to transport every bit of ore.

Panning for Gold

There are plenty of privately run establishments in Gold Country that will let you pay for the privilege of trying to strike it rich, but one of the best publicly operated places to try your luck is at Marshall Gold Discovery State Historic Park. Located in Coloma, it sits on the site where James Marshall found gold in the American River while working for John Sutter at his sawmill.

This park is special in that you can pan for gold and then walk through living-history exhibits that preserve the nature of the gold rush era. About 70 percent of the modern-day town is part of the state park, which should give you an idea about just how seriously these folks take their history. Learn more at *www.parks.ca.gov*.

Riding the Rails

The Yosemite Mountain Sugar Pine Railroad harkens back to the early 1900s, when gold was moved by railroad—and sometimes stolen by horse-riding bandits. Those days are re-created, bandits and all, during lunch and dinner rides along this railroad, with pricing packages available for adults and children alike. Details are available online at *www.ymsprr.com*.

Visitor's Bureaus, Chambers of Commerce, and Helpful Groups

BIGGER NORTHERN CALIFORNIA CITIES such as San Francisco, Fresno, and Sacramento have large chambers of commerce and visitor's centers, but there are plenty of more specific resources throughout the region. From the Oregon border out to Lake Tahoe and the Napa Valley Wine Country, these organizations can help you plan your vacation to make the most of every nook and cranny northern California has to offer.

Northern California Visitor's Bureaus

Access Northern California

This nonprofit organization is dedicated to helping people with physical limitations and disabilities travel safely and comfortably throughout northern California.
www.accessnca.com

American Canyon Chamber of Commerce

American Canyon is the second-largest city in Napa County and is often considered the county's gateway because it's located at the southern edge, north of San Francisco.
www.napavalley.com

Berkeley Convention and Visitors Bureau

This city on San Francisco Bay is well known for its academic and liberal communities. You can download a digital version of the annual visitor's guide.

www.visitberkeley.com

Burney Chamber of Commerce

About fifty miles northeast of Redding is the town of Burney, at the base of Burney Mountain in the Cascades. A major attraction is McArthur Burney Falls Memorial State Park.

www.burneychamber.com

Butte Valley Chamber of Commerce

Dorris and Macdoel are the main towns this chamber represents. One of the area's best-known attractions is a 200-foot flagpole, the tallest west of the Mississippi River. Fishing, hunting, and dog sledding are popular local activities.

www.buttevalleychamber.com

California Delta Chambers and Visitors Bureau

This organization represents the state's 1,000 miles of navigable waterways. There are links to marinas, hotels, restaurants, annual events, and more than a dozen local chambers of commerce for more detailed information about specific locales.

www.californiadelta.org

Calistoga Chamber of Commerce

Calistoga is the town at the northern edge of the Napa Valley, right in between Napa and Sonoma counties in the heart of California Wine Country. Hotels, spas, shops, and wineries are among the major attractions.

www.napavalley.com

Chester and Lake Almanor Chamber of Commerce

Part of Plumas County, the Chester and Lake Almanor area offers outdoor activities year-round. Snowmobiling and skiing in the winter give way to fishing and hiking every summer.
www.chester-lakealmanor.com

Chico Chamber of Commerce

Chico is a town in Butte County, about ninety miles north of Sacramento. The town is home to Bidwell Park, one of the largest municipal parks in the United States, and has served as a backdrop for popular movies, including 1976's *The Outlaw Josie Wales* starring Clint Eastwood and 1939's *Gone with the Wind*.
www.chicochamber.com

Citrus Heights Chamber of Commerce

Citrus Heights, about fifteen miles north of Sacramento, became an independent city in 1997 following nearly a hundred years as an unincorporated area of Sacramento County.
www.chchamber.com

City of Sacramento

The official Web site of the city of Sacramento includes links to the Convention and Visitors Bureau, links to popular tourist attractions, and all the information you'll ever need about getting to and from the city.
www.cityofsacramento.org

Corning Chamber of Commerce

Corning is in Tehama County. The city is also known as Olive City and is home to the Bell Carter Olive Company, said to be the world's largest ripe olive cannery. Tours are available, local businesses offer olive tastings, and there's an annual Olive Festival held every August.
www.corningchamber.org

Delta Loop Recreation Area

Located in the Sacramento and San Joaquin Delta area, the Delta Loop includes a ten-mile scenic drive as well as more than fifty attractions for campers, boaters, diners, and other visitors. *www.deltaloop.com*

Dunsmuir Chamber of Commerce

This chamber represents the towns of Dunsmuir and Castella, as well as the Upper Sacramento River area. Annual events include a summer music concert series each August, as well as the Dunsmuir Railroad Days celebration in July. *www.dunsmuir.com*

Eastern Plumas Chamber of Commerce

Representing Eastern Plumas County in the Sierra Valley, this group represents off-the-beaten-path businesses that are about 160 miles from Sacramento and 250 miles from San Francisco. The region is known for year-round outdoor sports activities. *www.easternplumaschamber.com*

Elk Grove Chamber of Commerce

Located in the southern part of Sacramento County, the city of Elk Grove was incorporated in 2000. It includes several protected wetlands and natural recreation areas. *www.elkgroveca.com*

Gilroy Visitors Bureau

Gilroy is located in Santa Clara County, near Silicon Valley. It's known as the garlic capital of the world and hosts a popular garlic festival every year in July. *www.gilroyvisitor.org*

Go Fresno County

This is the official Web site of Fresno County, and it offers tons of links to activities like the Fresno County Fruit Trail, a self-guided tour through the area's agricultural heartland.
www.gofresnocounty.com

Greater Redding Chamber of Commerce

The town of Redding is becoming known not just for vacations, but also as a destination for conventions. There are a large number of hotels, campgrounds, RV parks, cabins, and houseboat rentals to suit virtually any kind of traveler.
www.reddingchamber.com

Happy Camp Chamber of Commerce

Representing the towns of Happy Camp and the Klamath River Valley, this chamber represents the businesses that have sprung up within Klamath National Forest since the days of trappers and hunters.
www.happycampchamber.com

Healdsburg Chamber of Commerce

Located in Sonoma County, the town of Healdsburg offers wineries, breweries, shopping, lodging, and more.
www.healdsburg.com

Humboldt County Convention and Visitor's Bureau

Humboldt County is about 200 miles north of San Francisco, part of what the locals call the Redwood Coast. Eureka is the most popular city in the county, which also includes multiple parks and museums.
www.redwoods.info

Indian Valley Chamber of Commerce

The town of Indian Valley is in Plumas County and is known for its outdoor beauty and activities. Annual events include a crab feed and auction in February, as well as a solar cookoff festival in July.

www.indianvalley.net

Isleton Chamber of Commerce

"Crawdad Town USA" is located along the Sacramento River in the California Delta. It's a small community, population less than 1,000, but nevertheless is home to an annual Crawdad Festival held each June during the Father's Day weekend.

www.isletoncoc.org

Lake County Online Visitors Guide

Located about two hours north of the San Francisco Bay area, Lake County sits smack in the middle of Mendocino, Napa, and Sonoma wine counties—all known for their fine wines and restaurants.

www.lakecounty.com

Lodi Conference and Visitors Bureau

Lodi is a town in San Joaquin County that boasts more than sixty wineries, a performing arts theater, local antiques stores, and more.

www.visitlodi.com

Lodi Wine and Visitors Center

Distinct from the Lodi Conference and Visitors Bureau, this group is sponsored by the Lodi-Woodbridge Winegrape Commission. It represents more than 800 winegrowers and sponsors the annual event Zinfest each May.

www.lodiwine.com

Manteca Convention and Visitors Bureau

Located in the heart of the San Joaquin Valley, Manteca hosts events that range from Oktoberfest to a Teddy Bears and Tea festival for mothers and daughters in May.

www.visitmanteca.org

Marin County Visitors Bureau

Marin County is just over the Golden Gate Bridge from San Francisco, on the way to the Napa and Sonoma wine region. It offers everything from sprawling beaches to redwood forests, plus music, art, and film festivals galore. Its farmers' markets are world renowned.

www.visitmarin.org

McCloud Chamber of Commerce

McCloud has held an annual lumberjack festival for more than fifty years, helping to celebrate its heritage as an early timber trade town. There's also an old-fashioned Christmas celebration each year that includes Santa Claus arriving during a downtown parade.

www.mccloudchamber.com

Modoc County and Alturas Chamber of Commerce

The Modoc National Wildlife Refuge, most of which is located south of the town of Alturas, includes thousands of acres of hunting, fishing, and recreational grounds. The county's historical museum boasts a collection of handguns and rifles from the 1400s through the post–World War II era.

www.alturaschamber.org

Monterey County Convention and Visitors Bureau

Big Sur, Carmel, Pebble Beach—the locations within Monterey County are known the world over. The Monterey Bay Aquarium also has an international following.

www.montereyinfo.org

Mount Shasta Chamber of Commerce

Mount Shasta is part of the Cascades and is the second-tallest volcano in the United States. The town of Mount Shasta is nestled at its base, and the chamber offers a downloadable visitor's guide that lists local attractions, annual events, and more.

www.mtshastachamber.com

Napa Valley Conference and Visitors Bureau

This group's official Web site features an interactive map, winery information, restaurant listings, a calendar of local events, and more. There's even a special section to help you plan your wedding in California's premier Wine Country.

www.napavalley.com

Northern California Adventures

Sponsored by the Redwood Empire Association and the North Coast Visitors Bureau, this Web site features more than 400 miles' worth of California towns from San Francisco to the Oregon border. Nine counties are promoted, including Napa and Sonoma.

www.redwoodempire.com

Northern California Marine Association

This boating group helps to organize popular events including the annual water festivals and boat shows in Oakland, Sacramento, and Folsom.

www.ncma.com

Northern California Travel and Tourism Information Network

The Shasta Cascade Wonderland Association's Web site includes information from eight northern California counties, as well as special sections on select cities, attractions, and activities. There's also a calendar of events and free downloads of full-color catalogs. Something else unique you'll find on this Web site is a weekly fishing report for northern California, compiled by the Western Outdoor News service.

www.shastacascade.org

North Sacramento Chamber of Commerce

This chamber represents Point West, the Uptown District, Del Paso Heights, Robla, McClellan Park, and Hagginwood. Artists' shops, retail stores, and hotels are the main visitor attractions.

www.northsacramentochamber.org

Oakhurst Area Chamber of Commerce

Located in Eastern Madera County, the town of Oakhurst is near Yosemite National Park in Gold Country. It hosts an annual chocolate and wine festival in October.

www.oakhurstchamber.com

Oakley Chamber of Commerce

Located about an hour's drive east of San Francisco Bay in the Sacramento–San Joaquin River Delta, the town of Oakley hosts an Almond Festival every year in September.

www.oakleychamber.com

Oroville Area Chamber of Commerce

Oroville is a town in Butte County that sponsors an annual ten-day festival and serves as a home to water sports, horseback riding trails, and museums.

www.orovillechamber.com

Paradise Ridge Chamber of Commerce

Paradise didn't incorporate as a town until 1979, but the area's rich history dates back to well before the first white settlers arrived in the 1800s. Today, one of the city's most popular attractions is the Golden Nugget Museum.

www.paradisechamber.com

Plumas County Visitor's Bureau

Plumas County is just south of Lassen Volcanic National Park. Its main towns include Chester, Quincy, Greenville, and Hallelujah Junction. The bureau helps to promote farmers' markets, county fairs, and similar activities. American Valley Speedway, featuring car races, is also in Plumas County.

www.plumascounty.org

Quincy Chamber of Commerce

The town of Quincy is located on the western slope of the Sierra Nevada. It is the county seat of Plumas County at the top of Feather River Canyon. Self-guided tours of the historic buildings downtown are a popular attraction.

www.quincy-chamber.com

Red Bluff Chamber of Commerce

Tehama Country, as the chamber of commerce calls the county, is about ninety minutes north of Sacramento and serves as the gateway to Lassen Volcanic National Park and the Yolla Bolly Mountains. Downtown Red Bluff boasts more than 150 businesses in its historic downtown area, and you can download a free map that will take you on a walking tour of the local Victorian architecture.

Red Bluff: *www.downtownredbluff.com*

Broader area: *www.redbluffchamberofcommerce.com*

Redding Convention and Visitors Bureau

Redding calls itself the second-sunniest city in America, with 88 percent of every year's days being free of rainfall. Turtle Bay Exploration Park is a main attraction, as is the Big League Dreams Sports Park. Golf and whitewater rafting are among the outdoor activities the area offers.

www.visitredding.org

Rio Vista Chamber of Commerce

About forty-five miles northeast of San Francisco on the Sacramento River, the town of Rio Vista boasts a bridge designed by Joseph Strauss, who also designed the more famous Golden Gate Bridge. The town is known for having some of the best sportfishing in the state.

www.riovista.org

Sacramenities

Sponsored by the Sacramento Department of Convention, Culture, and Leisure, this Web site is a gateway to the city's events, attractions, and more. There's also an interactive events calendar, if you want to see what's happening during the time you plan to visit.

www.sacramenities.com

Sacramento Convention and Visitors Bureau

Maps, hotel packages, and other special travel offers are all available at this official Web site of one of northern California's largest cities. The "things to do" section is a boon for anyone planning a vacation in the Sacramento area.

www.sacramentocvb.org

San Francisco Convention and Visitors Bureau

There are sections on this Web site for pretty much any kind of travel you require, including discount packages, handicapped

accessibility, and gay-themed vacations. You can search for hotels by neighborhood and find everything from museums to golf courses to annual events.
www.onlyinsanfrancisco.com

San Jose Convention and Visitors Bureau

Founded in 1777, San Jose is the oldest civil settlement in all of California. It was the site of the first state capital and is now one of the largest cities in the state. San Jose averages 300 out of 365 sunny days each year—meaning just about any month is a good month to visit.
www.sanjose.org

Santa Clara–Silicon Valley Central Chamber of Commerce and Convention-Visitors Bureau

Attractions in this region include a theme park, a computer museum, a NASA exploration center, wineries, shopping, and more.
www.santaclara.org

Scott Valley Chamber of Commerce

The Oregon border towns of Etna and Fort Jones fall under the purview of this California chamber, which helps to sponsor an annual bluegrass festival each July.
http://users.sisqtel.net/svcoc

Sonoma Valley Visitors Bureau

One of the most popular places in California Wine Country, the Sonoma Valley is home to countless wineries, restaurants, and gastronomical delights.
www.sonomavalley.com

Stockton Convention and Visitors Bureau

This San Joaquin Delta city takes great pride in its cultural offerings, including theater, dance, music, art galleries, and a

world-renowned museum. Annual events in the region include the Almond Blossom Festival in February, an Asparagus Festival in April, and a Wine and Sausage Festival in June.
www.visitstockton.org

Surprise Valley Chamber of Commerce

Surprise Valley is about seventy miles long, running between California's Warner Mountain Range and Nevada's Hayes Mountain Range. The valley includes four historic towns: Cedarville, Eagleville, Fort Bidwell, and Lake City. Cattle drives are a regular occurrence, as are horseshoe tournaments, powwows, and rodeos.
www.surprisevalleychamber.com

Trinity County Chamber of Commerce and Visitors Bureau

Based in the town of Weaverville, this chamber's Web site has an extensive list of annual countywide events.
www.trinitycounty.com

Tuolumne County Visitors Bureau

Yosemite National Park is the main attraction in Tuolumne County, which also offers skiing, hiking, biking, river rafting, fishing, camping, gold panning, sightseeing, fine dining, accommodations, and more.
www.thegreatunfenced.com

Vallejo Convention Center and Visitors Bureau

Vallejo is thirty-five minutes from San Francisco and about fifteen minutes from Napa and Sonoma counties. It is home to the Six Flags Discovery Kingdom amusement park, the Jelly Belly Candy Company, and an Anheuser-Busch brewery.
www.visitvallejo.com

Visit California

This is the official Web site of the California Travel and Tourism Commission. It covers all of California, not just the northern section, and has an interactive map where you can click on a region of the state and learn about all it has to offer.
www.visitcalifornia.com

Visit Siskiyou

This group, representing Mount Shasta County and the Siskiyou County Visitors Bureau, offers links to multiple chambers of commerce as well as an annual calendar of events.
www.visitsiskiyou.org

Weed Chamber of Commerce and Visitors' Center

The city of Weed is located along the Volcanic Scenic Byway, about halfway between Portland, Oregon, and San Francisco, California. The visitor's center can direct you to local motels, restaurants, and more.
www.weedchamber.com

Willow Creek Chamber of Commerce

Willow Creek is a town in the heart of Six Rivers National Forest—home to countless sightings of the man-animal creature known the world over as Big Foot. Fishing, swimming, and rafting are among the local attractions, as is the annual Big Foot Days celebration.
www.willowcreekchamber.com

Yosemite Visitors Bureau

The world-famous Yosemite National Park is just one of the attractions you can enjoy in the Sierra Nevada and Madera County.
www.yosemitethisyear.com

Yountville Chamber of Commerce
This gourmand's paradise is known as the culinary capital of the Napa Valley. Renowned for its world-class restaurants in the heart of California Wine Country, Yountville offers family events and adult-oriented wine festivals alike.
www.napavalley.com

Yreka Chamber of Commerce
Yreka is about twenty miles south of the Oregon border, inside the Shasta Valley. It calls itself the Golden City and is the seat of Siskiyou County. Outdoor activities include golfing, fishing, hunting, whitewater rafting, and snow skiing.
www.yrekachamber.com

Lake Tahoe Visitors Bureaus, Chambers of Commerce, and Helpful Groups

Lake Tahoe Chamber of Commerce
This Web site offers a directory of links and resources, including travel guides, vacation deals, and maps of the local and surrounding areas in case you plan to drive from a major airport outside the immediate area.
www.tahoechamber.com

South Lake Tahoe Chamber of Commerce
You can request a visitor's information package, check out restaurants and lodging, look at a calendar of local events, and more.
www.tahoeinfo.com

Visiting Lake Tahoe
This Web site is a gateway to visitor's bureaus on both the north and south shores of Lake Tahoe. There are separate events calendars for each region, plus information about dining, lodging, and more.
www.visitinglaketahoe.com

Visit Reno-Tahoe

Offering information about Nevada-side as well as California-side attractions at Lake Tahoe, this Web site includes an events calendar, lodging and gaming information, and convention details. *www.visitrenotahoe.com*

Annual Festivals and Events

THE SUMMER AND WINTER MONTHS tend to be the busiest in terms of northern California and Lake Tahoe events, since that's when the weather tends to cooperate for outdoor festivals or winter sports extravaganzas. Still, no matter what time of year you choose to visit, you'll find a town or county waiting eagerly to show you a good time. From olive, wine, and chocolate festivals to snowshoe races and cowboy poetry shows, you'll never want for something interesting to do.

January

Historic Longboard Ski Revival Series Races
The Eureka Bowl in Plumas Eureka State Park is the site for these races, which feature skiers in 1860s period costumes racing on 9- to 16-foot skis down one of America's oldest recorded ski slopes. Prizes are given for racing and attire. The event is held in January, February, and March, depending on snowfall.
www.plumasskiclub.org

Martini Madness

Part of the December-through-March Olive Festival in Sonoma Valley Wine Country, this event brings together bartenders from Sonoma County wineries, restaurants, and other establishments in a contest to create the best new martini.
www.sonomavalley.com

February

AT&T Pebble Beach National Pro-Am

This annual golf tournament at the world-famous Pebble Beach course pairs some of the best-known professional golfers in the world with celebrity teammates.
www.attpbgolf.com

Cloverdale Citrus Fair

Held since the late 1800s, this annual event includes the Citrus Fair Wine Competition, promoted as the world's largest wine contest. More than 100 wineries participate each year with tastings in San Francisco that are open to the public.
Fair information: www.cloverdalecitrusfair.org
Wine competition: www.winejudging.com

Indian Valley Crab Feed and Auction

Sponsored by the Indian Valley Chamber of Commerce in Plumas County, this event includes an auction of many things—but not live crabs, as the name implies!
www.indianvalley.net

Lake Davis Sled Dog and Snowshoe Races

Typically held in February—weather permitting—this family-friendly weekend in the Sierra Nevada includes events and how-to demonstrations such as "how to ski and bike with your dog." Family pets are not welcome at the sanctioned sled dog races, but they are welcome at the official sponsor hotel, Chalet View

Lodge. You and your dog can snowshoe race in a fun half-mile event or a more serious 5K.
www.lakedavissleddograce.com

Olive Festival Passport Weekend
This annual event is the big finale to the three-month Olive Festival held in Sonoma Valley Wine Country from December through February. Multiple venues throughout Sonoma County host olive, food, and wine tastings, live entertainment, and more.
www.sonomavalley.com

Paws for Love
Held each year in the town of Healdsburg, this event benefits the animals of Sonoma County. It includes auctions of art painted by shelter animals, live and silent auctions of award-winning wines, live music, and gourmet food tasting.
www.pawsforlove.info

Plumas County Snowmobile Poker Runs
There are four snowmobile poker runs held each February in Plumas County: the La Porte Harold Schmidt Memorial Poker Run (sometimes held in January due to snowfall), the Chester Winterfest Poker Run, the Lake Davis Winter Holiday Poker Run, and the Bucks Lake Snowdrifters Poker Run. Each of the areas has snowmobiles available for rent.
www.plumascounty.org

San Francisco Ocean Film Festival
Held for the first time in 2003, this annual event highlights films that focus on ocean sports, environmental issues, the marine sciences, ocean exploration, and coastal and island cultural history. It typically takes place at a theater on the San Francisco waterfront.
www.oceanfilmfest.org

March

Dixieland Monterey

Monterey Bay comes alive with three days of Dixieland, ragtime, swing, and jazz at this event, which has been held since 1980. It started out as a supplement of the Monterey County fair but has grown into an event in its own right, drawing thousands of music-loving fans.
www.dixieland-monterey.com

Redwood Coast Jazz Festival

Held in Eureka since 1990, this four-day event includes Dixieland jazz, calypso, zydeco, swing, and more. Big-name headliners in the past have included acts like Big Bad Voodoo Daddy. A half-dozen arts centers and nightclubs serve as venues around town.
www.redwoodjazz.org

Surprise Valley Squirrel Roundup

Sponsored by the Surprise Valley Chamber of Commerce, the annual Squirrel Roundup was started in 1991 as a way to help protect alfalfa fields, crops, machinery, and cattle from ever-increasing numbers of squirrels. Hunters and their families typically attend from multiple states, enjoying not just squirrel hunting but also events like a barbecue, a silent auction, and a sing-a-long.
www.surprisevalleychamber.com

Vinton Cowboy Poetry Show

Held every year since 1986, this weekend-long event celebrates cowboy poetry, which has many definitions but typically includes rhymed, metered verse written by someone like a rancher who has lived a good deal of his life as part of the Western cattle culture. There's usually at least one featured performer, plus food and additional events.
www.cowboypoetry.com

Weaverville Chocolate Festival

Begun in 2004, this annual event features chocolate delicacies, demonstrations, sculpture, and recipes. There's also an official festival cookbook created each year, so you can take home your favorite decadent recipes.

www.northstate.org

April

Big Sur Invitational Marathon

Even if you don't want to run through Monterey County, you can cheer on the participants as they race along some of California's most scenic roadways. There's a twenty-one-mile fun walk, if that sounds more appealing to you, as well as other less strenuous events.

www.bsim.org

Gold Nugget Days

This event takes place the fourth weekend of April in Paradise, celebrating the discovery of a fifty-four-pound gold nugget worth $10,690 on April 12, 1859. There's a parade, contests, a donkey derby, music, a bean feed, and more. You can even pan for gold, but you probably won't find a nugget as big as that first one.

www.paradisedirect.com

Kool April Nites

Classic cars and drag races are the big attractions at this Redding event, which also features food, music, dancing, and a two-and-a-half-mile cruise loop where you can show off your own cool wheels on streets blocked off from local traffic. If you think you might want to take part instead of just watching, register early. Kool April Nites typically has to turn away several hundred cool-car owners each year.

www.koolaprilnites.com

Northern California Cherry Blossom Festival

More than 150,000 people typically attend this annual Japanese community event in San Francisco. There's a street fair with a food bazaar, children's activities, and live entertainment such as folk dancing and martial arts.

www.nccbf.org

Red Bluff Roundup

Held in Tehama County for close to ninety years, this weeklong countywide event includes a chili cookoff, a parade, pony rides, a car show, a wild horse race (governed by the Wild Horse Association), Western buggy rides, a bowling tournament, barbecues, and more.

www.redbluffchamberofcommerce.com

San Francisco International Film Festival

This event takes place during April and May of each year, upholding the tradition of excellence the festival has held since it began in 1957. It is promoted as being the oldest film festival in all of the Americas and welcomes some 80,000 people each year.

www.sffs.org

Sea Otter Classic

Often referred to as Bikestock of North America, this event features BMX bicycle racing, mountain bike racing, kids' events, Olympic champions, and gear of all kinds. It's held in the city of Monterey.

www.seaotterclassic.com

Sonoma Valley Film Festival

This film festival highlights independent cinema as well as local food and wines. It's held in the large plaza in the town of Sonoma, where visitors get to mix and mingle alongside moviemakers, wine growers, and celebrity chefs. Every movie screening begins with a food and wine tasting and ends with a question-and-answer session hosted by actors and directors.

www.sonomafilmfest.org

Stockton Asparagus Festival

This festival is always held the last full weekend in April. It includes live music, a deep-fry eating competition, spear-throwing and golf putting contests, wine and microbrew tastings, arts and crafts, and more. If you have ever wanted to try Asparagus Wheat Ale, this is the place.
www.asparagusfest.com

May

Artsfest

Held each year in San Francisco to showcase theater, dance, film, music, and more, Artsfest takes place over multiple venues throughout the city and broader San Francisco Bay area.
www.artsfestsf.org

Carmel Art Festival

Several dozen art galleries in the Monterey County town of Carmel host this annual festival, which also includes a youth art show and sculpture in the park.
www.carmelartfestival.org

Castroville Artichoke Festival

This Monterey County town "goes green" for a weekend in May to celebrate the artichoke with live music, cooking demonstrations, wine tastings, a parade, arts and crafts, children's games, and more.
www.artichoke-festival.org

Cinco de Mayo

The city of San Jose has celebrated this May 5 event since 1983. The downtown parade is sponsored by the San Jose *Mercury-News* and the San Jose Chapter of the American G.I. Forum.
www.sjgif.org

Feather Fiesta Days
This is a ten-day event in the Butte County town of Oroville, named for the Spanish word *oro*, which means "gold." The festival includes a parade, a car show, an art show, a chili cookoff by local firefighters, a craft fair, a flea market, and more.
www.orovilleareachamber.com

Kinetic Grand Championship
Wildly decorated and creatively people-powered machines travel from Arcata to Ferndale in Humboldt County during this three-day race event, held each Memorial Day weekend.
www.kineticuniverse.com

Mamaspalooza
Held every Mother's Day weekend at the Del Monte Shopping Center in Monterey, this event showcases goods that will help make any mom's life a little bit easier and maybe even a tad more fun.
www.delmontecenter.com

Red Bluff Recreation Area Nitro National Drag Boat Festival
The U.S. Forest Service allows this annual event, which features high-speed boats racing at more than 200 miles per hour. Records have been set on Lake Red Bluff, which is actually part of the Sacramento River.
www.rbdragboats.com

Redding Rodeo Week
The rodeo itself is just the beginning of the fun at this weeklong event. It also features a dinner-dance, a golf tournament, a street dance, a fast-draw tournament, a chili cookoff, and a parade. You may even get a chance to meet Miss Redding Rodeo.
www.reddingrodeo.com

San Francisco International Arts Festival

Bill T. Jones and Danny Glover are among the cultural elite who sit on the national advisory board for this annual event, which began in 2003. Academic symposiums and lectures are inter-mixed throughout the ten-day program with live performances at multiple venues across San Francisco.
www.sfiaf.org

Shasta Art Fair and Old Time Fiddle Jamboree

A celebration of the Victorian era and gold rush, this event usu-ally takes place during Mother's Day weekend. It includes arts, crafts, exhibits, food, and, of course, music by way of fiddlers.
www.visitredding.org

Sonoma Jazz

This internationally acclaimed festival happens every Memorial Day weekend with big-time headliners such as Harry Connick Jr., Tony Ben-nett, Michael McDonald, LeAnn Rimes, and the Robert Cray Band.
www.sonomajazz.org

Zinfest

Sponsored by the Lodi-Woodbridge Winegrape Association, this annual three-day event at Lodi Lake showcases local wineries of the San Joaquin County area.
www.lodiwine.com

June

Arcata Bay Oyster Festival

More than 70 percent of the fresh oysters eaten in California are grown in Arcata Bay, which has been hosting this festival since 1991. You can try all kinds of oysters, including raw, fried, barbe-cued, atop pizzas—you name it. Crowds typically top 15,000.
www.oysterfestival.net

Art and Wine in the Park

Held for nearly two decades, this Fortuna event includes regional California wines and beers as well as works by local craftspeople including photography, paintings, ceramics, and jewelry. Proceeds fund the local Rotary and its community projects.
www.discovertheredwoods.com

Calistoga Art in the Park

This event benefits Napa Valley youth art programs and features arts, crafts, a silent auction, local wines, food, and music.
www.calistogaartcenter.org

Crawdad Festival

Held during Father's Day weekend in the Sacramento River town of Isleton, population 840, this festival draws about 50,000 for Louisiana-style fun. In fact, the festival claims to host the largest consumption of crawdads outside Louisiana itself. It's been a treasured local event since the mid-1980s.
www.crawdadfestival.org

Cruisin' Paradise

Sponsored by the Paradise Chamber of Commerce, this long-weekend event includes a barbecue, a classic car cruise, a car show, a craft show, and an antiques fair. The event is sponsored by the Paradise Ridge Chamber of Commerce.
www.paradisechamber.com

Juneteenth Cultural Festival

The African American Community Service Agency in San Jose has worked for a quarter-century to host this festival, which commemorates the end of slavery in America. The weekend-long event includes music, sermons, and more.
www.sjaacsa.org

Monterey Bay Blues Festival

Held for more than two decades and considered one of the finest music festivals in the United States, this three-day event has three stages and boasts performances by big-name acts including Joe Louis Walker and Buddy Guy.
www.montereyblues.com

Plumas-Eureka State Park Living History Days

During three days in June, July, and August, volunteers dress in period costumes and re-create life as it was in the town of John-sonville during the days of California's gold mines. There's even a working blacksmith shop where you can watch souvenirs being made.
www.plumas-eureka.org

San Joaquin Fair

One of northern California's premier county fairs, this annual event is held in Stockton and includes live music, horse racing, carnival rides and games, agricultural exhibits, food, and more.
www.sanjoaquinfair.com

Super Bull Rodeo

Held at the Modoc District Fairgrounds in Cedarville, this annual event began in 1996 and features bull riding, "America's Most Dangerous Sport." The event is sanctioned by the U.S. Bull-Riding Championships and includes professionals from the bull-riding circuit. Music, dancing, and other fun family activities are part of the day, which also includes cash prizes in the thousands of dollars for the best riders.
www.surprisevalleychamber.com

July

Blues by the Bay
Held on the waterfront in Eureka since 1996, this two-day event includes seafood, microbrews, and other refreshment vendors, not to mention act after act of blues solo artists and groups.
www.bluesbythebay.org

California Rodeo Salinas
This rodeo in the Monterey County town of Salinas has been held for nearly a century. It includes professional steer wrestling, bull riding, calf roping, bareback bronco riding, barrel racing, parades, live music, food, and more.
www.carodeo.com

Carmel Bach Festival
Straddling the months of July and August, this Monterey County event has been going on for nearly seventy years. It features dozens of musicians from all over the world performing the classic composer's works at multiple venues throughout the city of Carmel.
www.bachfestival.org

Chester Wild West Rodeo
This weekend event began in 2004, but it pays homage to the 1920s and '30s, when a rodeo by the same name ran for some eighteen years. It's held at a portable arena on Olsen Meadows and includes a children's silver dollar coin hunt, barrel racing, wild steer riding, bull riding, and more.
www.chesterwildwestrodeo.com

Dunsmuir Railroad Days
Established in 1940, this long-weekend event celebrates the railroad history of the town of Dunsmuir. You can tour locomotives and train cars, enjoy hand car and motor car rides, check out

model railroad exhibits and craft booths, play in a softball tournament, and watch the event's parade.

Fortuna Redwood AutoXpo

This is the biggest annual event in the town of Fortuna, held since 1990 to showcase classic cars, antique farm equipment, and more. The three-day event includes a swap meet, tractor pulls, and a sock hop.

http://redwoodautoxpo.com

Fortuna Rodeo

Held in the town of Fortuna since 1921, the Fortuna Rodeo is a weeklong festival that includes raging bulls, courageous cowhands, a chili cookoff, a junior rodeo, a deep-pit barbecue, and more.

www.fortunarodeo.com

Gilroy Garlic Festival

The Santa Clara County town of Gilroy is known as the garlic capital of the world, and this annual three-day event boasts foods created with more than two tons of garlic. Held the last weekend of July, the Garlic Festival also includes live music, arts and crafts, and a garlic recipe cookoff.

www.gilroygarlicfestival.com

Hayfork 'n You

Held at the Trinity County Fairgrounds in Hayfork, this event includes mud wrestling, poker runs, wet T-shirt contests, tattoo contests, live music, RV and tent camping, and more.

www.hayfork-n-you.com

High Sierra Music Festival

High Sierra Music is based in Berkeley, but its biggest annual event is held during the week of Independence Day in Quincy. The festival is a four-day camping and music event that features

acoustic singer-songwriters, bluegrass, funk, electronic, rock, jazz, and more. More than seventy-five acts typically perform, and more than 10,000 people usually attend.
www.highsierramusic.com

Lumberjack Fiesta

Sponsored by the McCloud Chamber of Commerce, this long-weekend event includes amateur logging competitions along with a parade, dancing, a baseball tournament, a horseshoe tournament, and more.
www.mccloudchamber.com

Scott Valley Bluegrass Festival

The Oregon border area of Scott Valley first organized this festival in 2004 to introduce visitors to the area and raise funds for local scholarships. The town of Etna hosts the festival, which goes on for two days.
www.scottvalleybluegrass.org

Scottish Games and Celtic Festival

Held for four decades in the city of Monterey, this weekend event features world-class pipers and drummers, Irish dancers, food, crafts, a caber toss, and more.
www.montereyscotgames.com

Sonoma County Showcase of Wine and Food

This event features the offerings of some 100 different wineries. There are exclusive lunches and dinners, hikes through the vineyards with winemakers, and a "Taste of Sonoma County" finale that highlights the best food and wine the region's top producers have to share.
www.sonomawinecountryweekend.com

Taylorsville Solar Cookoff Festival

This Plumas County event includes professional and homemade "solar barbecues" alike, usually including some crafted from television satellite dishes.
www.indianvalley.net

Twain Harte Summer Arts and Wine Festival

Held for the past three decades, this annual weekend event features live music, food, wine, crafts, a vintage car show, and family-friendly performers. The Central Sierra town shuts down its streets for the festival, so you can't miss it.
www.fireonthemountain.com

August

Bear Valley Music Festival

Sit inside a 1,250-seat tent and listen to a full symphony orchestra, internationally renowned soloists, and opera stars in a High Sierra setting. This festival has been going on for four decades in Tuolumne County.
www.bearvalleymusic.org

Bridgefest

The Humboldt County town of Bridgeville hosts this annual event, which features a flying saucer contest and typically involves flying saucers, extraterrestrials, and curious humanoids swarming on and above the town's old bridge span.
www.redwoods.info

California Exposition and State Fair

Held each year at the Cal Expo fairgrounds in Sacramento, this two-week event typically draws more than a million visitors. There are concerts by well-known headliner acts such as Huey Lewis & the News, Lonestar, and KC and the Sunshine Band, plus horse racing, a wine and cheese garden, and countless exhibitors and rides.
www.bigfun.org

California X-Treme Summercross

Amateur and professional motocross riders alike have taken part in this annual event since the late 1990s. "Breathtaking, highfly-ing, daredevil events" are promised by sponsor NEC.
www.necsports.com

Corning Olive Festival

Held for nearly twenty years, this long-weekend event includes a parade, arts, crafts, food, children's carnival games, music, danc-ing, lawnmower races, a pancake breakfast, and a talent show.
www.corningchamber.org

Hops in Humboldt

Humboldt County microbreweries make their best beers avail-able for tasting and purchase at this festival in Fortuna. Home brewers, too, are given a chance to showcase their suds.
www.hopsinhumboldt.com

Humboldt County Fair

This ten-day event has been held for more than a century. Based in the town of Ferndale, the fair features horseracing, carnival rides, live entertainment, and livestock shows and auctions.
www.humboldtcountyfair.org

Organic Planet Festival

Begun in 2004, this Eureka event is held at Halvorsen Park in Humboldt County. It features live music, a garden tour, a fashion show, and more. The festival's goal is to "celebrate a natural and nontoxic world."
www.organicplanetfestival.org

Redwood Art Association Summer Small Works Exhibition

Held for five decades, this exhibition is located in a Eureka Old Town Victorian house. New and established artists present their

work for display as part of the Redwood Art Association, the oldest of its kind in Humboldt County.
www.redwoodart.org

Sierra Brewfest

What the festivals are to wine buffs in Napa and Sonoma counties, the Sierra Brewfest is to beer connoisseurs. The Brewfest is sponsored by Music in the Mountains, a group that produces events in the Sierra Nevada foothills. Dozens of microbreweries bring their best brands for tastings at the Nevada County Fairgrounds in Grass Valley.
www.musicinthemountains.org

Sonora Blues Festival

Blues fans have been trekking to the Mother Lode Fairgrounds in Sonora since 1986 to listen to blues soloists and groups perform at this festival. There are typically three stages for the daylong event.
www.fireonthemountain.com

Steinbeck Festival

This four-day celebration of author John Steinbeck takes place in Monterey County with talks, films, panel discussions, readings, bus and walking tours, and more. A simultaneous street fair offers fun for non-literature lovers, as well.
www.steinbeck.org

Thunder Rolls for Charity

Held at the Shasta County Fairgrounds in Anderson with proceeds going to various charities, this annual motorcycle event includes the "wall of death," which is promoted as riding motorcycles inside a giant wooden bucket at highway speeds. There's also a Poker Walk (like a poker run, but without really going anywhere) as well as live music on a main stage.
www.thunderrolls.org

Weaver City Street Rollers Car Show in the Park

This event takes place at Lowden Park in Weaverville. The weekend's festivities include live music, dancing, food, a quilt raffle, and more. *www.trinitycounty.com*

September

Acorn Soupe Tree of Life Gala

Coming up on its tenth year, this annual St. Helena benefit raises funds for environmental education and youth development programs. Collectable vintages are among the wines offered at auction, alongside getaways for food and wine lovers.
(707) 254-7284

Annual Puppet Festival and Workshop

Held at the Jarvis Conservatory in Napa City, this family-friendly event is pretty much just as advertised in its name. Tickets are usually $20 for adults and $10 for kids. For more information, call (707) 255-5445 or visit *www.jarvisconservatory.com*.

Autumn Moon Festival Street Fair

San Francisco's Chinatown section has been hosting this event for nearly two decades. Live entertainers, food vendors, craft merchants, and more fill the streets for a weekend of cultural family fun.
www.moonfestival.org

Big Foot Days

The town of Willow Creek is the self-proclaimed entrance to Big Foot Country, where people have reported sightings of the man-monster creature for generations. Labor Day weekend in Willow Creek includes a celebration of Big Foot with a parade, games, and more.
www.willowcreekchamber.com

Blues by the River

The Shasta Blues Society is instrumental in this annual Sacramento River event at Lake Redding Park. It's a lawn chair affair, so don't forget to bring yours if you think you'll need a break from boogying to the music onstage.
www.shastablues.com

Chico Airfest

This annual event is held at the Chico Municipal Airport in Butte County. It features military and civilian aerial demonstrations and displays, along with kids' activities.
www.chicochamber.com

Coast Guard City Celebration

The town of Eureka celebrates its designation as a U.S. Coast Guard city with baseball, golf, a reception, a search and rescue demonstration, and tours of patrol boats, buoy tenders, and helicopters.
www.redwoods.info

Cruisin' Calistoga Beer and Wine Festival and Car Show

The name of this event is a mouthful, and so are the chili, pasta, beer, and wine that are available for tasting as live music plays in the background at the Napa County Fairgrounds.
www.win-rods.com

Cruz'n Eureka Car Show

Hundreds of classic cars take part in this cruising car show on the streets of Eureka, which has hosted the event since its inception in 1993. A swap meet, a raffle, and a silent auction are also part of the fun.
www.redwoods.info

Gold Rush Days

Held every Labor Day weekend since 1999, this event features period artifacts, dancing, crafts, horse-drawn carriages, period musicians, wagon and pony rides, gold panning, and more.
www.discovergold.org

Harvest Festival

The Kiwanis Club of Napa sponsors this event, which is a quarter-century old. Wines and gourmet treats are available from local wineries and restaurants, plus there's live music, art for sale and exhibition, a silent auction, and more. The venue is typically Yountville Lincoln Theatre, about nine miles north of the city of Napa.
www.napakiwanis.com

How Berkeley Can You Be?

This festival in the city of Berkeley, just outside of San Francisco, has been held annually since 1996. The parade typically draws more than 20,000 spectators, and the festival includes live music, craft vendors, food, and more.
www.howberkeleycanyoube.com

Kaiser Permanente San Francisco International Dragon Boat Festival

For more than a dozen years, this two-day event has welcomed more than 100 dragon boat teams and more than 2,500 dragon boat paddlers from the novice to competitive levels. Live music, food, crafts, and children's activities round out the weekend.
www.sfdragonboat.com

Monterey Bay Birding Festival

Based in Watsonville, this event includes trips all around the Pajaro Valley, which is well known as the heart of Monterey Bay's world-class birding area. Trips are organized to places like Big Sur, Santa Cruz beach, and the Carmel River.
www.montereybaybirding.org

Monterey Bay Reggaefest

Held during Labor Day weekend at the Monterey County fair-grounds, this festival carries on for two days with two stages full of well-known and upcoming acts alike. Island-style cooking, arts, and crafts are also part of the fun.

www.mbayreggaefest.net

Monterey Jazz Festival

First presented in 1958, the Monterey Jazz Festival is one of the best known events of its kind in the United States. It features not just music, but also presentations, workshops, exhibitions, food, and more spread out across a twenty-acre fairground.

www.montereyjazzfestival.org

Oakley Almond Festival

This three-day event is held in the town of Oakley, in the Sacramento–San Joaquin River Delta about an hour's drive east of San Francisco Bay. It includes live music, a fun run, carnival rides and games, a parade, a car show, a cooking contest, and more.

www.oakleychamber.com

Oroville Salmon Festival

Held the fourth Saturday in September, this Feather River event includes tours of a fish hatchery, educational events, salmon tasting, a craft fair, and a farmer's market. The idea is to celebrate the thousands of salmon that make their way up the river each year from the ocean to spawn.

www.orovilleareachamber.com

Paddlefest

Started in 2003, this annual two-day event takes place at the Aquatic Center on Humboldt Bay in the town of Eureka. Canoe and kayak races and events are scheduled for adults and children alike. There's also live music, vendors, and refreshments.

www.redwoods.info

Paul Bunyan Days

Held every Labor Day Weekend at Fort Bragg on the Mendocino Coast, this long-weekend event includes a horseshoe tournament; a craft fair; a gem, mineral, and fossil show; a classic car show; an ugly dog contest; a Frisbee dog contest; and a logging show that features axe throwing, hand sawing, pole climbing, and more.

www.paulbunyandays.com

San Jose International Mariachi Festival

This two-day festival showcases the Mexican-American heritage of the city of San Jose. It includes live music, dance, food, drinks, and more.

www.mhcviva.org

Sebastopol Celtic Festival

This four-day event features artists from North America and Europe. Celtic crafts are on display and for sale, as are fine foods and microbrewery ales. There are children's activities, singing, and dancing galore.

www.seb.org

Street Rod Extravaganza

Held in the town of Chester near Lake Almanor, this annual weekend-long event includes a poker run, a poker walk, music, dancing, food, and more.

www.chester-lakealmanor.com

Surf-4Peace

Trinidad is the town that hosts this day-long surfing competition, featuring separate classes for long boards, short boards, men, women, and children younger than eighteen. Proceeds benefit the Humboldt Surfriders and the Redwoods Peace and Justice Center.

www.redwoods.info

Tapestry Arts Festival

Held in San Jose every Labor Day weekend, this event has run for more than three decades and features visual and performing arts with proceeds benefiting local arts programs. The event previously was known as Tapestry in Talent. Activities include hands-on art projects, rock-wall climbing, a hang-gliding simulator, food, music, and more.
www.tapestryarts.org

Taste of Lodi

This San Joaquin County event features as many as forty award-winning local wineries along with local foods, wine seminars, chef's demonstrations, and live music. If you want to pair your wine with another gourmet item, you can also visit the Port, Cigar, and Chocolate Pavilion.
www.visitlodi.com

Tulelake Butte Valley Fair

This five-day celebration begins the Wednesday after Labor Day in Tulelake, just four miles south of the Oregon-California border. More than 60,000 people typically attend, and the fair takes great pride in its family-friendly, no-alcohol policies. As county fairs go, this one is big, attracting main-stage talent like *American Idol* contestant Kelly Pickler.
www.tbvfair.com

Valley of the Moon Vintage Festival

Held in Sonoma County, this century-old event is one of the longest running in all of California, second only to the Rose Parade. It includes music, comedy, food, and more.
www.sonomavinfest.org

Wings of the Warners Festival

The town of Alturas hosts this annual bird-watching festival in conjunction with a hot-air balloon festival. The site is the Modoc

National Wildlife Refuge, and guided tours are available if you want to look around instead of up for a few hours.
www.alturaschamber.org

Woofstock
The Sequoia Humane Society raises funds through this annual event in Eureka. There are dog contests, canine demonstrations, a "Mutt Strut" through Old Town Eureka, pet-related vendors, food, and more. Live music in the past has included headliners like Iron Butterfly.
www.woofstock.org

October

Apple Harvest Festival
Fortuna hosts this daylong, citywide celebration with hayrides substituting for taxicabs as the preferred form of transportation between venues. Orchard tours, live music, an apple pie contest, children's games, a street fair, and more round out the day of family fun.
www.discovertheredwoods.com

Autumn in the Alps Quilt Show
Held in the scenic mountain hamlet of Weaverville since 2002, this town-wide quilt show spans the entire historic district. The host organization—Thursday Night Strippers Quilt Guild of Weaverville—promises a quarter-mile of quilts on display.
www.trinitycounty.com

Burney Falls Heritage Day
Columbus Day marks the date for Burney Falls Heritage Day, where you can visit McArthur Burney Falls Memorial State Park and see re-creations of old-time blacksmithing, weaving, candle making, and other pioneer trades and crafts.
www.burneychamber.com

The Civil War Revisited

Promoted as the largest Civil War re-enactment and living history event in the United States, this annual Fresno event is sponsored by the Fresno Historical Society.
www.valleyhistory.org

Copia Napa Harvest Festival

Usually at the end of October after the harvest and grape-crush rush, this is a weekend of wine tasting and friendly Olympics-themed competition at Copia in Napa City.
www.copia.org/harvest

Halloween "Spooktacular"

The V Marketplace hosts this month-long event with giant ghosts and hallway-menacing ghouls offering scares and screams for free to the public.
www.vmarketplace.com

Humboldt Pride Festival

Arcata is the host city for this festival, which was first held in 1992. It includes a film festival, a beer and wine festival, and a pride parade.
www.humboldtpride.org

Johnny Appleseed Days

Held the first weekend each October in the town of Paradise, this festival's heritage stretches all the way back to 1880, when it was known as the Harvest Home Festival. If you want to sample and buy apple pies, it's hard to find a better venue. You can also enter your own family's pie, cake, or other apple-oriented recipe in the apple recipe contest.
www.paradisedirect.com

Mount Shasta International Film Festival

This three-day, multivenue event showcases independent films from American and foreign directors, as well as documentaries. *www.shastafilmfest.com*

Napa Valley Lighted Tractor Parade

Need a little humor and history mixed in with your pre-Christmas holiday parade? Try this Calistoga event, which honors the region's agricultural heritage. *www.calistogachamber.com*

Oakhurst Fall Chocolate and Wine Festival

Inflatable rides, a car show, and a silent auction help to round out the weekend's worth of eating at this annual event in the Gold Country town of Oakhurst, near Yosemite National Park. *www.oakhurstchamber.com*

Rio Vista Bass Derby

Held for sixty-plus years in the Sacramento River town of Rio Vista, the annual Bass Derby is a three-day contest featuring sturgeon, striped bass, salmon fishing, and a kids' division. More than 40,000 people typically attend. *www.bassfestival.com*

Sacramento American Arts Festival

Featuring hundreds of vendors and artists, this annual exhibition in the Sacramento Convention Center highlights more than 15,000 original works by contemporary craftspeople and artists. Visitors get an opportunity to meet many of the artists who are selected to participate. *www.cityofsacramento.org*

San Francisco Fleet Week

This annual weekend-long event features demonstrations by the U.S. Navy's Blue Angels, a parade of Navy ships, fireworks, ship tours, and more.
www.fleetweek.us

Tarantula Awareness Festival

Timed to coincide with the creepy-crawliness of Halloween, this annual event at Coarsegold Historic Village in the Sierra Foothills near Yosemite National Park includes pumpkin decorating and dessert contests, a hairy legs contest, tarantula races, and a children's costume parade.
www.coarsegoldhistoricvillage.com

West Coast Monster Truck Nationals

Held at the Tehama County Fairgrounds in Red Bluff, this event is sponsored by the Major League of Monster Trucks. Watch trucks with names like Bigfoot, Avenger, and Sudden Impact in crushing, bone-breaking action.
www.mlmt.com

Western Open Fiddle Championship

Held the third full week of October, this Red Bluff event has been held since 1982 and draws fiddlers and other musicians from all around the world.
www.westernopenfiddle.com

November

Icer Air

Some of the world's best snowboarders and skiers descend on San Francisco for this weekend-long "urban big-air" event, which takes place on the city's naturally steep streets.
www.icerair.com

International Latino Film Festival

San Francisco hosts this three-week film festival, which has been going on for more than a decade.

www.latinofilmfestival.org

Pebble Beach Equestrian Championships

Held at the Pebble Beach Equestrian Center in Monterey County, this event is the grand finale of the horse show season in the area.

www.ridepebblebeach.com

December

Brighten the Harbor

Sponsored by the Monterey Peninsula Yacht Club, this event features boats decorated with holiday lights cruising round-trip from the city's Coast Guard Pier to Lover's Point. Awards are given for the best decorations.

www.mpyc.org

Butte Valley Chariot Races

These races are held on Sundays at Macdoel Downs, starting the first Sunday in December and continuing through the first Sunday in March.

(530) 397-3711

Olive Harvest Tasting at the Sonoma Barracks

This event is part of the Olive Festival in Sonoma Valley Wine Country. The festival starts in December and runs through March.

www.sonomavalley.com

Tahoe Adventure Film Festival

This festival highlights the best action and adventure sports films of the year. Look for images on the big screen of whitewater rafting, rock climbing, skydiving, snowmobile stunts, big-wave surfing, and more.

www.laketahoefilmfestival.com

Truckers Christmas Convoy

Held at the Redwoods Acres Fairgrounds in Humboldt County, this event features more than a hundred large trucks adorned in holiday lights. The parade winds through town on the second Saturday night of December. Attendance is free.

www.redwoods.info

INDEX